HEY!
DIDN'T YOU USED TO BE
JOHN DAWE?

True Stories From One of
Canada's NICEST Broadcasters

BY
JOHN B. DAWE

 FriesenPress

Suite 300 - 990 Fort St
Victoria, BC, V8V 3K2
Canada

www.friesenpress.com

ISBN
978-1-5255-9281-2 (Hardcover)
978-1-5255-9280-5 (Paperback)
978-1-5255-9282-9 (eBook)

1. BIOGRAPHY & AUTOBIOGRAPHY, PERSONAL MEMOIRS

Distributed to the trade by The Ingram Book Company

THOSE TO WHOM THIS BOOK IS DEDICATED

The following names are those of people no longer with us but who have had an impact on my life and times. I miss them in no small way and enjoyed re-living the memories as I wrote this book.

Judy Allan	George and Tula Allison
Constance Brown and	Rob Buckman
Jack Greenwald	Jerome Couelle
Doug Colvey	Joan Dawe
Jim Dawe	Victoria Ellins
Randolph Dawe	Bruce Garvey
Allan Fotheringham	David Graham
John Gorman	Ian and Mary Henderson
Bob Hughes	Dan Laffey
Katerina Kessler	Bob McAdorey
Laura LaPlante	John Meyer
George Mede	Florence Millman
Harry Meyerovitch	Dave Nichol
Patrick Nagle	Morty Pesner
Alan and Pauline Orr	Leanne Sanders
Jim Ritchie	Hal Shaper
Louise Scott	Ron Williams
Reg Thomas	John Zitko
Ed and Anne Zitko	

TABLE OF CONTENTS

INTRODUCTION

This book is an attempt to try to recollect the people and events that shaped my life. There are gaps galore in the chronology along with people and circumstances that involved me with them. That's because I have blanked out many memorable moments or have simply forgotten, not wanting to ask others for assistance out of fear of what they may tell me.

It is not a journey of which I am particularly proud; it's just a journey about one person's passage through life so far. I laughed out loud writing about many of the incidents; I wept describing others; while some had me shaking my head in disbelief that I could have done or said such a thing. There are many skeletons that will appear like half-worms in an apple core. But so be it. I apologise in advance to anyone who suffered from my thoughtlessness or lack of honesty, integrity and morality or by my stupidity. Especially my stupidity.

I am what I am and there's little I would change.

And by the way, as you will come to appreciate, I have travelled a lot but don't expect travelogue-type writing because that's not my nature. It's more an understanding of "being there" without describing the "there."

CHAPTER 1

The Beginning

I was eased from my mother's womb as she lay on the kitchen table in a rented house not far from a maintenance site in what was called York Township. It was just before noon on August 10, 1939. Less than one month later the Second World War began.

Having another boy must have been a disappointment for my father but neither he nor my mother, nor my three brothers for that matter, ever mentioned it.

My mother was accompanied by a doctor and friend-cum-midwife. Sometime later when I was particularly quiet, lying beneath some blankets, someone had the good sense to check me out and discovered a mess of blood at my feet. It turns out the umbilical cord hadn't been securely tied, so that was quickly rectified and there was no big alarm.

While four is a sizeable number of children to have these days, it wasn't in the thirties, and certainly not within families of Newfoundland origin where typical numbers of children per family averaged around ten. Both my mother and father came from large families.

My cousin Alonzo used to come to Toronto every winter to work, and every time he went home to Blow-Me-Down, there was another baby waiting to greet him. He had ten, I believe.

Sometimes Alonzo was accompanied to Toronto by his father and uncle, George and Herbert Porter. When they were with us, I had to sleep on the front porch. It was enclosed but had no insulation, and I could see my breath going to bed and getting up in the early hours to deliver newspapers.

Alonzo had a great heart but since I was seldom able to decipher all that he was saying, his Newfoundland outport accent being so bizarre, I wasn't able to learn much about his depth of character. He liked to drink beer, though, and to supplement his construction income so he could enjoy his favourite pastime, he used to go with me shovelling snow in one of the close-by upscale communities. I was the front man, making the approach at the door and agreeing to the price, while he did most, though not all, of the heavy work.

We did very well, Alonzo and me, and to this day I've never been able to understand why nobody in some 24 years had ever knocked at my door and offered to do the snow at my Rosedale home. A few times I had been approached while I was doing it myself, but by then I had the rhythm – and was getting exercise – and didn't want to retreat indoors.

Not long after the war began, my father decided he had to sign up to serve in the Canadian military. I know nothing about his motivation, though I suspect it had something to do with some of his workplace colleagues joining up and he didn't want to be seen as a slacker.

My father worked very hard as a steel rigger with Dominion Bridge, a company I myself would spend a summer working for in Elliot Lake about 15 years later.

Steel rigging seemed to be part of our heritage. The best in the trade are from Newfoundland along with some Indigenous tribes. The Mohawks were said to have rigged steel on most of the tall buildings in New York City. But in one of the photographs that now grace the Museum of Modern Art, there's a group of steel workers taking a lunch break on a girder. One of them is my father's brother, Uncle Jack.

Dad was about six feet tall, with a powerful body. He was also very handsome and the perfect match for my mother who was a beauty. And this is not a son boasting about his parents ¼ I have the photographic proof.

We didn't take many photos back then. I have a few and I'm sure my brothers have some, and even more came to light on the death of our mother when family friends shared their pictures with us.

One of my favourites is a picture of my father dressed in a double-breasted suit and standing outside the Weston Sanitorium, the place where tuberculosis patients were sent to die. When he went to join up for the war, a series of mandatory tests showed him to have what was then called consumption, but what we later knew as tuberculosis.

All this happened when I was about ten months old. At my age, I wasn't allowed in to see him on visitor's days and the only times I saw him at all were when he slipped away AWOL, I believe, on two occasions. So, I don't remember him. I knew he was generous, though, because he gave me a quarter once and he also made me a wallet with my initials on it.

I used to carry my favourite picture of him in my wallet, and it showed a tall, solidly built man with a somewhat pained look on his face. But the wallet was stolen from my office at Global Television News. Thankfully, it wasn't the wallet he made for me; I still have that.

When I think about how long I carried that picture, I'm amazed, because I really didn't know the man.

In effect, I never had a father to talk to, to teach me things and to counsel me, not forgetting all those nice-to-do things such as taking me to the ice rink or encouraging me to swim. I know for sure, though, that he loved me, and that was made absolutely and unequivocally clear to me on the morning of his death in 1947.

I have never discussed this with my brothers; my mother and I never discussed it after it happened. I was not able to put it into perspective until years later when my wife deepened her understanding of the mystical and the spiritual, as well as energy and the viability of the soul, and these things became an integral part of our life together, though I rarely, if ever, get involved in discussing it publicly.

It was late in October 1947. By this time my father had spent about seven years in the "San" as we called it. I was eight years old and shared a bed with one of my brothers at our house in North Toronto. I don't recall how often, if ever, I discussed our father with my brothers, but I know they were forced to go into a children's facility at the San as a precaution after Dad was confined there.

I had no understanding of the enormity of the dedication my mother showed toward my father until much later in life, when I learned that every day for those seven years she had visited him. For the first six years or so, we lived not far from St. Clair Avenue, from where she took a streetcar to the end of the line then walked a few kilometres to the San. She did it every day as far as I know. She also worked every day, so how she found the energy, heaven only knows.

If the journeying took its toll on our mother, she never let on. And she was, I understand, unwilling to unburden what weighed on her heart and mind to her children, or others for that matter. She had secrets that were only revealed many years later and, even then, they were never, ever discussed. She did, however, tell us from time to time that he was hanging on despite losing more than half his body weight after innumerable operations.

4

Later I learned that he was one of the unlucky ones at the San who was not part of a program testing a new drug to treat TB, a drug that ended up successfully combating the disease. It was an antibiotic called streptomycin and is still in use today, 75 years after its discovery. Instead of the drug, Dad got the placebo and, as his lungs became more affected, they simply surgically removed the tissue until he had barely enough left with which to breathe.

One morning that October, very early, around 4 a.m., I awoke crying and went to my mother's room, where I disturbed her much-needed sleep.

"Daddy's dead," I told her. "No," she said, "he's very sick but they promised to call if there was any change."

"No, no," I repeated, "he's dead. He came to visit me and he told me, and he said everything was going to be all right. I saw him and that's what he said."

Bleary-eyed and dazed, Mother told me it must have been a dream and encouraged me to try to go back to sleep.

I did but learned when I awoke again that morning that Father had died at about 4 a.m. and that the San didn't call until about 5:30 a.m. to tell Mother.

The incident, or premonition, was quickly forgotten and never discussed again.

Randolph Azariah Dawe was 39 years of age. He was buried at Prospect Cemetery and the spot was marked by a piece of concrete with a number on it: 1349, Sec 24. Cost: $23.25 (25% of that paltry sum "will be invested in the Perpetual Care Fund," the receipt said, and I sometimes wonder if they honoured that.)

Many years later I talked about getting a proper headstone but my idea was dismissed. Neither I, nor my mother nor brothers ever, to my knowledge, visited the gravesite after the funeral.

It was many, many years before I learned why.

CHAPTER 2

Mother

Memories of my early years are vague and only a few come to mind.

One was going to a camp for a week or so with my mother. It was called Bolton Camp and our going there was arranged by people in Toronto who had identified families in need of a summer break. The Neighbourhood Workers' Association had been founded in 1922, and part of its mandate was to identify low-income families who were in need of a short holiday. The families went to a former fishing camp a few miles from Bolton for a 12-day visit. The camp also became affiliated with the Toronto Star Fresh Air Fund.

I remember two things about that camp: First, we had porridge three times a day (I was a toddler after all) and it took me many years before I could enjoy it again. And second, I ran away for some reason and, to my chagrin, was caught by some Boy Scouts who had been called in for the search. I wasn't happy and vowed never to join Cubs or Scouts. I never did, though many years later I encouraged my own son to do so.

One memory that comes back to haunt me when I'm near or on the water occurred when I was a toddler. We had been taken to the public swimming pool on St. Clair West. There were a lot of people in the pool but not me. I remember getting the attention of my oldest brother, Jimmy, and while talking to him someone pushed me into the deep end. All I recalled was everything going black. I was told later Jimmy pulled me out and somebody worked to bring me around.

I never did learn to swim but I loved being on and in the water but only when my feet could touch bottom.

Another vivid memory was walking down a street hand in hand with my mother when I was about five years old. We passed a church and I told her that when I was older we would get married in that church. I remember her laughing at the comment – and believe me, she didn't laugh very often that I recall, certainly not back then. But to me the comment made sense because the dad I never knew was in hospital and everybody else I knew had mothers and fathers.

My mother was totally devoted to her four boys and raised us to respect and love each other. I remember so well how she would tell my wife that her boys never fought with each other, not ever.

My wife Shirley is the oldest of four children and she, too, was raised mostly by her mother, because her father was a commercial fisher on the west coast and spent most of his days at sea or maintaining the boat. She knew from experience that there just had to be conflicts in my family because she experienced them in hers.

But my mother was adamant: Her boys never fought.

I always agreed with my mother during these conversations because I could never remember a time when there was any nastiness in our relationship, and certainly no fighting, except when the older boys donned boxing gloves for fun.

There was lots of tension in our home, however, especially when mother remarried and we were living in a tiny North Toronto house with one bathroom. But Mother worked overtime to keep the peace and mediate any problems quickly and effectively. She needed the family unit to be tight, loving, peaceful and tranquil, if not serene.

I believe it was during those early years that I learned some of life's great lessons, the ones that hold you in good stead for the years ahead.

The most important of these was the Golden Rule: Do unto others as you would have them do unto you. Mother emphasized that more than anything and I have consciously tried to live by that code of conduct and I know my brothers have, too. I have wavered off course at times, though I hope never often enough nor far enough to cause any serious long-term hurt.

If I have one major shortcoming, it's a temper. Interestingly, it doesn't manifest itself on the golf course or on the tennis court, and rarely in a work situation or in public, for that matter. But in family situations, or occasionally with friends, my anger can erupt over the most innocuous of things.

I've always explained my occasional ill temper as my way of letting go rather than keeping it pent up inside, which can lead to other more serious problems. At the root of it is this: If I don't agree with something, it must be challenged, and challenging people is what journalism is all about. But to do so in personal matters is unacceptable.

I believe my mother knew this personal fault may have been in her boys' genes because another of her sayings that she mentioned time and again was this: "When ignorance is bliss, 'tis folly to be wise."

I was never one to debate issues because I could never acknowledge the other person had a view if it differed from my own, at least not without displaying disgust at an opposing view. Thankfully, that attitude changed sharply around the time I was living in Montreal. Still, it was many years before I learned from where that conceit may have evolved.

My father, I was told, had a terrible temper. I never saw it, of course, and my mother never mentioned it – except once when she witnessed my bad behaviour during a holiday, and then she mentioned it only to my wife Shirley. But I was to learn by the time I was 40 that my father had a strong jealous streak, among other shortcomings, and that my mother bore the brunt of this.

One of the big secrets in our family – and, yes, every family has secrets – was that my mother was often verbally abused and occasionally physically abused by my father while he was confined in the San.

I know he loved my mother, as he did his boys, but as his body deteriorated and he knew an early death was imminent, he lashed out at the person he knew best and saw most often.

My mother never shared her experiences with us or anybody else as far as I know, but she was close to one of my dad's nephews and he knew some if not all of the stories. All the more remarkable, then, that Mother continued to travel daily to the San and, more often than not, carried homecooked meals for him.

In the short period after Father's death, something happened to convince her to find another husband. Her decision disappointed my father's family and that hurt my mother, but she did so anyway. Frankly, the local Dawes were never that supportive of us and, after my father died, they were noticeable by their absence, most of them, at least.

With everyone gone now, it is difficult to know the facts, but I was always led to believe that she remarried out of necessity to keep the family together, out of fear that her financial circumstances wouldn't permit her to provide the home she wanted for her boys.

I was always under the impression, too, that she was at risk of having her boys split up and put into foster homes, but my brothers assure me that was not the case. Still, if life was hard for her while Father was living, it was as tough after he died.

The house where I was born was rented and Mother was able to provide for us and pay the rent, although I never really knew how she managed it.

We weren't lacking for anything that I can think of, and we even got to spend some time out of the hot city during a few summers. Life changed, though, when we moved north of Yonge and Eglinton. How that house in North Toronto came to us encapsulates one of the great family stories and, in particular, says volumes about my mother.

One of the many jobs my mother held while my father was in hospital was working for a public health nurse named Mrs. Laroche. She lived in a tiny bungalow on Craighurst Avenue, eight blocks north of Yonge and Eglinton, where she took in a boarder, usually an elderly person requiring constant care, who had no family of their own. While Mrs. Laroche worked, my mother would clean the house and care for the boarder.

My father was apparently very upset about this and his biggest concern, apparently, was that mother could contract some infectious disease from Mrs. Laroche, who was working with poor and impoverished people in Toronto.

Occasionally, mother would take me and the other boys with her and one of the great treats we got was homemade ice cream, which Mrs. Laroche made in those silver metal ice cube trays that had an ice cube separation mould with a lever. I can still savour the taste. It was the best ice cream ever because commercial ice cream had filler in it and we were convinced it was sawdust – it sure had the texture of sawdust.

Anyway, Mrs.Laroche had strong, grandmotherly feelings about us and we loved her, too. I think Mrs. Laroche saw herself in my mother, a determined person dedicated to those less fortunate.

One day in 1945 or thereabouts, she told my mother that if anything ever happened to her, my mother was to go to the desk and search a certain drawer for some papers. Mrs. Laroche must have known she hadn't long to live because some six months later she died.

When my mother found the papers, they included a copy of her will in which she left the house and personal effects to Mother. When Mother later joined the lawyer and Mrs. Laroche's brother for a reading of the will, the brother became angry, saying he had just paid $175 for the funeral and was left nothing.

My mother excused herself, walked across the street to a bank, and withdrew almost all of her meagre savings. She handed the money to the man, who took it, said nothing, and stomped out of the lawyer's office never to be seen or heard from again.

So there we were, now living in our own little house, kind of a magical little house in a completely different neighbourhood just off Yonge Street, with every conceivable kind of shop, cinemas, a bowling alley, churches of all denominations, a private girl's school along with public and high schools. Very "WASP" compared to where we came from.

Of course, home ownership came with a price. There was an outstanding mortgage for a start, not much, but a mortgage nonetheless. Then there were taxes, insurance and utility bills, not to mention the cost of coal and later heating oil.

Mother also had to get a job because her main income had derived from caring for the Laroche household, and Father was still in the hospital.

It wasn't long before she was working for The Little Pie Shoppe, a North Toronto institution for at least 60 years. Long hours in the baking room didn't deter her still travelling to Weston to see Dad, even though the trip was much longer than before.

We boys went to John Ross Robertson Public School with Jimmy, the eldest, later moving on to Northern Secondary to learn a trade while the rest of us went to North Toronto Collegiate Institute.

All of us did odd jobs delivering for the local drug stores and most of us had a paper route. My first route was to deliver a fairly large number of both the *Toronto Daily Star* and *Evening Telegram* newspapers when they cost three cents each. You can imagine how much I made. I did those after school but I didn't do it for long.

Without knowing why, a boy took offence at my doing the paper route he had just lost – and one day he hit me on the head with a hammer. It was diagnosed that there was no serious damage (although I have a few theories about that) but I can still feel the ridge in my skull that the blow created.

Larry and Frankie had routes delivering *The Globe and Mail* and I got one, too. It meant getting up at about 4:30 a.m., which says a lot about why I'm a morning person, since I did that for about 11 years.

We all had other jobs, too. In other words, we kept busy and never put any pressure on our mother for spending money and the like. In my case, there was a five-pin bowling alley just north of Yonge and Eglinton where I set pins for a paltry sum, but it all helped. For the most part, we were enjoying our new lifestyle and new community.

When Father died, his death didn't bring much change since he had been confined in hospital for so many years. There were other pressures, though, and about a year or so later mother remarried.

Wally LaPlante was a carpenter from Northern Ontario, a divorced man with two children, a boy and a girl. He was a very different man from what I understood my father to be, and he had issues that didn't lend themselves to enjoying a serene lifestyle in our tiny, magical house.

Mother hung in there with him for more than 40 years, spending much of their last decade together taking care of him as he battled disease. During that time they also went to live in Montreal and in Windsor where Wally found work when things were slow in Toronto.

Mother was never out of work. She continued to work at the bakery for a long time and she spent a comparable time working at a dry cleaning shop around the corner. She said it kept her in touch with the community and the world.

She and I had a special bond. It may have evolved from my being the youngest, ending up spending the most time with her. We did two trips together over the years and both were memorable beyond belief.

The first was a lengthy visit to Newfoundland by train in 1949, the year of Confederation. Memory fails to reacquaint me with the reason we went to the place of her birth, but it was probably because there was illness in the family. I was chosen to go because the other boys had commitments.

So much of what happened on that trip is lost now but some experiences stand out. I don't recall the train trip or the ferry crossing, except that moment of sadness in my mother when she realized I had left my jacket on the train. She had wanted me to look nice for her family and this was a special treat for me.

I do remember the train trip from the boat terminal because we were travelling on a narrow gauge railway line that was affectionately called "The Bullet." On many occasions we had to stop to allow families of moose to cross the tracks. And if I stuck my head out the window between cars, I had to be careful not to get soot from the coal-fired engine stack in my eyes.

My mother's birthplace was an outport on Conception Bay called Blow-Me-Down, so called because of a very high rock structure that sided the cove. There were only a few houses in the place, as colourful as what we've come to know about Newfoundland, and the centre of activity was a long wharf. A visit to that dock tested your nostrils because it was home to several barrels of smelly cod's liver. Still, I spent many, many hours on that dock, fishing for what they called Tommy Cod (small codfish) and flat fish; catching them was a no-brainer because they were so plentiful in the shallow waters.

The thrill of thrills, though, was going out with the fishers to bring in what was called the "traps." These were very large gill nets that were positioned in known codfish gathering areas of Conception Bay, after which the men would go and drag the nets into the skiffs along with the bounty of cod. I was only ten years old and average size, but I was gaffing fish as big as me and hauling them into the skiff. What an experience.

It's rare to see codfish that big these days as the cod fishery is still subject to quotas because of over-fishing, and what they do catch hasn't had a chance to grow so big.

Going to and from the traps and on other outings we saw whales, too. In fact, my mother and I on a number of occasions took a skiff out to jig for squid or fish for cod and we often saw minke whales surfacing, sometimes very close to our boat. I don't remember seeing any icebergs, but Conception Bay used to get its share of those monsters, too.

I spent about two months there but never really got to know my cousins, aunts and uncles well. Our worlds were so different. My grandparents were not there, either. In fact, I never met a grandparent on either side of my family.

Confederation would bring changes to the lives of Newfoundlanders, though, mostly positive changes as I recall, the Children's Allowance being the most important since it brought much-needed income to the families.

One interesting side note to the trip. As a youngster in Toronto who was able to earn a small amount of spending money by delivering prescriptions and groceries, not to forget my paper routes, I had access to funds for treats such as candy. Well, that wasn't the case in Newfoundland, so getting a candy, or "sweets" as they called them, was a big deal, and what they got was limited to hard candy – boiled sweets – from Britain.

I made a pledge while there to try to bring more sweets into their lives and, every Halloween for a half-dozen years later, we took a huge selection of our trick or treating rewards and sent it to our Newfoundland family by parcel post.

The other trip my mother and I took together was somewhat different. In 1966 I had left journalism and was working for an international airline when I got engaged. I realized that once I was married I wouldn't be able to use my travel benefits for anyone other than my wife and children. So, I proposed taking Mother on a trip.

When I first asked her where she'd like to go, she said South Africa, and I agreed that would be a great place. Unfortunately, South African Prime Minister Hendrik Verwoerd was assassinated that September and we had to change our plans.

"OK, where in the world would you like to go?" I asked her.

"Around it," she replied, thinking she was making a joke. But that's exactly what we did, with short stops at San Francisco, Honolulu, Tokyo, New Delhi and Tel Aviv, with long stays in Hong Kong and London. She talked about that trip for years afterward; I never saw her so happy.

After my stepfather died, my mother threw herself into her work with even more enthusiasm. But she also quietly decided she wanted to do more, including travel.

My brother Larry had taken her to Newfoundland and, for reasons that aren't clear, she had no desire to return to her birthplace. But she enjoyed going to Thunder Bay, where my eldest brother Jimmy was living with his family, and to Minneapolis where my brother Frankie lived with his wife and two children.

She also travelled with Shirley and our son Jonathan to Vancouver where she met my in-laws for the first time. She was enthralled with the place. Shirley and I had been married for about 20 years and this was the first time my mother had met her parents and other family.

Mother worked almost up until the day she died. In the final few years, it was not-for-profit work for a local church, which had a club for seniors that met regularly. Mother bought all the food for those gatherings, cooked it and lugged it over to the church, which was about two blocks away. Paradoxically, she was older than most of the people in the club, called, affectionately, "The Smilers Club."

Until taken from us by congestive heart failure, Mother was in great shape and extraordinarily active. She and a neighbour would walk from Craighurst Avenue down to the Eaton Centre, about eight kilometres, then return on the subway. And they did this more than once a week in the good weather.

All her life, my mother asked for very little from any of us. She was seemingly driven by one thing: To keep her boys and the expanded family a cohesive unit.

If I inherited an ill temper from my father, I gathered other, mostly positive qualities from my mother, things such as being practical, independent and self-sufficient, giving rather than taking, and everything in moderation (the latter I often failed miserably at). But she also had an obstinate streak, and that she passed along, too.

For her, a healthy body led to a healthy mind and that's why her meals were legendary among our friends. Our little home was always open to anyone in need of shelter, a place to hang out, a meal or a good dose of family values. But she was constantly being tested, usually by circumstances over which she had no control; and I precipitated some of them.

CHAPTER 3

First Life's Lesson Looms Large

The Second World War had been over for a year or so when I returned home from public school to an empty house. My brothers – Jimmy, Larry and Frankie – were out and my mother was working as she did every day. I cannot recall what was happening in the world that day since there was only one thing on my mind: I was hungry and there was nobody to help a seven-year-old find a bite to eat.

It would be hard to miss anyone in our tiny home. The house had but two bedrooms and one bathroom, an unfinished basement and a wide, open backyard. In the beginning, we were five living in that house, my mother and her four boys. Not long after she remarried following my father's death, her husband brought his two children from a previous marriage to live with us and, in between, we always had some of my mother's family from Newfoundland bunking in during the winters. For long periods each year for more than a decade we had as many as 10 people living in the house at one time.

Still, on this particular day I was alone and I was hungry. It must be said now, however, that hunger was something I never truly experienced, not at home in any case. Despite our humble circumstances, especially in those early days, my mother was always able to put good, nutritious food on the table.

But on the day in question I was hungry and alone, and I began to forage for something to eat. It didn't take very long to find a banana that had been sitting out on a plate by the sink and it was ripe.

I knew enough about bananas (though nothing about their nutritious value) to know that when the skin gets very dark, the flesh is very sweet and I realized I had to look no further for sustenance.

Sometime later as my mother worked feverishly in her tiny kitchen and the family was coming together for dinner, my mother called out: "Boys, did any of you see the banana I left by the sink?" I admitted it was me who ate it and learned more than one valuable lesson that would stay with me forever.

My mother was a terrific cook but her specialty was baking. She had bought that banana at a discount because it was past its prime and had planned to use it to make banana bread.

When I admitted taking it, she thanked me for my honesty and then said: "What I want you to understand is that that banana may have filled your tummy for the moment but it was meant to make bread for the entire family." I felt horrible and couldn't face my brothers, who, bless them, said nothing.

Bananas were very special for my mother. She considered them a big treat because in her youth, living in a Newfoundland outport, bananas were a big deal, as big as or bigger than oranges and lemons and other fresh fruits, all of which had to be imported by ship into the then British colony and transported by vehicles along non-existent roads to stores that could only handle a few of the precious, delicate morsels.

When she migrated to Canada she learned to make banana bread and banana cream pie, although she was famous in our circles and beyond for her lemon meringue pie, mainly for its subtle tartness.

I will never forget the look on my mother's face when, in 1966, during a trip around the world, our second stop was Honolulu. Just outside the airport terminal building she spied a banana plant laden with fruit. She literally ran to the plant and embraced it, displaying the biggest smile I had ever seen on her face up to that point.

Bananas have remained a special part of my diet, too.

CHAPTER 4

Go Jump In The Lake

Mother had incredible patience, which, for a woman alone caring for four young children with few resources and even less downtime, was remarkable. She also had a keen understanding of human nature and didn't react adversely to changing circumstances or situations.

Moving from a rented house in a blue collar, immigrant quarter of Toronto to our own home on the cusp of a white- collar quarter brought new demands on our behaviour. You could not, for instance, take short cuts through people's properties without causing a huge fuss. In one case, someone called the school to complain about local children on their property and the school, while not able to identify the culprits, sent letters to the most suspect families. The practice stopped immediately because part and parcel of the threat was a visit to the principal's office and a few minutes of pain and anguish in the form of "The Strap."

The possibility of getting the strap was a huge deterrent to bad behaviour in my early years at John Ross Robertson but, in my eight years there, I still managed to get the punishment three times. One of these still bothers me to this day.

Like all schools, John Ross Robertson had a boarded hockey rink and on occasions when the ice was soft, the school didn't want anybody on the ice, and that included on the boards. One day some friends were chatting beside the boards and I happened to drop something onto the ice. Just as I climbed over to retrieve it, I was spied by a teacher and immediately taken to the office for "that punishment."

Naturally I didn't think the punishment fit the crime and my complaints brought a doubling of the encounters with the strap. Corporal punishment such as the strap was outlawed a few decades later and, since in the 21st century there seems to be a lot of re-thinking of old policies and attempts at reconciliation coupled with apologies, I've been waiting for the school authorities to issue their apology for employing the strap in my day. None has been forth-coming, needless to say.

As I write this, I cannot recall the other two episodes with the strap but I do know I was a targeted student, even though my activities were more entrepreneurial than sinister. I did some deals involving trading cards for which some cash traded hands. Some parents complained and the practice halted, although not one of my customers copped me out.

I told Mother all the things that happened at school and I can't recall her ever getting angry with me, even though she must have known I had a naughty streak. I tend to think she liked me for being honest, even though that honesty evolved out of a most embarrass-ing situation.

One thing I did and lived to regret was taking a commemorative medal from a hallway display case on a dare. I took it (a Winston Churchill medal) but got too scared to return it. I tucked it away with some other things and forgot about it. More than 60 years later we were moving again, and I found a box I hadn't looked at for decades. There amongst myriad mementos was the tiny case holding the medal.

For a long time I pondered what to do with it. I settled on returning it to the current principal in an anonymous envelope with a short note explaining its appearance. At least, I thought, the school could have some fun telling the local media about it; and maybe a story for the children?

Well, nothing happened to my knowledge, but at least my guilt was somewhat mitigated.

Something else happened to me at the outset of my years at John Ross Robertson. It wasn't traumatic but it warrants telling.

Post-war Toronto acted the same as other communities in North America when it came to assisting the immigrants who poured out of Europe after the war of 1939-45. Food, clothing, goods and money were collected in a variety of ways, and at John Ross Robertson there was a constant stream of fundraising activities.

In my first year there, probably in the first month, our teacher asked us to bring a dime to school the next day for something or other. I hadn't started earning money yet (that happened a year or so later) so I had to ask my mother for a dime.

The request caught her in a bad moment: she was exhausted and faced getting the dinner ready before heading out for her daily trip to the San to see our father.

"I don't have a spare dime. Tell her to go jump in the lake," she said, and the next day I dutifully did just that.

I was fortunate enough to be in a skipping class for Grades 1 and 2. As it happens, I didn't graduate to Grade 3 the next year but stayed on a slower path in my formal education.

CHAPTER 5

Life at John Ross Robertson P.S.

Aside from one or two things mentioned earlier, not a lot occurred at John Ross Robertson. I met some wonderful people there, some of whom I am still in touch with some seven decades later.

I was a mediocre athlete at JRR: I played some volleyball, baseball, and did some track. My one achievement was making the relay track team, which went on to win third place in the city championship that year. I qualified for the team by running without shoes on a cinder track (common back in the 40s and 50s) and winning a heat. I'll never know why I didn't damage my feet doing that.

I used to pole vault, too, but could never rise above six feet, even though I tried harder at that than anything else.

Academically I was an average student, although some of the report cards I saved always seemed to say I needed to try harder, to work harder.

There was one occurrence, though, that in retrospect presaged my comfortability with an audience.

I cannot recall the exact grade, probably six or seven, but we had in our class Anne MacDonald, daughter of the renowned Canadian poet, Wilson MacDonald. One day she proposed to our teacher that we have a poetry reciting contest. The winner would receive a hand-scribed book of her father's poems.

The chosen poem was "The Black Crow." Everybody felt my rendition was best and I won the book. Sadly, it disappeared from our home a few years later.

I'd like to share that poem with you:

The Black Crow

A black old crow
Sat on a tree
And he swore at you
And he swore at me.

And the only cuss
That he knew was "Caw"
But he cussed that cuss
With great eclat.

But another bird
Cried "Caw-Caw" slow
And I said "He's swearing"
But a bird said "No."

"That's a preacher bird
And he's only saying
The same words slow
So they sound like praying.

"Our words are the same
If you swear 'em or pray 'em
But it's all in the way
The black crow says 'em."

Wilson MacDonald

Another interesting thing that happened to me was being photographed by the *Toronto Daily Star* while lolling on the school grass just after summer break began. The photographer had me looking for four-leaf clovers. The picture appeared in the *Star* but I never kept a copy.

The theme of the article was something about "what kids do when school's out for the summer." This was the final summer I was able to loll anywhere as subsequent summers became key money earning periods.

One event I can't shake from memory was that day in March 1953 when the school informed us that "Uncle Joe" had died and many of us wept at the news. Uncle Joe was Joseph Stalin and the full extent of his tyranny hadn't been disclosed. To those involved in World War II, he was an ally and his passing was upsetting. It wasn't long afterward, though, that details of his murderous ways made it into the western press.

I used to walk between our home on Craighurst and JRR, but sometime in the late 40s I was given a bike by my Uncle Charlie Porter.

My mother's brother Charlie was one great character. He lived with his wife Maude on Balliol Street where he kept ferrets in his back yard for hunting rabbits. They had lost their only child, Richard, to leukemia, and Charlie became a thoughtful uncle to his sister's boys. He often took us up to Holland Landing to fish for perch and catfish with the most basic equipment, and we always came back with enough for at least one meal. Every time I travel between Highway 400 and Airport Road along Highway 9, I pass the spots where we fished, just beyond some of the richest soil for growing vegetables in Canada.

Charlie had a business that installed lath, drywall and insulation in houses. Lath was basically thin wooden slats that served as the foundation for plaster in walls and ceilings ... and it was soon replaced by what we now call drywall.

One summer, when I wasn't caddying, I went to work for Charlie. He had the contract to finish the inside walls and ceilings and to insulate houses in a new development just north of John Ross Robertson P.S. To this day I can still feel the itchiness I experienced putting that insulation into blazing hot attics. We never had a shower at our home and it was always a terrible chore cleaning up after work. It's no wonder I lasted just part of one summer doing that kind of labour.

But around this time, Uncle Charlie presented me with a bike, the likes of which you'd never see today. In his travels he must have collected parts of bikes and ended up creating this multi-coloured unusual one-speed bike that I cherished for years. I have no idea how I did it, but I could ride that bike without stopping up Yonge Street, well beyond Sheppard and back again. Anyone who knows how steep the hill is at Hogg's Hollow will know what a feat that was with a one-speed bike.

I used that bike for my morning paper routes that I did for a decade. But before that, I delivered prescriptions for Lillico drugstore at Sheldrake and Yonge and later, groceries for the Red and White store on Yonge between Craighurst and Albertus. I ended up working after school and weekends for Bill Maslen's Red and White store for many years, and that experience served as a foundation for just about everything I was to do in life.

Red and White stores were independently owned, community-based grocery stores that were killed off beginning in the 50s by the proliferation of big grocery stores, or supermarkets, as they were called, that had the buying power to reduce prices well below what small stores had to charge to cover costs.

I learned a lot about supply and demand, the psychology of customers, the importance of marketing, and loyalty in all its many flavours, among other things. That I ended up in jobs that relied heavily on people-orientation is no mystery.

CHAPTER 6

Life After John Ross Robertson P.S.

It was tough leaving JRR to go to high school because I was going to North Toronto Collegiate Institute and all my friends were going to Lawrence Park Collegiate or elsewhere. I knew also that JRR was happy to see the end of me. I had been bad or unruly enough to get the strap three times, and I'm sure the school had an inkling that I was behind some other things that I considered entrepreneurial (using today's term) at the time but they considered it exploitation.

The best example I can think of is my dealing in trading cards. In the post-war era there were quite a few trading cards available related to the war as well as to sports. Some of them came in bubble gum packages and, because I was earning money doing a paper route as well as delivering groceries, I was able to buy a lot of chewing gum to get those cards. I ended up with a lot of duplication, some of which duplicates were somewhat rare, so I sold those duplicates to kids at a high premium; that behaviour was more than frowned upon.

All I know for certain about the school's view of me is that not long after I left, the JRR district southern border was changed from Craighurst, where I lived, to Lytton, one block north, and middle class not working class. Some claim the change was made to prevent the children of the football player "Cookie" Gilchrist from going to

JRR but I can't confirm that. He was a Black football player, a really good one, who with his young family moved onto Craighurst and drove a truck he used for business that had written on the sides: "Lookie, lookie, here comes Cookie."

Black families were rare in what we called North Toronto in those days. Our neighbours were in shock once in the late 50s when I decided to hold a birthday party in the back garden and invite some new friends from a funky jazz club I had been frequenting called the First Floor Jazz Club on Asquith Street, just north of Bloor. It was an after-hours club that rivalled the House of Hambourg, which was an older, more traditional after-hours club where the likes of Peter Appleyard and Moe Kaufman played. I'm not certain it was the presence of Blacks in our garden for the party or the fact that we had strung lights and had jazz music blasting well into the night that upset the neighbours, but I do know we had to break off the festivities earlier than I had hoped.

I don't remember there being any Blacks at NTCI when I started there, moreover, there weren't many ethnic groups represented, especially visible minorities that we were used to seeing in the community where I was born.

There weren't many Jews at NTCI either but, because the school had an excellent music program and a German class, we attracted some keen Jewish kids from other schools such as Forest Hill Collegiate. One of them was a character named Ed Cowan. He was the producer one year of an annual variety show at the school called "Maytime Melodies." I cannot remember what year it was, probably 1955/6, but Ed called for auditions to perform in his show.

My best friend Danny Ghikadis and I thought that was a good idea so we both entered our names. We had to learn the ballad "If They Asked Me I Could Write a Book" and we both worked hard to perfect it. In fact, I was certain I was going to make the cast, but when the announcement was made, neither Danny nor I was on the list, which included almost all Jewish names and which I found disconcerting at the time. Danny and I eventually had a good laugh at that but I promised I'd never let Ed forget it.

My other most notable Jewish friend at NTCI was Billy Lipson. I could not believe how well this guy dressed but I soon found out why: His uncle was the manufacturer of Lipson shirts, one of the top if not the top line of men's shirts back in the 50s

When I started high school I knew I wanted to get involved in sports. Although I was still delivering newspapers and working after school, I did try out for the bantam football team under some coercion from my friend Danny, even though I was on the small side.

When I met the Coach, Syd Reynolds, he asked me if my brother Frank was going to play Junior football and I replied, no. Why not, Syd asked, and I stupidly pulled another "jump in the lake" response and replied that Frank wasn't a fan of the coach, Bob Gladish. That got me into deep trouble for quite some time with everyone involved, especially Bob Gladish. (Frank did play junior and senior football at NTCI and at University of Toronto where his Victoria College team won the coveted Mulock Cup.)

Despite my size, I also went out for basketball, a sport I loved but I was really too short to be an effective player. Over the years at NTCI, though, I hung out with many of the football and basketball players, one of whom became a life-long friend. His name was Bob Hughes and he ended up having a significant role in my life.

My oldest friend, though, is Danny Ghikadis, who lived a few streets over from me on Briar Hill. We hung out a lot and, in the first year or so, we were joined by Ian Henderson. Ian, however, left when his banker father was transferred to Montreal. We lost touch for a number of years but re-connected when I moved to Montreal in 1960. Like Bob Hughes, Ian had a big influence on my life.

As you may have gathered, I was not academically inclined. Certain teachers and courses I loved, such as history, but I had a lot of issues with discipline and lacked the patience to study properly and memorize things.

One teacher I remember, Sam Huntington, who taught biology, told me just prior to yearend that the mark I'd get on my report card would not reflect my understanding. He said he knew from my questioning and my responses to his questions that I had absorbed more about his subjects than those who simply memorized things. I believe he was right, and I know he set me on a path of appreciation of nature and all living things along with a deep respect for the environment.

My history teacher was a Mr. Kelly. He was, I believe, a Briton, whose enthusiasm for history captured my interest and I performed better in his class – and on his tests – than I did in any other subject. That interest in history held me in good stead when I became a reporter and worked in marketing.

My Grade 11 English teacher's name was Miss Henderson. In response to something stupid I said to her in class, I was graded just below 50 in English literature and in grammar, bringing my overall average for that year to a shade under 60%. With two failing grades, that meant I failed my year. And that would be a life changer.

If I was a rebel before, failing Grade 11 turned me into a full-fledged one. My less than enthusiastic interest in academics waned further; I wasn't allowed to play organized sports; and my friends generally moved on as I lost the respect of many school chums, and even my family was disappointed. Unless you've experienced something like failure at an impressionable age, you wouldn't understand how traumatic it was for me. But the trauma did not last long because I was determined to continue learning about life and having fun.

Too much fun, sometimes. I was suspended a few times: Once

for wearing jeans, which in those days were banned; and a second time for laughing too much in class. My mother had to take time off work to go to the principal's office where she looked him straight in the eye and said: "I'm happy he has something to laugh about."

CHAPTER 7

Life Inside NTCI

I wasn't much of a student, academically, that is. I was definitely more interested in girls (shocking, I know), my other friends, working, and earning money. Sports played a minor role in my life, but it was through relationships in football and basketball that I met some people who would figure prominently in my later life.

The three most important guys at school were Dan Ghikadis, Ian Henderson and Bob Hughes. Among the girls, the most lasting relationship was with Marilyn McCabe. I was her first date in high school, but she fell for my friend Dan, then later met and married a friend from public school, Ray Blair. To this day they remain among my closest friends.

My friendship with Ian Henderson looked like it would be short-lived since he was only at NTCI for a couple of years, but when I moved to Montreal, we renewed our friendship and were like brothers for more than 40 years.

I don't remember how I met Danny; it was probably at school, but we we've been close friends for more than 60 years, with a few absences along the way. Generally, we'd walk to school together; I'd pick him up at his home at 22 Briar Hill Avenue. Dan's family operated the New Service Linen Supply Company that provided linen to restaurants, bars and hotels in the city. I raise that because whenever I visited his home, his mother was always ironing the company linen. She was fast and took the chore in stride.

I'll never forget how she watched – well, listened mainly – to the McCarthy Hearings on TV that were sensational in their approach to rooting out the perceived communist threat in the U.S. as the Cold War heated up just after World War II and just before the Korean War. Those were scary times and Bea Ghikadis revelled in it.

We didn't have a TV in our home until the late 1950s. Until then I occasionally watched it at Danny's, at the Pinkney's up the street (mainly "Hockey Night in Canada") and at our next door neighbour's, Mrs. Clark, who always had her hair done and wore a dress when Ed Sullivan's show came on because she was convinced he could see her.

During those walks to school, Danny and I would pass many girls making their way to St. Clement's School, which was close by. I took a fancy to one of them, so I started smiling at her, then saying good morning and then, much later, asking for a date of sorts. I had no car and little time for dates, but there were always school dances and the like. Anyway, those early get-togethers with this girl named Hope were forgettable, but eventually we became intimate and for my first sexual experience I couldn't have asked for a finer partner.

I remember vividly one occasion when a neighbour friend took us to his girlfriend's family farm in late May. It was a sunny and warm day and, taking a hint, Hope and I went for a walk in the woods. There was still some snow and ice in the thickets, but we eventually found a huge pine tree under which there was a deep bed of needles – an ideal spot for making love. We took off our clothes and enjoyed each other for a while when we suddenly heard a train whistle. We jumped up and ran into the meadow in time to see the train. The engineer waved and shouted unknown things at us but seemed to take delight in watching two nude kids hooting and hollering in the sunshine.

I always felt Hope and I had a special relationship and one day, a few decades later, I managed to learn where she was living and telephoned her. A woman answered the phone and I said, "Hope? It's John Dawe."

"What do you want?" she replied, and the conversation ended a few seconds later. I was shattered.

One of the most unusual relationships I had during those years was with a boarder at Havergal College named Katerina Kessler. I'm not sure how we met but we became fast, platonic friends and she enjoyed visiting our family home. I can't remember how she arrived at our house, but I know I walked her back to Havergal a number of times and it was quite a hike, especially in the winter. But we had fun times.

I could never figure out why Katerina and I had developed such a good relationship because our backgrounds were as different as night and day. But we enjoyed each other's company and we each talked a blue streak.

I always knew nothing serious would come of my relationship with Katerina, but one day she contacted me after being back home in Colombia for a break and asked me to join her at the Selby Hotel on Sherboune, just below Bloor. I was a bit taken aback as the invitation seemed unusual, but I went anyway, thinking, I guess, that we were about to get seriously involved. (The Selby Hotel had a reputation and not a good one, if I remember correctly.)

Well, aside from talking about our hopes and aspirations, some necking and petting, not much happened as I, for sure, was in no position to make any commitment. One of the things I remember distinctly was that she said she would never marry for money (and she came from a wealthy Colombian family in Bogota).

A few years later I received in Montreal a forwarded letter from her, inviting me to her upcoming nuptials to a Robert R. Snodgrass in the chapel at Harvard University. I never went because I frankly couldn't afford to do so. Katerina changed her given name to Kay and went on to become an award-winning printmaker, ending up in California.

Katerina was a great individual, what my wife Shirley would call a rich hippy. The reason I was so attracted to that kind of person (aside from the fact that she was a knockout) was because of someone I had met at North Toronto Collegiate a few years earlier.

Her name was Tania Tchernoussoff, the first Ukranian I came to know. Doubtless, Tania was the first free spirit, real eccentric I was to meet on my life journey, and there have been many. She was a cousin to Natalie Nesterenko, who was the great hockey player Eric Nesterenko's sister, both of whom went to NTCI.

Tania was an outsider, Slavic looking, and gifted with a sense of self and fun. We never really dated as such but hung out a lot. I've always wanted to find out what happened to her but it's like she left the radar screen in the late 50s and never returned.

Most of my pals from the early years at NTCI faded from view after I failed grade 11. But as I repeated that year, I made friends with a new group of mainly sports-oriented students. I wasn't allowed to play sports that year, having failed, but I stayed close to the football team as manager. I was fortunate to form many relationships with some terrific boys and girls, some of whom remained friends for life.

CHAPTER 8

Life Outside NTCI

One thing that struck me that first September when I started high school was how tanned most of the boys were. I eventually learned that most of these kids either didn't work during the summers or they worked at outside jobs where they could develop great tans. Many of them, of course, had cottages or went to camp.

That was never an option for me and, frankly, I enjoyed working during the summer to earn money and to help my mother out. I continued to do my paper route until 1959, just before heading to Montreal.

I delivered a route on Blythwood Road for just one year. It was considered a small route, starting at Yonge Street and heading east. Just beyond Blythwood P.S. I had one customer who lived in the original farmhouse and ran a nursery on the property just east of what is now the Sunny View School. Beyond that were open fields all the way to Bayview, unlike today when it's completely built up with detached housing. I had to travel from the farmhouse to Bayview to deliver one paper to the gatehouse of an estate situated just north of Sunnybrook Hospital. Every morning I saw lots of wildlife on that long journey, including foxes.

On the corner of Blythwood and Yonge, where Sporting Life now sits, was a service station and car dealership called Hyland Motors. I worked at Hyland Motors for a couple of years, pumping gas and greasing cars. I never had a driver's license, but I occasionally would drive a car, but stopped after two incidents. Once I took a car out for a spin and made too sharp a turn when bringing it back. I damaged the door and the owner, a working colleague, was livid. The other time I was returning a car from the workshop on the second floor when I stepped on the clutch instead of the brake, going around a corner, and flew into a display of oil cans, sending many through the air, and stopping only a few feet short of a huge glass window of the showroom.

Shortly afterward I left, not because I had to but because I let down my boss, Dave Gourlay, who was just the nicest person to work for. He eventually left to work at the Canadian Broadcasting Corporation, but by the time I got to work there he had retired.

When I wasn't working at Hyland Motors or at the Red and White store, I was a caddy at Rosedale Golf Club. I got to know some of the members well because I developed quickly into a Triple A caddy, and that meant I got a lot of the highly desirable carries. I was a favourite of one man who brought the same guest every summer, a white-haired southern U.S. gentleman who I understood was Chairman of Coca-Cola. After each round, this man would flip me a quarter (25 cents) and suggest I go buy a Coke. I never complained about tips but his were the cheapest.

Another great carry was Bill Twaits who either was or became Chairman and CEO of Imperial Oil in Canada, the country's most powerful oilman. As it happened, I also delivered The Globe and Mail to the Twaits family home on Hillhurst Avenue.

I met Bill Twaites' wife Fran and their two daughters, Judy and Sherry. Judy's and my paths would cross years later when my family moved from Montreal to Toronto in 1978 and I met Judy at a restaurant. It turned out she and her husband David Allan had a son similar in age to ours and they ended up going to the same schools for a while. But more importantly, our two families became fast friends and remain so to this day, sadly without Judy who died far too young of cancer.

Also living on Hillhurst was the Trevalyn family. One year they gave me as a Christmas gift, a Canadian silver dollar enclosed in a leather pouch inscribed "Here's Luck from the Trevalyns." Believe it or not, I still have that silver dollar and the pouch.

The only other story worth mentioning occurred early in my ownership of that route. I delivered newspapers heading west up the south side of the street, starting at Avenue Road almost to Bathurst Street then back down the north side. As I was a third of the way along the road one morning, I noticed someone getting out of a car and throwing something into some bushes on the opposite side. As I was returning, I saw that the person had hidden three car radios he had stolen from cars along the route.

Since I was almost finished delivering that morning, I bundled the radios into my two bags and took them home. This was a major chore – if you knew the size and weight of those car radios from the early 50s, you'd know what I mean.

When I got home, my mother suggested I take them to the police station, about six blocks south of us, and tell them what had happened. I did that and gave them a description of the car (vague) and the person (more vague). A few weeks later the police contacted me to tell me who the theft victims were. One of them was a customer who paid for their annual subscription directly to the *Globe* so I went up to their door and identified myself to the person who answered. He merely said "Thanks" and closed the door. There were some life lessons in that snub, but I won't get into that.

I continued to deliver newspapers during all but one of the

summers I worked on construction. I'd get up at around 4:30 a.m., deliver my papers, then come back home for breakfast, and change into work clothes to show up at two jobs over two summers. For one, I was a carpenter's apprentice working on the Ontario Health Insurance Plan building on Yonge near Eglinton. That building has now been replaced by a condominium, but it must have been hard to take down because it was an unbelievably solid building of reinforced concrete and brick.

Reinforced concrete has generally replaced steel girders in constructing buildings today, but there was a time when you only saw steel being used. The men who worked on those buildings, bridges and the like were steel riggers. Both Dad and Uncle Jack worked for Dominion Bridge at some point and, when I went to Elliot Lake to find work, the Dominion Bridge boss at that time, John Craw, was someone who had worked with my Dad and uncle. He hired me on the spot. I was not quite 18 but strong for my age; I had to be.

One of the jobs the Bridge had was the construction of a headframe for the Consolidated Denison Mine, a renowned uranium mine that created the fortune of founder Steve Roman. The headframe houses the cables that allow the miners' cages to penetrate deep into the mine shafts and to bring ore back to the surface. It's made of structural steel that's lifted into place and secured by a minimum number of bolts to allow the structure to go up quickly and efficiently. Later, a crew would follow the erectors to "bolt-up" the joins; I became a member of that crew.

By the time I joined the bolt-up crew the structure was more or less complete and towered some 225 feet into the air and was said to be the tallest headframe in North America. There were no lifts or ladders allowing the workers to ascend the structure; they had to climb like a monkey up the biggest support steel girders using boots with cork soles to allow grip. I took to this chore immediately and really enjoyed climbing the steel and walking along beams that were maybe six inches wide, sometimes with 100-pound tanks of oxygen or even heavier acetylene tanks on my shoulder.

A steel joint had, say, six holes for bolts. Three of those were filled by the erecting crew and the rest by our bolt-up crew. Sometimes the joints didn't line up and it was necessary to burn a bigger hole and that's why we needed the tanks of gas. Once a joint was completed, one of us would use a non-corrosive paint to protect the steel bolts.

It was necessary to leave the headframe to go to lunch in the commissary, a very large place that catered meals for all the different mine workers. It was operated by a firm called Crawley MacCracken that did mine catering and worker housing across Canada. Climbing down and back up after lunch was okay but I didn't want to do it often, say, when I needed to relieve myself. Instead I'd just find a quiet spot to one side and let go.

I remember vividly one day when I was at the top of the headframe and needed to pee. I proceeded to do so while standing on a six-inch beam. I could see the stream heading toward the ground, only to be picked up by a gust of wind and thrown right back into my face, and I had nowhere to duck. I never tried that again from the top.

Although I can't handle heights well today – frankly, I steer clear of them – my precarious workplace didn't bother me then. In my first week on the job, however, I dreamt I was falling off the steel and was awakened by a security guard who had heard me fall out of my top bunk onto the floor, where I remained sound asleep.

The mining camps attracted a diverse group of workers, the ones who prepared the facilities for the mining and milling: They were big, small, tall or fat and spoke a wide range of languages. They were also a tough group, but in my summer, I didn't witness one fight.

The Crawley MacCracken crews were even stranger. But they had some habits that were scary.

Elliot Lake had no outlet for alcohol and the only way to get some was to drive to Blind River, down on Highway 17. The men with cars would go to Blind River and bring back cases of beer, which they had to smuggle into the camp and hide. The catering crews, though, didn't have vehicles and took to meeting their cravings with after-shave lotion or the alcohol used in lamps. I remember one morning leaving our tent very early and having to step over one of the men, called bull cooks, who had passed out from drinking Aqua Velva; the bottle was close by.

I saw a lot of things that summer I worked at Elliot Lake.

The road leading from Highway 17 to Elliot Lake was gravel and, in many parts, the bed had to be raised because it travelled through bogs or other wetland. In those deep gullies beside the road were some remarkable skeletons of vehicles, mostly cars. Some of those workers made a lot of money, which they would use to buy the latest cars, then drive those cars at top speed along the road, often missing a turn, or swerving to avoid a deer or something and ending up in the deep ditches. They'd usually leave the cars there, and that made them vulnerable to scavengers who would take anything they could detach, including tires, seats and engine parts.

In 1986 during a road trip to Vancouver with my family, I diverted up that road to show them Elliot Lake and the mine where I had worked. Many of those skeletal cars were still there, almost 30 years later.

When my job at Dominion Bridge finished, I returned home, carrying with me a large amount of cash. For safety I kept it in large bills in my boot. I wanted so much to arrive home and, after going through the door, take that roll of bills and throw it into the air to show my mother how successful I had been. By the time I got home, my sweat had permeated the bills and what I threw in the air never separated and came down with a thud. Image ruined.

It was still only late July, early August, and at home I was bored. In a flash I was back in Elliot Lake and was able to find work as a surface labourer for the mining company until I had to return to school.

During that time, I met a fellow named David Ogden, from Toronto, who was a driver for the mine owner Stephen Roman. One day he regaled me with some anecdotes about Mr. Roman and one of them concerned the water he drank. I know that sounds crazy and it did to me, too, because Mr. Roman only drank bottled water from Italy. And this was 1957 when it wasn't readily available in stores. I told David I didn't believe him, so he took me to Mr. Roman's gorgeous home and showed me the storage room laden with cases of San Pellegrino. I took a bottle because I was compelled to try it and David was curious, too. I immediately spit it out because it tasted like water with rust in it (that's how I described it at the time). I was used to the pristine water from Quirk Lake.

Later in life, however, natural spring soda water became a mainstay in our fridge.

*Mother with her boys at the beginning of her long journey raising four
boys alone. From left, Larry, Frankie, Mother, me and Jimmy.*

First mode of transportation, c 1941.

Rare photo of Mother and Father before his hospitalization a few months after I was born.

Kathleen Graham helped out while Mother was away caring for Dad and Larry was hospitalized for observation. Left, Jimmy, Kathleen and Frankie with me up front, c1941.

*Dad on the day in 1940 he entered Weston Sanitorium which he never
left except for two AWOL episodes and his passing in 1947*

My one and only visit with Santa Claus at Eaton's with family friend Susan Morgan, c 1941

I was not my normal happy self in this c, 1953 family photo. A few years later I was the tallest.

Football rebel at North Toronto Collegiate.

Dressing for Havergal College formal dance in late 50's. The brush cut didn't work for me.

My oldest friend Dan Ghikadis.

I was Marilyn McCabe's first boyfriend at NTCI in 1954. She left me for my friend Danny, then married an old friend from JRR, Ray Blair. We're still great friends.

Golfing at Myrtle Beach South Carolina with two of my oldest buddies, Ian Henderson, left, and Bob Hughes.

CHAPTER 9

The Royal York Hotel

On another summer job, I joined a union as a student (unions encouraged students to work on jobs, hoping they would take to the trades later in life) and worked as a hod carrier on the construction of a new wing for the Royal York Hotel. I was a member of the hod carriers union but worked solely for a bricklayer. The longest job was tiling the inside of the new elevator shaft.

It must have been my lucky summer because something happened that could have killed me but only caused a few scratches.

We were installing tile in the elevator shaft and were working on about the eighth floor this one day, when the scaffold gave way and I fell about 20 feet. My bricklayer wasn't there, and I had been piling bricks for that shift on a scaffold that had been erected by labourers. I only fell a relatively short distance because just two weeks prior, the government agency, the Workmen's Compensation Board, had changed some labour safety practices, including the use in elevator construction of full wooden plank floors on which to build scaffolds. Previously they just ran a few planks across the opening. When I fell, I thankfully relaxed somewhat and only suffered some scratches. I was very lucky.

Ironically, that east side addition to the Royal York Hotel in 1958 failed to motivate the hotel's owner in 2019 when it decided to renovate another of their hotels, the Chateau Laurier in Ottawa. Their plan for an addition to that iconic hotel next door to Parliament Hill was to be a modern glass and steel structure that was, in the opinion of just about everyone except Ottawa City Council, an eyesore and a travesty.

At time of writing the plan was still up in the air, but critics could have saved a lot of debate by simply pointing out what was done to the iconic Royal York Hotel back in the 50s. The new wing in Toronto was an exact replica of the original design built in the 20s, giving the building integrity and balance.

A year after working on the Royal York expansion, the hotel would be the venue for another experience. That story unfolded in 1957, the year I worked as an apprentice high steel rigger in Elliot Lake, northern Ontario.

I have mentioned that Elliot Lake had no outlet for alcohol and the only way to get some was to drive to Blind River. The men with cars would go to Blind River and bring back cases of beer. I went on one of these trips and it resulted in meeting a young woman called Marilyn Johnson, who attended a close-by camp for wealthy young ladies, many of whom came from the United States. We struck up a friendship, platonic, that would be short-lived.

Marilyn was from Grosse Point, Michigan, where her family lived on an estate made possible by her father's involvement in bringing fibreglass technology for cars to Detroit, at a time when there was a push to reduce car weight and increase gas mileage.

My brother Frank who, along with some friends, had also worked at Elliot Lake, met the camp girls, too, and that fall he and the boys drove to Michigan to see them. It was an exaggeration to be sure, but Frank said the drive into Marilyn's house at Grosse Point took about ten minutes. Befriending Marilyn was one of only a few times

I flirted with the wealthy of the day. She was really cute but had bands on her teeth that made kissing almost painful, so we seldom did. Nothing else ever happened but we became close friends and wrote each other weekly.

In September 1957, she wrote to tell me she was coming to Toronto for a visit with her mother. They would stay at the Royal York Hotel and I was invited for lunch in their suite.

It was an embarrassing situation for me because I didn't know how to handle myself in the face of such opulence. I can still remember the look on Marilyn's mother's face when I watched the waiters bring the lunch into the dining room of the suite. Lots of silver and crystal for what was a basic soup and a sandwich offering.

Needless to say, this trip taught Marilyn a valuable lesson, one that I'm sure her mother had predicted. I don't think it needs spelling out here.

As I think about my times at the Royal York Hotel another memory comes flooding back.

In 1959 my oldest brother and I had taken a motoring trip to Vancouver, just the two of us. I really wasn't a driver (as you may have gathered from earlier comments) but he thought it would work out anyway.

It was a great adventure. We drove mostly through the United States because the TransCanada Highway system hadn't been completed and the American roads were just so much better. We had little money and decided to sleep in the car until we got to Vancouver, where our brother Larry would put us up in his shared apartment.

Our first night on the road we got one helluva scare. We were in northern Michigan and had gone to an A&W for some fast food, which we ate in the car and then proceeded to sleep. At about two or three in the morning, we were awakened by shouting and then lights filling the car, followed by, seriously, machine guns at the windows.

As it happened, two convicts had escaped from a nearby prison and a widespread search for them brought a few carloads of deputies to the roadside rest area where we had parked. It was a scene right out of a gangster movie. They quickly went on their way after some brief conversation, but it was a very scary half hour or so for us. It didn't deter us, though, and we saw some amazing things on our journey, including the petrified forest in North Dakota.

At one point we were driving in a straight line through farmland for what seemed like forever. It was late summer, and the corn was high. The road in this one area was raised above the farmland so there was a deep shoulder. We saw the most beautiful woman wearing very little, walking on the opposite side of the road. We honked as we drove past and she waved so Jimmy stopped the car and reversed to have a chat. As we stopped, we saw she was smiling, but what we hadn't seen was the leash she was holding, which she tugged, and two very spirited Doberman Pinschers appeared from the deep shoulder. We got the hell out of there very fast, waving to the woman who was having a good laugh.

The other notable thing that happened was that I experienced a dramatic change in the temperature for the first time. I'm pretty sure it was in Montana. It had to be more than 80 degrees Fahrenheit on the prairie, and we had no air conditioning. In the early evening, we dropped into a valley and I swear the temperature was 40 or less. I couldn't believe the change. Later in life I would experience a similar temperature change in an African desert.

We got to Vancouver and settled in for a few days and I remember only one thing about the time spent there. We had gone out drinking beer one Saturday afternoon and I over-indulged, so when we got back to our brother's apartment, I proceeded to fall asleep on the floor. Jimmy, meanwhile, went to pick up his date for that evening, a woman he had met while working in B.C. a few years before. The next thing I remember was this absolutely stunning woman towering over me and urging me to get up, to which I replied, "Fuck you," and went back to sleep.

That woman was Anna Finlayson and she was supposed to be my date that night. Instead we never spoke again until she came to Toronto a few months later for the Grey Cup festivities. She was there as Miss B.C. Lions and ended up winning the Miss Grey Cup title. She called me from the Royal York Hotel, which was Grey Cup Central in those days, and said she had a game ticket for me.

How great was that? She asked me to come down to the hotel and meet her mother, her chaperone for the whole event, and I readily agreed. When I got to the hotel, though, I couldn't get through on the house line and the front desk did not allow me on the upper floors. When I tried to sneak up, the house security grabbed me and, literally, threw me down the stairs. I eventually got the ticket, but it was after the event. I still have it.

CHAPTER 10

Remembering the Hugger

Many relationships were formed with some terrific boys and girls at NTCI but the one that stayed into my senior years was with Bob Hughes. When I said earlier that Bob Hughes deserved a chapter, I should have said he deserved an entire book, because few people I have known have had a life like his.

We rarely talked about his growing up prior to NTCI but I do know he was born in Dundas, Ontario, an only child, whose father was in the navy and, I believe, died at the end of the war. He lived with his mother, Esther, but received guidance from a man who was a shipmate of his father. This man worked in Great Lakes shipping and I remember Bob telling us about a job he had, working in the galley of one of the lake boats. It was during this time that Bob discovered booze, something that would lead him into situations that the rest of his friends could only experience through novels or the movies.

I should say here and now that Bob was tall, in great physical shape, thanks to his involvement in sport, and very handsome, not to mention having more charm than anyone deserved at such a young age, hence his nickname, "The Hugger." He played goal in hockey and was fearless. He was a forward in basketball, a wide receiver in football and was outstanding in all of them. It goes without saying, the girls adored him.

One time we double-dated and went to the Northeast drive-in theatre over near Agincourt. Bob had this hot girlfriend and she had a friend who became my date. I managed to secure a pint of whiskey for us, but neither girl wanted any, and Bob was driving so he refrained (he was smart that way). We weren't far into the forgettable movie when Bob and his date started to make out, and I took that as a sign to make moves, too. My advances were rebuffed and, having had a few drinks to embolden me, I quietly left the car.

I don't know what I was thinking. I was about ten miles from home – about 16 km – and there was no public transportation. So, I walked, had a nip, then walked, had a nip, then walked, until I made it to Fran's restaurant, our hangout at Yonge and Eglinton, some four hours later. I wasn't there long when Bob came in and gave me absolute hell for leaving and ruining his evening. I was sober by this time and only laughed, saying it was good to see a friendly face.

Bob heard the siren call of making money as an insurance salesman. Before he completed Grade 13, he left NTCI and began leading what we called then "The Good Life" – car, apartment, money, girls, you name it. At one point he was living in a Rosedale coach house he shared with another fellow.

Bob always had the great girls and one of them was a well-known model named Ulla Moreland. She had movie star looks and the two of them were the best- looking couple in town. A real power couple.

We never double-dated again and we lost touch for several years as Bob burned the candle at both ends, and I went to school and worked the rest of the time. But our lives would become intertwined many years later.

CHAPTER II

Angry Young Man

Failing Grade 11 was a huge learning experience. I had made a mistake by trying to be a smart-ass and paid a price.

My friends, of course, moved on and while my relationship with Danny didn't change that much, it was different. He and the others went on to bigger things while I repeated a year and suffered the humiliation of failure.

Offsetting this partially was that I got to know groups of different people, a tad younger but full of fun, so the year wasn't a total waste of time. I wasn't allowed to play sports, which was OK because I needed to work anyway, but I did participate in games as a coach's assistant of sorts.

It was with this group that I played what we affectionately called "The Rosé Bowl" (as in the wine) over the Christmas holidays at the NTCI field. It was a football game with tackling but no pads. Stupid, really, because one or more of us could have been badly injured. But the wine made us loose, I guess.

I excelled at pass defence and in the following season my pals asked the coach to let me play defensive safety, but he refused. Bob Gladish held a grudge a long time.

On one occasion I remember a tall, strong fellow named Ed

Ociena got the ball and charged through the line. There was only me between him and the end zone, so I threw all caution to the wind and held my ground. I stopped him cold and he never let me forget how surprised he was at my foolhardiness but praised my guts. Ed went on to play in the Canadian Football League – for Calgary, I believe.

Having the right clothes was always an issue at NTCI but the culture was changing, albeit slowly. I remember one of my pals organized an Ed Norton Day when he encouraged all the guys to wear clothes similar to those of the television character played by Art Carney in "The Honeymooners" – t-shirts and overalls. It caused quite a stir.

Around the same time, we struck against a school policy and we all left the building, either forcibly or on our own. Not long after, the main body went back in but I didn't. Many years later, one of my pals from those days, Dinah Christie of TV and cabaret fame, told me: "We all looked back and there you were on your own, smoking a cigarette and refusing to budge while we all trudged back in."

I left high school with a diploma but not senior matriculation. For that I needed to pass an exam in trigonometry. Maths always gave me trouble ,but I found trig the worst. Still, I needed it. So, in June 1960, I arrived at a University of Toronto facility to write that exam a second time. I walked into this huge space filled with what seemed like hundreds and hundreds of desks, paused, then turned around and walked out. I just couldn't face it.

A few days later I was on a train for Montreal where a construction job awaited. My plan was to make enough money to go to the University of British Columbia. Why UBC? My brother Larry lived out there in a house and promised me a couch to crash on until I could get established. It was a great plan.

Great, that is, until I discovered the delights of living in Montreal.

There was no way I could leave the city for Vancouver. So, armed with my papers I went to the McGill University registrar's office to apply there. When they saw my marks, they smiled and showed me the door.

Undeterred, I ended up going to Sir George Williams University (now Concordia), taking three, night courses. Unfortunately, that didn't last long because by then I was working at the *Montreal Gazette* and my journalism career had its scratchy start.

But I'm getting ahead of myself again. A lot happened before that.

CHAPTER 12

Montreal – The Beginning

After an uneventful train trip, I found myself in downtown Montreal on University Street, looking at a wonderful building that housed the Zeta Psi Fraternity where I was to live for about three years, even though originally I was going to be there only temporarily while I got my life together in preparation for Vancouver.

My brother Frank, who is a Zete, was already there for the summer and I was welcomed by the fraternity because they were always interested in having residents to help cover their costs. Little did they know I would become a fixture for so long.

Initially, they must have had their doubts. Fraternity brothers, as they're called, are generally drawn from the middle or upper classes. In Montreal it appeared to be all upper class. Yet, here I was, an outsider who left early in the morning dressed like a tradesman and returned in the evening looking, well, dirty. Construction can be, after all, a dirty job and I was a bricklayer's apprentice, which meant I mixed mortar and carried it and the bricks to the bricklayers using a hod. In Toronto I was a member of the Hod Carriers Union but in Montreal that wasn't necessary.

The job itself was interesting. We were re-bricking a huge wall that covered the south side of what was left of the Windsor Hotel.

This renowned hotel on Peel Street opposite Dorchester Square (now Boul. René Lévesque) had suffered a fire on its south side so it was demolished and the land sold to developers of the Canadian Imperial Bank of Commerce tower. It meant the south side of the hotel had to be finished both above and below ground, giving the bricklayers plenty of work.

I was paying $25 a month for my shared room at the fraternity and that included breakfast five days a week. What I normally did for dinner after work was stop at the Rymark Tavern just up the street where I could eat like a king for very little money. Occasionally I would eat things I'd never touch at home, like pig's feet and sauerkraut.

Best of all, though, I could have a quart of beer, and while I was enjoying one of those one evening, I was invited to join a table of "suits," guys who worked in offices and who met there most days.

Well, one beer led to two which led to three and that was it for me, but during that gathering, I was inducted into their group. They called themselves "The Apache Killers" and because I had gotten a buzz on early, I was considered a scout. Membership in this group was confirmed by a handwritten form that could only be written on the back of a package of Export A cigarettes. I still have that.

In the day, that was a fun thing but, of course, I knew little then about most things, and certainly nothing about Quebec's treatment of Indigenous people, nor their long- time attitude toward them. There were no Apaches in Quebec and it was all a figment of their imagination. Today we would call it racist, but then it seemed genu- inely amusing.

One evening we were joined by a celebrity hockey player who was staying at the Mount Royal Hotel across the street. He didn't drink any more, having sworn off a year or so before, but knew the guys from those days when he would drop into the Rymark on arriving in town for a game at the Forum, Montreal's hockey mecca.

The player was Eric Nesterenko. Eric played for the Chicago Blackhawks. I had gone to high school with his cousin Tania and fleetingly knew his sister Natalie. I always used to think the world was such a huge place, but I was beginning to understand that it was very small, indeed.

Another noteworthy event took place while I was working at the hotel. It concerned a speech there one afternoon by Prime Minister John Diefenbaker. It was at a meeting of the Canadian Club, and to get the Prime Minister to speak was an honour. The construction team was told that we could work up to the time he was scheduled to speak but then we had to lay down our tools and find something else to do.

Only a year before, Mr. Diefenbaker had cancelled the Avro Arrow project and, although I knew nothing about the politics of the decision at that time, I knew it caused a lot of grief in Ontario with tremendous job losses, not to mention the loss of prestige, because we were developing a fine reputation for excellence in the field of avionics. Canada had become home to a large number of aviation engineers from Britain and Europe who had left after the war to find work in North America. We attracted thousands of great minds.

These great minds were lost to Canada with the cancellation and almost all of them went to the U.S. where they worked for, among others, NASA. Canada lost its extremely advanced industry. Interestingly, experts were saying that the Arrow could have been as useful in 2018 with electronic upgrades as it was then.

We could have had a superior aviation industry. Instead, the government opted in 1962 to buy Bomarc missiles with nuclear warheads from the U.S. as our contribution to North American security. They were obsolete and scrapped nine years later.

The Arrow cancellation was a blow. I felt I had to say something since the perpetrator was in town but getting close to him was impossible. Instead I did something foolish.

I had been told what time Mr. Diefenbaker was going to start his speech. I waited a few minutes to allow for a delay and then opened up in the hotel basement with a huge jackhammer that was used for breaking up concrete and brick. The noise was deafening and since I was immediately below the room where the speech was being given, it caused an uproar.

I half expected to be fired but wasn't. I never paid attention to the media in those days so I didn't know if the action made it into any reports. I knew and that was enough for me.

That job finished right about the time winter began to settle in. The thought of working on construction didn't appeal and I was told I was eligible for unemployment insurance. So, I quit and applied for UI. It was perhaps the most humiliating thing I had ever done or would ever do. I received one cheque for $25, but getting it forced me to lie and to humble myself before public servants. I swore I'd never do it again.

Part of my survival technique was to use an electric frying pan my mother had given me to heat up canned Chef Boyardee pasta and other canned foods. I had to be careful because residents were not allowed to have such devices in their rooms. I can still conjure the smell of that sauce with all those additives.

The biggest blow to my ego at the time but one that taught me another great life lesson occurred when I was convinced to use an employment agency to find a job. At the northeast corner of Ste. Catherine and Peel streets, the Ace Employment Agency was headquartered in a small second floor office above the retail stores. It was called Ace... I kid you not.

I didn't have the clothes to think about getting into retail, which I favoured because of my past grocery store experience. The counsellor ended up making an appointment for me at a company in the rag trade.

The next day I put on my only sport coat, nicely pressed pants and a recently ironed shirt for an interview I confidently knew I could master. And I did. The owner of the clothing company was overweight, poorly dressed and smoked a cigar in a messy office. While I stood in front of him, I noticed a sign over his head: Caveat Emptor, it read.

"What does that mean?" I enquired.

"You don't know Latin?" he responded. "Buyer beware," he continued.

He then proceeded to explain that the job was as a shipper in the basement. It was menial work, he implied, but really important. "We have to get our orders out right and on time. If you do well, you can move up to sales." It paid about $40 a week.

We chatted for a while and he rose to shake my hand, indicating I had the job and he'd see me the next day. I was elated. But the positive mood didn't last. Later that day, Ace called to say the job had been filled by a recent immigrant who was prepared to do it for $25 a week. I never forgot the guy or that sign or the fact that there was always someone out there hungry enough to work for less, if it meant working at all. It was a competitive world and I had to get used to it.

I was feeling a little depressed, so I reluctantly decided to go back to Toronto. When I discussed things with my mother, she gave me advice that at the time seemed ludicrous but today would make a lot of sense: "If you want security, become a policeman, a fireman or a garbageman. What you'll have is a secure income and benefits."

The thought of doing any one of those jobs was abhorrent to me. After Christmas I went back to Montreal armed with the first and only loan I ever asked of my stepfather, some $200. I wasn't back long when another Zeta Psi House resident, Jim Van Vliet, who was a sports reporter for the *Gazette*, told me that his friend John Meyer, the financial editor, was looking for a department junior.

The only thing I knew about journalism was that I had spent more than a decade delivering *The Globe and Mail* and, for a short time, the *Toronto Star* and the *Telegram*. I knew something else, though.

A friend of my brother Larry's had been a reporter but had left journalism and was now in public relations. He was a great raconteur who always regaled us with fascinating stories, and I thought he had a job that would suit me to a tee.

That came to mind when Jim told me about the job, so the next day I went to meet John Meyer. We hit it off and I was hired for the sum of $25 a week. That was more than enough to allow me to book the dinner plan at the fraternity, five days of dinners a week for a modest monthly fee of $15.

Having a job and living with some good friends meant the world to me. I'd never had a car and really didn't need one because I walked everywhere or, when absolutely necessary, took taxis or public transport. And everything I needed in my world was within walking distance of my room, including my workplace.

More about the beginning of my journalism career at the *Gazette* later. But first I have to digress to open up about something that was almost as important as my first job.

CHAPTER 13

Meeting Elizabeth

While I was living at the Zeta Psi house, I met some guys who liked to play English rugby. They invited me to join them and I readily accepted. Montreal at that time had a few teams that played each other and against anyone else who enjoyed rugby, which meant some U.S. universities.

We went to Dartmouth College in New Hampshire for the first foreign outing. I don't remember too much about it other than that we had a terrific time. But the next U.S. visit was to New York City to play New York University.

For those who knew, rugby wasn't about playing the game as much as it was about drinking beer afterward. I don't remember anything about that game but what happened afterward changed my life. That's because I met Elizabeth McAulay.

Try to picture this: You wake up from a deep sleep to find yourself on a hard floor with all your clothes on and in a surrounding that's completely foreign. The hangover isn't that bad. What the hell was I doing there? Where the hell was I? Who was the person looking at me from above?

Elizabeth took her time to explain that we had met at the tavern where the teams had regrouped after the game. We'd talked, and since I'd got separated from my mates, she'd invited me back to her flat on Bleeker Street in Greenwich Village where she'd prepared a spot on the floor for me to crash. And crash I did, obviously. Nothing had transpired between us, in fact, and I had been a perfect gentleman, which is why she didn't hesitate to help me.

We talked for a long time about a lot of things when I suddenly remembered I had driven to New York with two of my friends and I had no idea where they were, how to reach them (no cell phones then) or how I was going to get back to Montreal with no money. It was a panicky situation, but I remained fairly cool, thanked Elizabeth for everything, and went out into the street to look, heaven knows where, for my friends.

It's hard to believe, but a few minutes later as I'm walking the streets of the Village, I see my two friends, who were out looking for me! Obviously, there was a guardian angel on my shoulder and as far as I was concerned, it was Elizabeth.

Soon after we got back to Montreal, I wrote to her in what would be the beginning of a friendship that I resisted encouraging further because it would never have worked. Elizabeth came from a very wealthy family and I had had a few too many relationships with young women from wealthy families that ended badly.

Still, in a way, Elizabeth became my "Henry Higgins," introducing me to some literature she loved, explaining its significance, and turning me into someone who wanted to learn about more sophisticated aspects of life: literature, of course, but classical music, dance, live theatre and film (not movies, about which I was well aware).

Without question, the most important literature Elizabeth introduced me to was *The Prophet*. I believe it's the third most popular book ever written, after the Bible and the Quran (Koran).

The Prophet is a book of 26 fables written in English by the Lebanese American poet and writer Khalil Gibran. The fables cover all aspects of life and offer simple but thoughtful ideas for living the many stages of a full life. It is spiritual but not moralistic or judgmental and is one of the most quoted books at weddings and funerals.

Coupled with the Golden Rule, *The Prophet* offers a guide to living a rich and honourable life. While I cannot claim total adherence to the teachings, I have tried my best to live up to them.

In effect, Elizabeth set me on a path of expanding my interests and being open to new ideas. I started in earnest to write poetry but most of it was pedantic and simplistic. But she said she enjoyed it and found herself responding in kind. But I never did pursue most of Elizabeth's literary recommendations because to do so would take time I didn't feel I had. I did purchase and enjoy *The Unquiet Grave* by Cyril Connolly but failed in my attempts to read fully and understand Jean-Paul Sartre's *Being and Nothingness* or the novels of his lover, Simone de Beauvoir. I had a superficial understanding of existentialism but couldn't grasp it completely.

At one point, Elizabeth got frustrated that I wasn't responding to her letters quickly enough and she decided to come and see me.

She came to Montreal and asked me to meet her and her aunt and uncle at a French restaurant that was top of the food chain, as we say, in Montreal. It was called Café Martin and I didn't know a soul who could afford to go there. Anyway, I arrived and the maitre d' escorted me to a private room upstairs where my hosts were waiting. Much of what happened that night is a blur, but I do know it brought to mind my experience with my young Michigan friend and her mother at the Royal York Hotel in Toronto several years previously.

The evening was the beginning of the end for our relationship. We did stay in touch and Elizabeth wanted to give it more time, but she ended up going abroad to study and work. The last piece of mail I received (and sadly cannot find) was an announcement in the

New York Times of her engagement. The photograph captured her extraordinary beauty but also the class and poise that scared the hell out of me.

How do you quantify the influence of a friend on your life? It's hard to put into words but you just know that you're a better person for having known that person. Their interests become your interests, so communication becomes richer. You see the world through different eyes and events through different distillations. Debates that had two sides turn into discussions with many sides. When your friend reaches deep into their being to share knowledge and experience, you are enhanced beyond belief though you may not realize it until later.

I'll never forget Elizabeth.

CHAPTER 14

Non-brothers in the House

Living at a McGill fraternity house had its advantages. It was cheap, centrally located and within walking distance of my work, and there was a constant flow of interesting people to meet and befriend. Some of these people had a big influence on me, such as the great actor Walter Massey, a sports journalist named Jim Van Vliet, and a medical student named Al Scriggins.

Walter took me under his wing and taught me about live theatre. I saw every one of his performances at the Mountain Playhouse, an English theatre on the top of Mount Royal that once had William Shatner as its business manager. One production was a musical called *The Boy Friend* and to this day, I still remember most of the words to two of its songs: "I could be happy with you"… and … "All I want is a room in Bloomsbury."

It wasn't long thereafter that the theatre closed (more for political reasons than financial – having an English-language theatre on top of the city's iconic mountain didn't wash with the French-Canadian majority). Walter ended up doing film and TV roles but, for me, it wasn't the same. He was a founding member of Canadian Actors' Equity and he was a cousin of the great Hollywood legend Raymond Massey. We stayed in touch while I lived in Montreal but lost contact with my move to Toronto in 1978. Walter died in 2014 just shy of his 86th birthday.

Jim Van Vliet was an eccentric sports journalist with the *Gazette*. He did two things for me for which I will be eternally grateful: He introduced me to John Meyer, financial editor of the *Gazette*, who was looking for a junior in his department. I won the job and that set me on a course that led to extraordinary work experiences, world travel and celebrity status. But that's well down the road. Jim also introduced me to his sister.

Caire Van Vliet expanded my understanding of other literature and art, mainly printmaking. She founded Janus Press in California in 1955 and became a leading typographer in the United States as well as a teacher of drawing and printmaking in Philadelphia. Jim introduced us and we became pen pals for many years. Not long after we met, she moved to Vermont and I used to visit her there after I became a landowner in northern Vermont in 1976. I have most of her letters and a few tiny woodcut prints that I had framed and still enjoy.

Jim left Montreal while I was still there and ended up reporting sports for the *Cleveland Plain Dealer*. He always carried too much weight and smoked heavily, leading to an early death. Claire is still living in Newport, Vermont.

Al Scriggins lives there, too, or rather did in the 70s. He studied medicine at McGill because he wanted to open a family practice in a small Vermont town where he would live with his wife "Bones" (her true name was Gigi) and their children in a house with a white picket fence. He did all of that, but his wife died at a young age and the dream was shattered.

Al took me on as a project to teach me about classical music. I had loved all kinds of music my whole life but here I was, 21 years old, and I knew nothing about classical music.

Al accompanied me on a classical journey starting with the great symphonies. I wasn't learning about structure so much as mood and feelings. I could feel the passion in Bach and Tchaikovsky. And when he played the "Polovtsian Dances" from Borodin's *Prince Igor* I swooned as I heard one of my favourite tunes: "Stranger in Paradise" from the musical *Kismet*. The writing was attributable to two Americans, but the melody was a direct lift from *Prince Igor*.

A few others from those days at the Zeta Psi House have played key roles in my life.

My closest friend became David Nunn, a well-travelled young man from Vancouver whose family operated a funeral home business on Cambie right across from city hall. He wasn't working at about the same time I wasn't, so we spent a lot of time together. He, too, knew a lot about classical music.

Through David I met David Graham, the youngest of the large Graham clan that lived in a huge home on Point Grey in Vancouver. David spent a lot of time on business in the east, so we saw a lot of him and were devastated by his early death. Another delightful character I met then was Peter Brown, of Vancouver, who accumulated wealth and prestige through a stock brokerage business. John Culter was another Vancouver boy living at the Zeta Psi House for a while and we kept in touch mainly through Facebook.

There were others from Vancouver, too, but this group became very special to me because when I got married, none of my family attended the wedding in Vancouver, so I prevailed upon David Nunn to be my Best Man and the others to be ushers, which they all readily agreed to do.

Once, when things were really desperate, I did something that I think emboldened me on many other occasions that called for unusual strategies. The Zetes were having one of their famous parties – probably the Milk Punch Party – but as residents we were allowed to attend parties as long as we behaved. It doesn't matter how poor you are, when you've got friends, there will always be a beer or two available, at least in this house.

We were enjoying a beer and talking about the guests when one of my buddies directed our attention to this absolutely gorgeous girl. He told us she was just terrific, smart and lots of fun, a cheerleader and one of the most popular girls on campus. He looked at me and said, "I'll give you $5 if you go over and bite her on the ass."

I was pretty much broke, with just enough to pay my rent, so five dollars was a lot of money in those days – about $40 today – so I said, "Sure."

I walked over to her, somewhat nervously, tapped her on the shoulder and said, "Hi, I'm John Dawe and I'm poor as a church mouse. There's a guy over there who'll give me $5 if I bite your ass."

Much to my surprise, she laughed and said, "Sure, here, but don't break the skin," and stuck out her gorgeous backside in full view of the guys. Her name was Claudia Hulme and I'll never forget her kindness.

Another time someone took me to a McGill lecture being given by the American novelist Norman Mailer. In his speech, which I found narcissistic, he referred to something I'd never heard before. He suggested that all of us have built-in "shit detectors" and these come into play when watching a film, reading a book and so on.

We were among the last to leave the lecture hall and found ourselves face to face with Mr. Mailer. I thanked him for his speech and said my shit detector had been working overtime all night.

I had forgotten his reputation for being pugilistic. He clenched his fists and had to be constrained, else I believe he would have belted me. Probably with some justification because I was being rude, if nothing else.

CHAPTER 15

Some of the Women in My Life

What we used to do at the weekends if there were no other plans was call up the nurses' residence at Royal Victoria Hospital and invite the nurses down for a party. The Zete House had a great party room and sound system. We had a beer machine and those who could afford it bought wine by the gallon.

I met some fabulous girls that way, although not one of whom did I get to know intimately, but we had great times, nonetheless.

One was Leslie McGrath, whose politician father, James McGrath, of Newfoundland, was instrumental in helping the Norwegian explorer Helge Ingstad in his quest to discover whether Vikings had inhabited North America as far back as the year 1000.

Helge Ingstad, his wife Anne Stine and daughter Benedicte had travelled to Montreal in the spring of 1961 to join their boat, the *Halten*, which had earlier come from Norway. It was berthed in Montreal harbour and being outfitted for their journey of discovery.

I met the Ingstads at the harbour and we got on famously. They asked me if I would like to join them on their journey and I made one of the few decisions in my life I came to regret; I said no. My reasoning was simple: I badly needed to work for some income and such a project would be a luxury.

The Ingstads went on to discover the extraordinary Viking settlement Vinland at what we call L'Anse aux Meadows at the tip of the Great Northern Peninsula of Newfoundland, thereby proving that the Vikings had discovered and inhabited North America about 500 years before Christopher Columbus.

Leslie and I kept in touch for several years, too, and I used to remind her I was one fellow she'd never forget. The reason? One day while we were visiting the Ingstads, we took a little tender out for a row in the harbour. She was rowing and I was admiring a very sharp seaman's knife I'd found in the tender when a wake from a ship hit the boat, and while I was grabbing the side to steady myself, the knife slipped into Leslie's leg. She still had a noticeable scar several decades later.

One of the other nurses I spent a lot of time with was Laurel Whitty, an American, who was blonde and bubbly, a great soul who went by the nickname Lolly. We spent hours talking and walking the McGill campus. Our best moments were lying on the grass and looking at the night sky for satellites and shooting stars. Satellites were in their infancy and still a wonder of the world, so we took great delight in spying them. We shared dreams, hopes and aspirations: One of mine was to travel extensively and that became a reality in ways I could not have imagined.

There was one other nursing student I will simply call Judy, whom I tried hard to court. She was from Alberta and a remarkable, dark-haired beauty. We spent a lot of time together, but nothing ever came of it (we used to say "I never even got to first base"). I did notice, though, that her classmates weren't all that friendly toward her and I thought it was jealousy because of her star-like beauty. It wasn't until after graduation and I was in touch with one of the nurses that I learned, when they were packing up to leave residence, somebody saw that a large chest that Judy had kept locked and guarded in her room was open. She lifted the lid to find it filled with cashmere sweaters and other articles of clothing that had gone missing from many of the girls.

I relate this anecdote mainly because for me it was a lesson in how appearances can be deceiving, and it was a lesson well learned.

At some point during this time, I met my first French-Canadian girl. I cannot tell you her name, but I will call her Celine. The chemistry between us was remarkable. We did all the things young people do when they're dating and don't have money or a car. In other words, we talked a lot, walked and danced to records at the frat house.

At a point some two or three months into our relationship, Celine said something to me in French and I couldn't believe what I was hearing.

"Johnnie," she called me with the cutest French accent, "je suis vierge and I don't want to stay that way." We discussed this for a quite a while that night, with me explaining the gravity of such a big step, believe it or not. It took me several weeks to finally acquiesce and it wasn't something I was comfortable doing.

A few weeks later Celine fessed up to why she'd decided to lose her virginity and with me. In short, it had to do with peer pressure from girlfriends and, perhaps more important, she didn't want people in her community to find out, so an English boy she trusted would be ideal.

Celine and I saw less and less of each other after she confessed her reasons for wanting her entry into womanhood, as she called it. It would in fact be several months before I heard from her again and the news was disturbing.

She needed my help because she'd got "into trouble," at least that's how she described it. She had nobody to turn to for financial help. She was really distraught, so I knew she was being truthful, but

I still had to see her in person. She came to the frat house and told me a story that I suspect is all too common.

She and some friends had accepted an invitation to go to someone's cottage in the Laurentians one weekend. There was lots of drinking and the boys (as she called them) got aggressive and demanding. The girls, she said, resisted but to no avail, and more than one of them was brutalized and raped.

I was in shock but expressed some doubts about her story. She told me to lift the back of her sweater, which I did, only to see awful bruising and welt marks from blows. She also had serious bruising on her upper arms, all of it still fresh-looking after the two months that had passed. I remember tearing up as she told me how hard she had to work to keep the incident from her parents and friends. But worst of all, she told me she was pregnant. She needed to get an abortion, and fast, but she didn't have the financial resources.

I was working but making only a puny salary and still living at the fraternity house. The only way I could get her the $250 for the procedure, which she assured me was safe, was to sell some shares I had just bought to start a financial portfolio. The shares were in a small company I learned about through my work at Canadian Pacific Railway. I had bought 100 shares at 50 cents each and they were now worth $2.50. I sold them and gave her the money.

Celine was most grateful and promised to repay me somehow. I never had the heart to tell her later that those shares rose to $21 each when the company was taken over a year later by none other than the CPR.

We only saw each other once again when she gave me something she thought would satisfy her debt. It was something I couldn't use and later gave away. Sadly, she called me looking for that item, saying she'd made a mistake, and was devastated when I told her it was gone.

The last time I heard from Celine was about 20 years later. I was working for Global News and she was now married to an anglophone, living in Ontario and watching me daily. She called to reconnect but I was going through some heady times back then and didn't take the time to chat.

I felt I did the right thing in helping Celine, but I regret now not remaining her friend, one of the most sensitive women I've ever met.

That memory, though, brings to mind another for which I am also truly regretful. It began while I was working at the *Gazette* as a junior in the financial editorial department and I joined the Montreal Men's Press Club, which was housed at the Mount Royal Hotel.

I wasn't much of a drinker, but it bolstered my ego to belong to a club where a lot of my colleagues from the *Gazette* hung out, along with those from the *Montreal Star* and a few other publications, and a host of public relations practitioners who were the biggest spenders.

I was there one weeknight when a member brought three women in to have a drink. One of them was a very attractive divorcée – I'll call her Claire – and I successfully hit on her. She gave me her number and when I called a few days later, she invited me for a drink at her place, a 20-minute bus ride away. In those days at the *Gazette* I was making $25 a week, so taxis were out of the question and I walked everywhere, except to Claire's place, which was really convenient by bus.

Claire had two young children and we got on well, though, to be fair, I was usually there late, after they were in bed. The relationship lasted a fairly long time, but circumstances forced its closure. Still, we remained friends and kept in touch until I joined an international airline and began to travel extensively, and then the relationship faded.

One day in the 80s, though, my phone at Global News rang just as I was about to tape an update. It was Claire. Her voice was soft and sombre, and she told me she was dying from breast cancer. She had just a few months to live and she wanted me to know she had followed my career through her children, one of whom lived in Toronto, and she felt so proud of my achievements. She had always been very supportive of me and encouraged many right moves. I felt horrible but couldn't speak because the producer was now beckoning me to get to the studio.

By the time I returned her call, some weeks later, I regret to say, she was gone.

There would be other relationships that would come and go but most had happy endings and I kept in touch as friends for many years in some instances. Though not always.

I had met this classy French-Canadian woman from Outremont. We used to meet downtown because I didn't have a car, but on one occasion she wanted me to come to her home, I thought, to meet her parents. Well, I was totally wrong because when I arrived at this Outremont mansion (her family name was household-known), I was shown in but had to wait in the foyer and never met the parents.

But I didn't care because I was smitten by this woman's beauty and charm. We were never intimate, and she ended up going to Paris a few months later for an extended period.

As it happened, I, too, went to Paris, alone, in May 1963, for my first time in Europe and I had enough time to contact her. A day or two later we had dinner at a wonderful restaurant, which I could ill afford, and agreed to meet the next night for a repeat outing. Here I was, alone in Paris, staying at a funky little hotel on the right bank and after a day's outing, I returned to find a note waiting for me. It read "annulée pour ce soir." For some reason I kept that slip of paper and I still have it.

I was heartbroken and never saw my friend again in Montreal.

But fate can play tricks on you and one day, many years later, Shirley and I were visiting friends who had rented a fabulous beach house in Maine. They came to meet us and gestured at a woman on the veranda of their cottage who was their guest.

I was shocked to see her again. She was even more attractive than I remembered and had what Shirley rightly called a rich hippy look with long, naturally greying hair and a loose-fitting gingham dress.

When we were introduced, she showed no sign of recognizing me. We hadn't known each other all that well but I thought even our short time together was memorable, especially the dinner in Paris. But, alas, she only said she vaguely remembered our meeting years before but that was it, no details. I, of course, was inwardly devastated that she could forget me so easily.

CHAPTER 16

Starting On a Career

My initial role at the *Gazette* was that of a "gofer." I was the junior in the financial editorial department led by editor John Meyer ,and it was my role to go for, or do, this and that, whatever was needed. I had signed up for evening courses at Sir George Williams University but was going to the *Gazette* at 8:30 in the morning to open the mail, check the wire services and generally get the office ready for the editor and reporters to start their day.

Under John's tutelage, I began to re-write wire copy and to understand what makes a good story. I got so wrapped up in that, along with spending much time with the fellow who made up the financial pages, that my day extended into the evening hours and I eventually gave up my academic studies at Sir George Williams University.

I truly loved being a part of the *Gazette*. I try to tell people that I could still smell the molten lead from the composing room of the paper several decades after leaving. It's all done digitally on computers now, which is too bad because those *Gazette* compositors were just the greatest characters to work with. I delivered newspapers as a kid; I worked for a newspaper. I still love that business and I hope it survives its current crisis.

One of the nicest people I met at the *Gazette* was Eileen Kerr, who not only ran the library but was the book editor and responsible for fillers on the editorial page. Eileen was instrumental in nurturing my newfound love of literature by allowing me to do book reviews, and when they appeared with my name at the bottom, it was a huge thrill.

She also encouraged my poetry writing and published at least two of my short poems, again giving me a great thrill at seeing my name in print on the editorial page.

I was working at the paper for about a year, making $25 a week, when the Managing Editor, Alan Randall, came to our office one day and told me he was raising my salary to $35 a week but, more importantly, he wanted me to join the city newsroom and become a general reporter. I turned him down because I really wanted to stay with John Meyer and work on the business financial beat.

That decision didn't sit well with the general news guys who didn't think much of the financial pages, even though at the time they were the most important in Canada because Montreal was the financial centre of the country.

While I was honing my reporting skills at the *Gazette* I was assigned to cover a meeting of the Canadian Club at the Windsor Hotel, where the finance minister of British Columbia was giving a speech about the province's takeover in 1961 of the private electricity generator, B.C. Electric, to form B.C. Hydro. This was a big deal – and controversial – because B.C. Electric was controlled by Montreal's Power Corporation. There wasn't a lot new in the speech, but some words used by the minister to describe the government's action were considered vital to lawyers in a civil suit against the B.C. government a little later.

I was working for the Dow Jones organization at the time and I received a subpoena to attend a Vancouver trial as a witness for the plaintiff. I was flown first class to B.C. and put up at the Hotel

Vancouver. I attended court for two days, accompanied by my brother's girlfriend, who was a stunning flight attendant with Canadian Pacific Airlines. Her name was Margaret Whipper. The mention of her beauty only becomes relevant because, on that second day, it didn't appear as though I was going to give any testimony, but the judge intervened.

He said something to the effect that he wanted to hear my testimony, knowing full well that on leaving the courtroom I'd be "taking out the only bit of sunshine in the room," referring to Margaret because she was wearing a white dress and looked like a movie star.

The trial had come up not long after I had joined the Montreal bureau of the iconic Dow Jones company of New York. Because I had turned down the opportunity to work as a general reporter, the relationship between me and the *Gazette* newsroom cooled. Then, one day, I heard that Canadian Dow Jones was looking for a financial reporter because theirs had moved to Vancouver to open a new bureau. I thought, what the hell, and called to make an appointment with the manager, Doug Colvey.

Doug was a grizzly journalist, a lovely, gentle man, who also had a stutter. We talked about my experience at the *Gazette* and he told me the job would be the junior in the department, handling stories emanating from the stock exchange across the street, among others.

He indicated he was interested in me and said he was prepared to pay me $75 a week. I looked at him in disbelief and said: "$75?!!!" and Doug said, "OKKKAAAY, NNNINETTTTY DDDOLLLARS." In one fell swoop I went from $35 to $90 a week.

There's one story during my short stint at Dow Jones that I don't tell very often. It had to do with anti-Semitism in the financial industry.

Montreal Jews excelled in the rag trade and retail, but others did well in food and drink. This community amassed large holdings but little of it made it into Montreal or its financial markets, which were the centre of Canadian finance back in the 60s. When I was looking for stories one day, I found out why but, sadly, I never got to write about it.

In the early 1960s, a Jewish stockbroker tried to buy a seat on the Montreal Stock Exchange, but he was blackballed, meaning, he failed to win over other members of the exchange. When I heard about this, I suggested to my boss I investigate and do a story on it. He turned me down without a full explanation. Undeterred, I made a call to someone whose name I got from a friend. The person I called was Jack Reitman whose family ran the Reitman chain of retail stores.

Jack Reitman invited me for lunch. I began by asking him if he had heard about the Montreal Stock Exchange's action against the Jewish broker. "Of course," he replied, "we all know, and it was more or less expected."

Jack went on to explain that the slight was typical and years before, that kind of behaviour from the financial establishment had led the Jewish community to do most of their investing in New York markets, either directly or through the New York-based brokers who had branches in Montreal, such as Bache and Company. He went so far as to say "there were many millions of dollars annually going into New York markets instead of Canadian markets" and "that was a shame for Canada."

I confirmed the essence of this claim with a friend who worked at Bache. He told me the vast majority of his and the firm's clients were Jewish. He further said that there was a natural flow of money and culture between Montreal and New York and very little between Montreal and Toronto or the rest of Canada.

Jack Reitman also implied that Toronto Jews acted similarly at that time, but I did learn a few years after our conversation that a

Jewish firm achieved a seat on the Toronto Stock Exchange and, ironically, it wasn't long before Toronto became the centre of finance in Canada. Coincidence? I think not.

Over the ensuing four or five months there was a confluence of factors that led to my being told by Dow Jones to take as much time as necessary to find another job. First of all, I was out of my depth and having too good a time with my newfound wealth. The two senior reporters were stable family men and I represented a different culture. But the key motivator was a corporate decision.

I had been hired to replace a reporter named Jake Doherty, who had taken his family to Vancouver to open a new Dow Jones bureau. He had been there only about six months when the private U.S. corporation decided to go public and, to please the underwriters, the balance sheet was impacted positively by the closure of eight bureaus around the world, including Vancouver.

Doug said in effect that Jake was a family man and we owed it to him to bring him back. I heartily agreed, especially when Doug said I could take as long as necessary to find another job. He wrote me a letter of recommendation that was the most positive I had ever seen, let alone received.

It took a few months, but I got a job in public relations, the place where I'd thought I wanted to be so many years before.

(In a twist that I never discussed with Doug or anyone from the office, Jake came back but was immediately courted by *The Globe and Mail* which, a few years before, had launched the Report On Business, which almost overnight became the journal of record for Canada's financial industry. Jake, incidentally, continued his upward path to become publisher of a number of important Canadian newspapers. He passed away of Alzheimer's in November 2018.)

While I was working at the Dow Jones news service, I learned about a low-cost charter flight offering a two-week trip to Paris. It was open to members of the Montreal Stock Exchange and their friends. Dow Jones had strict rules about accepting gifts, so I cleared my participation with the boss, and he agreed it wasn't a favour to me, it was just a cheap charter flight that was becoming common in the industry. It would be my first trip abroad, so I had to get a passport, learn about currency, read up on the destination, and so on. Since I was alone and didn't know anyone else on the trip, I was going to be very casual with one haversack as baggage.

The fact that my first overseas trip was to Paris was serendipitous. One year when I was at high school, they had done posters of all the football players, and mine had one of those thought bubbles over my head showing a cut of a fashion model and a drawing of the Eiffel Tower. I guess at the time most of my thoughts were about beautiful women and travelling. Who would have thought?

My friends were very happy for me and one of them said I simply had to go to London where she would arrange for me to stay with a friend. The idea was compelling, and I readily accepted.

As luck would have it, on the flight I sat beside a young man in the investment business named Duncan Smith. He was a lot more worldly than me but he, too, was new to Paris. He did, however, have the name of a friend and a telephone number. The friend worked at the Canadian Embassy. Her name was Jeanine.

When we arrived, we had no idea where we would stay, so Duncan called Jeanine. He was in a phone booth of sorts, and after a few minutes she asked him where we were staying. He held his hand over the receiver not wanting to appear ignorant and asked me the name of a hotel. I looked up at the buildings nearby, saw a sign and said "Le Figaro." He told me she laughed at that and said: "Call me when you're settled." What a classy woman. *Le Figaro* is, of course, the name of a French newspaper.

I ended up staying at a fabulous small hotel on the right bank, near Place de la Concorde, on rue Boissy D'Anglas and the hotel was named after the street. It was so reasonable and fabulous I couldn't believe my luck. When I went into the room, I saw a sink and another device on the floor that I had never seen before, a bidet.

On my first day I walked the entire day and came back exhausted. I figured the thing that looked like a toilet would be ideal for washing my feet and that's what I used my first bidet for. It worked well, too.

I eventually linked up with Duncan, and Jeanine had us over to her flat for drinks and to meet some friends from Montreal. These were French women from Westmount who were in Paris with a mission – to meet and marry a wealthy Frenchman or other European. I know I keep talking about the gorgeous girls I've met but, believe me, these two were the real deal – What Montreal was always famous for – and they were great personalities to boot. We had a good time and I saw them again, but it was all in fun.

I did an amazing amount of walking in Paris and I discovered things I never knew existed. One day I saw some people going into a beautiful old building that turned out to be the Musée Rodin. I had no idea who that was but once inside and seeing the garden and reading about Rodin, I fell in love with his work and ended up spending the entire day there. Rodin remains one of my favourite artists of all time, and it was because of that experience I began a love affair with sculpture.

The Rodin experience led me to visit the Louvre where I "blew my mind," as we used to say, on the sculpture "Victoire de Samothrace" at the top of the stairs near the main entrance in 1963. Later I spent some quality time with "Mona Lisa" but it was Eugène Delacroix's painting "Victoire Guidant le Peuple" that gave me the greatest thrill. (On my last visit to Paris a few years ago, I sat with that painting for an hour, fighting huge crowds, to re-acquaint myself with its majesty and remember what it engendered in me at the time.)

The other institution that astounded me with its novel exhibiting style and the quality of its offering was the Jeu de Paume, home of the great Impressionist painters. Each painting was imbedded in the wall and that lack of framing gave the impression that the paintings were floating and complementing each other. It was extraordinary. I've seen such a display once or twice since but on a minor scale.

The Jeu de Paume no longer houses the Impressionists' paintings. It's now a gallery of modern and postmodern photography and media. Close by, though, is the Musée de l'Orangerie and it has a wonderful selection of Impressionist paintings, including the permanent collection of eight huge "Water Lillies" murals by Claude Monet.

My favourite food in Paris was a baguette with cheese and ham, eaten on a bench along the Seine, followed by a single pression, or draught of beer. Oh, my, I can taste it now ... And one of my favourite spots was a bench on the Seine in full view of Notre Dame Cathedral. I really loved that building with its flying buttresses.

But I had promises to keep and had to leave Paris for London for a few days to see friends of friends in Montreal and to meet up with an old girlfriend who now was living on the Thames in a houseboat.

I took the boat train from Paris to London and arrived tired and sweaty in the middle of London looking for an address I had been given. The numbering system didn't make sense, odd and even numbers were mixed, and I was about to give up when this couple wearing white sweaters and slacks and carrying tennis racquets came by and I asked them if they knew where number 15 was. They were the ultimate London snobs who said nothing but pointed across the square to one of the fine, attached townhouses.

I was a little apprehensive but knocked on the door. This lovely woman opened it and said, "Oh, you must be Geraldine's friend John. You look tired; let me draw you a bath." She did and showed me my guest room, then said she had to go out. She wanted me to rest up because we were going out for dinner with a group of people.

I didn't know what to say except thank you. I was a bit embarrassed because I had no clothes for this lifestyle, but at least those I had were clean. She left and I was enjoying my first-ever giant English bathtub when I heard a knock on the door.

What to do? Well, I got up, wrapped a towel around me and went to open the door (just like the song, "Splish Splash" from the 50s). There standing before me was a vision of beauty that literally took my breath away. She had on a grey pleated skirt, a cashmere (maybe angora) sweater and a headband – I'll never forget the headband.

"Oh," she said, "I was looking for Sally."

I said Sally had gone out, that I was a visitor from Canada, and would she like to come in and wait.

"No, thank you," she said, smiling at the towel. "Just tell her Jacqueline popped by, Jacqueline Bissett, and I'll talk to her later."

Sally told me later that Jacqueline was a model friend who was hoping to be in the movies. I never saw her again on that trip, or ever, but I did see her in many movies. She played Steve McQueen's girlfriend in *Bullitt*. I always held her up as the epitome of British beauty until I met Honor Blackman.

Sally was a beauty, too, but she was dating an actor and I wouldn't dare overstep my welcome with my hostess. In fact, that night we had dinner with a group of actors, including her beau, John Thaw.

I wrote some diary entries (though not many) on this trip and one of them said this John Thaw was destined to be a great actor. As it happens, he was and was best known for his long-time role as Inspector Morse in the TV series. His many movies included *A Year In Provence*. He died aged 60 at the turn of the century. He had married Sally Alexander and had a child, a girl, who herself is an actor. They later divorced.

Other actors in the party were a popular television star named Stephanie Beaumont and Corin Redgrave of the renowned acting family.

I did spend some time with my friend on the houseboat near Cheyne Walk but the rest of my time in London was a bit of a blur. I did like it, though, and vowed to return to get to know it better. Little did I know then that I would be spending six glorious months there, living the high life in Chelsea, the absolute centre of Swinging London.

But before that, I had to return to Paris and then Montreal, feeling that I had only scratched the surface of my experiences and I wanted more.

CHAPTER 17

The Glamour of Travel

After leaving Dow Jones I joined Canadian Pacific Railway as a press representative in their public relations department. I was working in one of the most iconic buildings in Canada, Windsor Station, for a giant company that was about to become one of the great multidimensional corporations in Canada.

One of the perks of the job was having a railway pass that gave me unlimited travel on passenger trains. I used my pass quite a lot because I was missing my family in Toronto and it was so convenient to pop up to see them.

On one occasion, though, I ran into my old friend from North Toronto Collegiate days, Ed Cowan. I recalled my audition for his "Maytime Melodies" production and we made light of it. Ed had just opened or was in the throes of opening the first ever public relations company associated with an advertising agency (which made a lot of sense since both were key elements of marketing) and when he heard I was practising PR at the Canadian Pacific Railway Company, he offered to hire me in his new firm. It would have meant leaving Montreal and becoming a glorified salesman for the service, so I turned him down. Ed's company went on to great things, as did Ed himself.

My work took me to places such as Kentville, Nova Scotia, where the CPR subsidiary, the Dominion Atlantic Railway, had an operation hauling product from a gypsum mine.

It was while I was travelling to do the gypsum story that I found myself on the Princess Helene ferry that served Saint John, N.B., and Digby, N.S. The entire ship went silent when a voice came over the loudspeaker to announce that John Fitzgerald Kennedy, President of the United States, had been assassinated. I was alone and found it hard to share my feelings with strangers. I knew his death was significant but how significant it was didn't sink in for a long time.

I also travelled into the interior of northern Maine where the CPR hired a local hunter named "Bucky" Robichaud to keep the beaver population under control. Why? Because those animals were constantly building dams that would erode the railway track beds, rendering them dangerous and creating serious delays on their main line to Atlantic Canada.

What I didn't like, though, was seeing so many dead beavers littering the swamps alongside the tracks. I asked Bucky why he didn't harvest the pelts or meat, but he merely shrugged and said there were just too many. That bothered me a lot because it seemed like such a waste, but I did understand the need to control the beaver activity because that line across Maine was a vital link in the CPR network.

The most exciting assignments, though, involved Canadian Pacific Steamships and their Empress ocean liners. Along with a photographer (I always travelled with one of a team we employed) I travelled by train from Montreal to Saint John, New Brunswick (travelling through the areas where Bucky Robichaud kept the beavers in check) to stay at the Admiral Beatty Hotel. The next day I would board the *Empress of Canada* ocean liner that had arrived from Britain and was en route to Montreal. I would enjoy First Class accommodation for the last night out lavish dinner and party.

It was a way for me to learn more about CP's diverse transportation systems and it allowed me an opportunity to meet some of the prominent passengers in first class who, I hoped, would agree to an interview that I would write up and distribute to the media in an effort to promote travel by ship.

The most interesting story involved, naturally for me, a beautiful woman. Christine (not her real name) was both the director of entertainment and one of the performers of cabaret shows on the ship. I did that trip three or four times and hit on her from day one. She was very English and loved the attention but never yielded to my boyish charm. Never, that is, until her last voyage.

I couldn't believe that she'd finally agreed to meet up after she was free of her duties to have a drink and … whatever. She gave me her cabin number, which I stored in memory, and proceeded to have a superb first-class meal with vintage wines. I even had a nightcap at the steward's insistence, forgetting I was already a bit tipsy.

Sometime later, I quietly and stealthily went to the first-class cabin area where Christine was waiting. I knocked on her door and nothing happened. I knocked again and moments later an elderly woman dressed in a nightgown angrily asked me what the hell I was doing there and what did I want. I quickly left the scene and went to my cabin where I cursed my stupidity for not writing down Christine's room number.

The next morning, we arrived in Montreal. Arrivals are always a very busy time for everyone but I tried to find Christine to apologize for not showing up. When I found her, she dragged me to a quiet spot, looked me straight in the eye and said, "Do you realize that was my last trip and I wanted it to be special. Instead I went to bed angry and going to bed angry – and randy – is never a good thing." We never spoke again.

The bosses loved my work, so much so that I was suddenly

promoted to be the number two person at the CPR's large Toronto PR bureau, out of which the staff handled PR for railways, shipping, hotels and its airline business.

What a job! I was taken aback that they thought so much of me but also deeply saddened because it would mean leaving Montreal, where I was enjoying the "swinging 60s" in Canada's liveliest city.

CHAPTER 18

The Big Step

On the day my boss Barry Scott offered me the transfer to Toronto – for a bigger job, more responsibility, more money, and tremendous prestige – I found myself in the Montreal Men's Press Club.

My face always gives away my moods and when I ordered a beer the bartender asked why I was so glum. "Just preoccupied," I told him, not wanting to spill the beans right then and there. A little later, one of my pals came in and asked me pretty much the same thing. This time I told him about the job, the transfer and that I really didn't want to go.

My friend, who was older, wiser and very much in tune with what was happening in Montreal media and PR circles, said, "I know of a great job going and you'd be perfect for it. They haven't found the right candidate and they're desperate because one of the bosses from London is here for the interviews and has to leave in a couple of days."

The job was Public Relations Officer, Canada, for British Overseas Airways Corporation, BOAC (which is now British Airways), a renowned international airline that, like Air Canada, was a crown corporation and had routes throughout the world.

Two or three things about that job struck me immediately. It was several paygrades above what I was making at the time. I had never before functioned as a manager with budgets and staff responsibilities and was somewhat naïve about the inner workings of management. And it was in an undertaking that hadn't yet peaked as "the" glamour industry to work in.

"No," I told my friend, "there's no way they'd hire me."

"What have you got to lose?" he said. "Here's the number of the guy to call."

I thought more about it that night and decided, "He's right, what have I got to lose?"

The next morning, I called the BOAC Personnel Manager who had me explain my experience over the phone because there was no time for a mailed-in resume. I was a bit shocked when he said, "Fine, can you come for an appointment later this afternoon?" I said yes.

Those who know me understand that in those days I always dressed to impress. I didn't have a lot of clothes but what I had were good quality and very smart. That day I was wearing a three-piece dark blue pin-striped suit.

You can imagine how nervous I was as I was ushered into the general manager's office to meet him, the personnel manager, the sales manager, and the second in command of the London headquarters PR department. The general manager for Canada was wearing the same suit as me, the guy from London had on a dark blue pin stripped suit as well, and the two others were in dark grey suits.

They quizzed me about my education (not a major determinant in those days), my working background and my aspirations. I had already decided I wouldn't be getting the job, so I answered their questions forthrightly.

I was asked if I had ever organized a press conference. I replied, no, but I had attended many and thought I could get up to speed in no time. This was one of many questions for which I could have fudged or spun the answer to my advantage, but I didn't. I was truthful. I had nothing to lose.

The next day I was offered the job and discovered that the salary was not far off what I had targeted as a teenager in Toronto ten years before.

I accepted it, then called my mother to explain why I wasn't moving back to Toronto. She was disappointed but understood. She knew nothing about the airline industry; she had never travelled outside Canada except to the United States a few times, mainly Buffalo, by car.

The issue I now faced was telling my boss at CPR. I had been there under two years and, while you couldn't call us friends, we had a mutual respect for one another. When I told him, he was disappointed I wouldn't be going to Toronto but delighted I had achieved such a good position.

"Who's it with?" he asked.

"BOAC," I replied. His smile faded and he said something to the effect that I was going to have problems with them. I gave him my two weeks' notice and later learned why he was so skeptical.

Canadian Pacific Airlines, an integral part of the Canadian Pacific group, had applied for routes between Canada and Britain but were turned down by BOAC, who had a trans-Atlantic pooling partnership with Air Canada, basically a monopoly on the best routes and they didn't want CPA in competition. The government ministers in Canada and the UK involved in such things agreed, so CPA were left to concentrate their efforts on other parts of the world that were less travelled and more difficult to promote at that time.

My CPR colleagues gave me a nice send-off. I kept in touch with a few of those former colleagues through the Press Club, but it didn't take long for my world to change significantly.

On March 15, 1965, the Ides of March, I arrived for work at another iconic Montreal building, Place Ville Marie. As was my habit, I walked to work as I always had because my living quarters were usually only about six blocks away – ambling downhill going to work, a little tougher climbing back home.

When I moved out of Zeta Psi Fraternity it was into a tiny flat in a rooming house at the southeast corner of Prince Arthur and Aylmer streets, between St. Lawrence and the McGill ghetto. It was really cute and, for me, ideal. You entered into an eight by ten feet bedroom, popped through bright red swinging café doors, down two steps into a small living room with a tiny kitchen at the end to the right and a bathroom to the left. Very compact, very easy to keep clean and perfect for a bachelor.

A lot of interesting things happened in that building and I came face to face with some aspects of life I had only read about.

A very pretty young McGill student lived on my floor in a lovely, slightly larger flat. She had wonderful taste and one wall was filled with overflowing bookshelves.

One day a few months after we had met, I heard a lot of racket from her flat and, when I went to investigate, there was an older woman and another younger woman ripping the bookshelves off the wall and generally tearing the place apart. I didn't want to interfere, so I retreated. A few days later I learned that my sweet young neighbour had committed suicide there and her distraught family took out their anger and frustration on the flat.

After the student's death the flat was fixed up and rented to a young married couple who were both attending McGill. They were from the United States and the young woman was the daughter of a renowned *Time* magazine photographer. Vickie and Ben Pope were the best neighbours you could ask for and we shared a lot of good times together.

They were sad when I told them I would be leaving because I had been offered a sublet for a fabulous flat, but I assured them it was only going to be a few blocks away and we'd stay in touch. We talked about the new digs and what I had and didn't have. A few days after that conversation, they were travelling in their van to the Eastern Townships and Vermont. Somewhere they found a beaten-up brass bed that they cleaned up, reconstructed and gave me as a housewarming present.

I can't tell you how moved I was by this extraordinary gesture. I had lucked into the ground floor of a McGill-owned brownstone. It had two giant rooms with high ceilings and a fireplace in each. A huge bay window overlooked Peel Street. There was a small but highly workable kitchen and a lovely bathroom. Ben and Vickie's bed became the centrepiece of the second room and I never closed the sliding door, so everyone who entered the flat marvelled at the size of the rooms and laughed at the dominance of the big brass bed.

CHAPTER 19

The High Life Begins

As I was settling into my new office on the 16th floor of Place Ville Marie (PVM) and meeting my new colleagues, I was getting some looks that made me a tad uncomfortable. I knew I was very young looking for the management role I was about to embark on, but I exuded confidence and that should have dispelled any questionable feelings.

It wasn't until a few years later that I learned the reasons for that early reaction. The man I was replacing had been forced out after an incident in the autumn of 1963. It seems he kissed his wife goodbye one Friday afternoon and left to take a flight to Toronto for business meetings, saying he'd be back on Sunday evening. When he did arrive back as scheduled, his wife fainted on seeing him come through the door.

The chap had allegedly been booked on Trans Canada Airlines (now Air Canada) flight 831 that evening but the flight never made it, having crashed into a field near the town of Ste. Therese, killing all 118 on board – the worst ever air disaster in Canada at the time.

In reality he had spent the weekend with his mistress in Montreal.

His wife had alerted BOAC management that he had been on that flight, so arrangements had begun to take shape for his funeral service and burial. When apprised of his whereabouts, the airline encouraged him to resign. His wife, however, forgave him and they remained together until his death.

That all happened some 16 months before I was hired. In the meantime, Canadian management had felt they could get the job done with existing marketing staff and a very bright PR department assistant named Laura Zagolin. But big developments in the industry and in the company were looming and it was deemed necessary to fill the slot and thus I was hired.

I had a lot to learn, too, and Laura was a superb teacher. She, of course, was disappointed not to get promoted but there was no way a woman would get the job with a British company in that era, even though other airlines had women in those positions, notably Alitalia and Swissair, not to mention Trans Canada Airlines, that year renamed Air Canada.

Laura confided to me she had been studying for a new career and would only stay on as long as necessary to bring me up to speed on everything and everyone. She soon graduated as a classical music conductor.

So one of my first tasks was to find a replacement for Laura. The successful candidate was a divorced mother of two, Madeleine Petit from Chicoutimi. Madeleine was really something and we got along well but it took me a few years to fully understand the mind of the French-Canadian woman. I was young and single and well paid, and Madeleine acted as much like an older sister as a secretary or assistant, protecting me from all kinds of risks and temptations. When I had lunches that lasted too long or were too liquid, she'd cover for me without hesitation and with much aplomb.

The only time I handled myself like an idiot with Madeleine (well, okay, maybe there was more than one time but this was the worst) was one Friday when she said she had to go get her hair done because she had a big date that night. It meant I could not have my normal very long Friday lunch downstairs at what we called "The Swamp," which was officially called Les Escargots. Since many Montreal business people began their weekend at noon on Friday, there'd be little for me to do in the office.

I did go for a quick bite with my pals (that means about an hour in Montreal) and begged off staying for more rounds to handle any phone calls. It was important in those days to be close to your phone. We were an international airline, and something could happen somewhere at any time, as the 1963 TCA crash attested. In my 15 years with BOAC, later British Airways, we had no accidents, only a hijacking when those were all the rage among terrorists. But other less critical things could happen, such as flight delays, so we had to be at the end of a telephone line at all times. Would that we'd had cellular phones then …

The afternoon slogged along, and my creative juices were not flowing, so boredom quickly set in. I kept looking at my watch. Madeleine had left at 11:30 and it was now 1:30, then 2:00, then 2:30, 3:00, 3:30 and, as each half hour passed, I got more annoyed.

She came back around 4:00, looking like she'd just stepped out of a movie and mimicking Sophia Loren. She had had her hair done, nails, facial, everything that French-Canadian women considered necessary for their well-being and their role in the world.

And how did your diarist react? Like a bloody fool, I chewed her out for taking advantage of me (I had done the same to her many times). Well, she held her ground initially but finally gave in to tears. I felt like the jerk I was. Some friends in the office consoled her but I finally suggested she go home because my stupidity has caused her *macquillage* to run.

Suffice it to say, it never happened again. I gave her as much rein as she needed and she never exploited it. We had a terrific working relationship for about a decade when she ended up travelling to Australia and marrying a Qantas airline pilot she had met on vacation. She did some amazing entrepreneurial things there, too, using her beauty, charm and smarts to advantage in a male-dominated world.

The reason I wanted to highlight Madeleine at the beginning of my journey into life at BOAC is to stress how vitally important it is in public relations to have a competent, trustworthy assistant. I travelled a lot both for business and pleasure (when you worked in the airline industry, you could travel anywhere anytime for next to nothing or free, and that included hotel accommodation) and I needed someone totally reliable to look after things in my absence.

My first trip was to Toronto to meet the managers and staff in our most important market. The next was a trip to London to meet my colleagues in the press relations department at BOAC headquarters, Victoria. I don't remember much of that trip because it was fraught with learning names, roles, reporting lines, security matters, and so on. What I did learn, though, was that the staff there had been hoping one of them would get the Canada job when it became available, rather than it going to to a local. I soon learned there was quite a gap in the pay structures between the U.K. and North America and a number of the lads in London savoured the prospects.

I enjoyed working with the headquarters PR staff, even more so when I was posted to London for a six-month secondment in 1967. But there was one with whom I developed a special relationship. His name was Ron Williams and he was tall, portly, balding, wore glasses and smoked incessantly, in other words, the perfect ex-journalist now in the world of suits.

I'm not sure why we hit it off, but our backgrounds were not dissimilar. He had worked for a news agency as I had, albeit for a short time. He had a great sense of humour and loved women. He loved making the rare visit to Montreal where the European flair of the city and the women had him enthralled for the duration.

Ron died in a car accident in 1970 after accepting a ride home from a colleague who had insisted that he hadn't had too much to drink after work. Ron for three years had been my main liaison at head office and my working relationships with London were never quite the same with him gone.

CHAPTER 20

Routine Work

After joining BOAC, I realized the most important work was getting to know the airport operations, including our management and staff and the security authorities who would have to clear me for special passes. It wasn't a chore for me because I enjoyed meeting people, especially those who were tolerant of my inability to converse at length in French.

But meet them I did, and it was a good thing because about one month later I was faced with my first airport arrival with a media circus.

The Rolling Stones made their first American tour starting in Montreal in April 1965 and they arrived in Canada on board BOAC. The media had been whipped into a frenzy over this visit and the plane was met by a throng of reporters and photographers. It was my job to keep them at bay.

The one aspect of that experience that stayed with me was the disdain, real or contrived, that the boys had for some fans who had travelled economy class on their aircraft and who had gathered at the foot of the first- class stairs to greet them. Well, maybe it wasn't "the boys" but rather Mick Jagger, who referred to the "ugly" fans at the bottom of the stairs. The girls couldn't have cared less as they were getting a close up look at a group that had already achieved legendary status.

Later in 1965, BOAC introduced a new service from London to Chicago via Montreal, utilizing the British-built VC10 aircraft. There was media interest in that inaugural visit of the VC10 to Montreal mainly because on board that first flight was one of the great beauties of the film world, Honor Blackman, who was renowned for her role as Pussy Galore in in the 1964 classic James Bond film, *Goldfinger*.

As the aircraft was being refueled, I rushed on board to find Ms. Blackman and ask her if she would kindly agree to coming onto the tarmac to have her picture taken. She readily agreed and, after the press got their photos, one of them took a picture of me with her and I've treasured that ever since.

Early in the new year, the Royal Family was making a fueling stop at Vancouver en route to the South Pacific, and there was much interest from the media to see them, so I flew to Vancouver to handle that; in the process I met Prince Charles and Princess Anne while their mother and father were busy with protocol matters. Neither was very friendly and, being teenagers, probably bored. The one surprising thing about Charles was his poor complexion. I had suffered from acne, too, and knew how self-conscious it could make a teenager feel.

One airport event that almost got me and some colleagues in a lot of trouble involved the notorious Great Train Robber, Charles Wilson. He had been found living in a Montreal suburb in the 60s and was being extradited to Britain. I had no idea he would be travelling on a BOAC aircraft until someone in the media contacted me. I didn't know because the police forces there and in Britain were cooperating to get him back quickly and they didn't want any fuss, so anonymous names were used. I had the complete trust of my colleagues in management, so I was able to confirm what flight he was on to a very large contingent of British press who booked the same flight.

When the police authorities heard about this, they switched Wilson to another flight leaving slightly later. I only found out about the switch by chance and I got assistance from our airport operations people to halt the first flight, which was taxiing for takeoff, and bring it back so the media could get on the right flight.

A day later I received a telegraph from London saying that the Chairman had had many favourable comments from the media about the cooperation they'd received from me at Montreal airport. To be mentioned in dispatches like that was a big deal. And thankfully the police authorities never raised the subject.

My work with BOAC brought me into contact with many journalists and business people. Allan Fotheringham and I, for instance, became friends over martinis at the Hotel Vancouver. It was one of my first visits to that city and it was my job to get to know the journalists that made a difference. I had arranged to have a drink with the city editor, Patrick Nagle, whom I had known in Montreal, and he brought along Allan, a renowned columnist. I was never a martini drinker and those served at the Hotel Vancouver in small fishbowls were dynamite. I was still nursing a second one and feeling it when those two were on their third or fourth.

Patrick had worked for *Weekend Magazine* until it folded and then joined the *Vancouver Sun* as city editor and later Southam Newspaper Group, eventually ending up as their roaming correspondent in Africa, Eastern Europe and western Canada. One of the greats, he died far too young several years ago.

Allan, meanwhile, went on to become one of the most controversial columnists for *Maclean's* magazine, a TV star with the CBC, and author of many books. He was one of my first tennis partners when

I joined the Toronto Lawn Tennis Club. His death in August 2020 was a real blow.

One of my most memorable encounters in London happened on a Friday in the early 70s. My friend Bob Hughes asked me to join him for a coffee meeting with Leonard Cohen and his group, who were in town prior to the Isle of Wight pop festival that weekend.

The discussion concerned a free concert Cohen would give that night at a mental hospital in Camden Town. The group was quite nervous about doing the concert, but it was Cohen's decision to do a free concert for every paid concert they performed. The hospital treated a relatively small number of those who were getting shock treatments, which offered little hope for full recovery.

I could certainly understand the group's reticence to perform that night for what they expected would be a small audience of 30 or 40 people. The sound equipment was elaborate and, in fact, some had to be set aside because there was no time to set it up properly.

While we set up the equipment on the stage of what I thought at the time was a quaint meeting hall, Cohen and his group practised a few numbers off to the side. Meanwhile, the audience began to arrive and filled every seat with standing room only in the aisles.

When Cohen finally took the microphone, there had to be at least 150 people in the hall, and he seemed to be overwhelmed by the number. He stood alone on a stage in front of an audience that was noisy and fidgety and wondering what they were doing there. When Cohen started to play and sing, they still didn't quieten down. So, he simply stopped singing and talked to them.

He talked about what medications they were on, uppers and downers, indicating he had tried them all. He talked about his experiences in such an intimate way the crowd gradually began to hang onto every word. Once he had them, he began to sing again and, for the next hour or so, between his singing and their loud applause, you could have heard a pin drop. It was almost eerie. All of us standing in the wings were amazed.

There was the odd outburst, but these were shouted down. When Cohen asked for audience participation, he got a lovely lady on the makeshift stage to dance. The audience clapped and the clapping lacked coordination, adding to the strangeness of the words he sang. It was highly unlikely the audience understood his words, but it didn't seem to matter because he had created an extraordinary empathy with them.

The concert lasted an hour and fifteen minutes. Afterward, when he was able to say a few words over the drone of applause, the hospital director said that in his 18 years at the hospital, never had so many patients turned up for a concert, never had a concert lasted so long, never had the patients stayed until the end, and never had the patients been so appreciative ... and all for someone about whom they knew nothing.

I have never experienced such silent adoration, nor would I again. In everything I read about Cohen after his death, there was never a word about this "policy" so I only assumed it wasn't so much a policy as a one-off decision at a moment of introspection or opportunity. But what a thrill for me to have been there.

CHAPTER 21

My Relationship with London

Not only was I lucky enough to be intimately involved in the most glamorous industry of the 60s, but I was also able to call London my near-second home since I travelled there regularly on business or for pleasure.

When the media referred to London as the centre of the Swinging 60s, they weren't kidding. It was the place to be or to be seen. What made my visits so exciting was the exposure I had to the swinging London movers and shakers through my relationship with Bob Hughes.

Bob had met and married a divorced South African woman of means named Joan Becker and they were living in the epicentre of this exciting city. She underwrote his transformation from male model with a fabulous personality and drop-dead good looks to a well-equipped commercial photographer (and later, film director). Joan had three children and was well linked to the London Jewish community, who were the most dynamic players in what London had become.

Hal Shaper, a friend of Joan's, was one great charismatic personality. He was a lawyer from South Africa whose love of music brought him to London, where he excelled as a lyricist working with some great composers for films such as France's Michel Legrand and America's Jerry Goldsmith.

Hal's ticket to ride had come in the form of a song he wrote for an English singer, Matt Munro, but which was picked up by Frank Sinatra and turned into an international hit. It was called "Softly As I Leave You." On the strength of that one song, Hal created a thriving music business and produced a number of bands, while continuing to collaborate in songwriting for some of the top names in music such as Bing Crosby, Elvis Presley, and Barbara Streisand, to name a few.

Hal lived modestly in Chelsea but had a fabulous address on Cheyne Walk. His flat was small but when his friend Dougie Cullinan (of the diamond fame) came to visit London, he slept on Hal's couch.

Hal was extremely well connected and treated me as a curiosity. We became fast friends a few years later when, probably under the influence of too much wine, I suggested he decide once and for all whether he was gay or straight, because his behaviour was sometimes unsettling. At the root of this comment was my fondness for his latest girlfriend (named Charlotte but he called her Charlie) whom he cheated on with occasional dalliances.

For some reason Hal did decide he was straight after all and in 1972 he married Susan, an actress, in a ceremony for which I flew to London.

But I'm getting ahead of myself. Whenever I went to London, I spent time with Bob and Joan. They eventually split but we were able to maintain a relationship with both of them.

When I got married and took Shirley to live in Chelsea for those glorious months in 1967, it was akin to a very long honeymoon. But Shirley, who was renowned for not being a cook, was taken under the wing of Joan who would take her to her new digs in Onslow

Square and teach her how to make some traditional classic dishes such as boeuf bourguignon.

It was both amusing and curious how many times Shirley would go to Joan's, make a fabulous meal then transport it back to our flat on Chelsea Manor Street for us to enjoy with or without guests. I should add that my wife became an extraordinary cook and still is.

Shirley remained close to Joan and when a friend, Janis Stewart, came to live in London she introduced her to Joan, and they became fast friends. A couple of events occurred as a result of our friendship with Janis.

First, we discovered an incredible restaurant called 235 King's which was, needless to say, on the famous King's Road. Food was fabulous but what made us go back time and again was a crème brulée that even to this day has not been matched by any restaurant anywhere in the world.

Our server at 235 was Gale Benson, a friend of Janis's. She was like an angel – her manner, the way she walked, everything. She was also the daughter of a politician and well versed in politics. We spent quality time with her mostly at 235 King's Road.

Gale eventually fell under the spell of a Black revolutionary called Michael X, a criminal, who, after being bailed out of jail by the singer John Lennon after his arrest for extortion, fled to his native Trinidad where he started a commune. Gale followed him there but to everyone's horror she was murdered by Michael X, who was eventually executed by hanging.

A movie was later made called *The Bank Job* that included as a subplot the story of Gale Benson. She is alleged to have been a spy for Britain's MI6 and was with Michael X to investigate his ties to Princess Margaret, the Queen's sister, and find any material related to that relationship.

After Bob and Joan divorced, he moved into a fabulous

studio-cum-flat in Chelsea and was doing well as a commercial photographer. I have mentioned Bob's addiction to alcohol but in London that spread to drugs. Never once did I see him partake in anything stronger than hashish, but he told me cocaine was his downfall financially.

On one of my visits to London, Bob was hosting an old friend, a Canadian actor. I didn't know the actor other than by reputation and his work in film and TV. But we got along well and this one night we got into hashish.

Now, it must be said, I had never before tried hashish or marijuana, for that matter, so this was a new experience. It took about two tokes for me to start laughing and I laughed for the balance of the night. At one point we went out to dine and Bob chose a Chinese restaurant that served a mean Peking Duck. As we ate the meal, I kept saying I felt like King Midas eating gold because the hashish had enhanced the flavour of the duck (and the hoisin sauce) so much.

Bob and I spent a lot of time together in those days. He never achieved the status of, say, a David Bailey, but advertising firms loved him because he produced what they needed and on time. I often told him he was too nice to his clients and they took advantage of him.

I remember once I arrived at his Chelsea flat on a Friday afternoon and he asked me for help. A client needed a weekend shoot for a presentation on Monday morning and other fashion photographers were either busy or too much into their weekend activities to bother.

Bob's plan was simple. He didn't have access to the modelling agencies late on a Friday, so we had to improvise. We'd go to some of the department stores and pick out the best-looking young women and offer them a chance to have a portfolio that might change their lives. Together we found a half dozen, mostly at Selfridges, and Bob photographed them the next day. He made the Monday deadline and got the assignment.

On another occasion Bob was going to have eight or nine clients over for dinner and he asked me to go with him to buy the groceries and wine. We went straight to the Harrod's Food Hall to buy this wide variety of foods that he'd cook himself (he was a good cook, having learned all the tricks from his ex-wife Joan).

He bought foods in the order he'd be serving them and when it came to dessert, he wanted to serve melons. It was the wrong season for English melons, but he found some from somewhere in southern Europe, maybe Spain. He picked up ten tiny ones and put them in the basket. I said, "You're joking, right?" "Why is that?" Bob asked. "They're 7£ each!" I said. "So what! I like them," he replied and that's what he served. This was back in the late 60s, early 70s, and the exchange rate was $3 Canadian to 1£, so each melon cost $21!

Bob eventually remarried, this time to one of the most beautiful women in the world, a Danish model named Maren Greve, one of fashion icon photographer David Bailey's favourite models.

Maren once took me to Les Ambassadeurs Club in London for lunch. She was wearing an extremely tight jean suit and there wasn't any eye that didn't follow her everywhere she went that afternoon. At the time, Maren had the distinction of being the only model to have an entire European *Vogue* magazine issue devoted solely to her.

After they married, they went to live in Marina del Ray, California, where Bob was hoping to break into film direction in a big way. He did a few television show directorial jobs but it never worked out; neither did the marriage. Maren returned to London and Bob ended up in Long Island, New York.

My wonderful muse, Elizabeth McAulay.

Mayhem at McGill's Zeta Psi Fraternity house often involved John Culter, left from Vancouver and "Corky" Fry from England.

In the winter of 1960 we rented a cabin with no running water on Chemin Boise, Ste. Adele.

Benedicte Ingstad graces the bow of "Halten" in the spring of 1961 just before setting off for Newfoundland and the discovery by the Ingstads of a Viking settlement from the year 1000 at L'Anse aux Meadows.

My CPR colleague Herb Brooks accompanied me on my first PR assignment on the Empress of Canada. It was a tough job but somebody had to do it.

This is the track maintenance rail car that took beaver hunter, Bucky Robichaud, and I to the wilds of northern Maine to witness mainline track bed damage from beaver dam flooding.

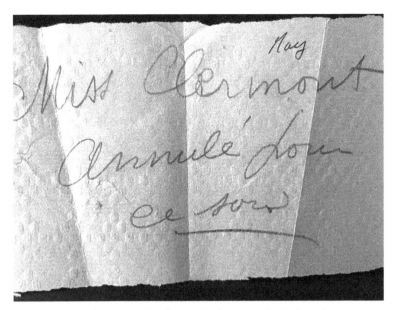

The actual 1963 note from the Paris hotel concierge that broke my heart.

My first flat on Prince Arthur St. W.

My art collection led Shirley to think I was gay.

My first encounter with a global celebrity was meeting Honor Blackman, aka, Pussy Galore, in 1965 at Dorval Airport.

Mirella Fares predicted I would marry Shirley.

*G.S.McDougall hired me in 1965. He was BOAC's Manager,
Canada and a renowned Canadian military aviator.*

*Brother Frank discovered me on The People Tree at Expo 67
Montreal. I was in London and had no idea.*

Our gorgeous wedding party on May 13, 1967, outside Holy Name Parish, Vancouver.

Happiness is loving my in-laws. From left, Anne, Ed, me, Shirley, Carley, Kate and John.

CHAPTER 22

That Life-Changing Moment
at Peel and Sherbrooke

Having had all these wonderful experiences travelling to London and other exotic places on business and pleasure, I was still enthralled with living in Montreal.

If London was the centre of the hedonist life for world players, Montreal was the place to be in Canada. It was the era of the Quiet Revolution, of free love, of women's liberation. The city was filled with expatriates from Europe and elsewhere and the numbers grew with all of the preparations for Expo 67. You had to be there. Journalist Peter Desbarats of the *Montreal Star* declared the 60s belonged to Montreal and there was no argument about that.

To have such a glamorous job and a glamorous lifestyle in Montreal in the 60s was just about the ultimate in living. In Toronto, business people took maybe 45 minutes for lunch, usually at their desks. In Montreal one had to go to a restaurant and it usually took at least an hour and a half. If you were walking down the street and saw a beautiful woman, you would smile and say, "Bonjour." More often than not, the greeting was returned.

My lifestyle didn't allow for any long-term relationships with women. Expat girlfriends would leave after several months so long-term affairs were never possible, nor desired. But I tended to keep in touch with all of them, much to the amusement of my male friends.

On one occasion, while visiting London, I went to a party and met this incredible woman who, under deep questioning, confided she had been married to an Egyptian film director. Her name was Mirella Fares.

She was of mixed ethnicity, having an Italian mother and Egyptian father. I had no idea how old she was but on hearing she was divorced and looking to start a new life somewhere, I suggested, under the influence of a few drinks, that she come to Montreal. I was floored when she agreed.

Naively, I thought I could get a discount deal to bring her to Montreal for a few weeks of job hunting and sightseeing, but there was no way. She would arrive sometime in June 1966 for three weeks.

A few weeks before her arrival, fate threw me a curve ball that, fortunately, in the end, I hit out of the park, thanks to a remarkable woman and a lot of luck.

It all happened on a very windy and rainy day in May. I walked to and from my office at Place Ville Marie, whatever the weather, all year long. I never drove a car until I got my first license in 1976, so walking and public transportation were still my thing, along with taxis, of course.

I lived in a wonderful flat on the first floor of a magnificent town-house owned by McGill University. It was on the east side of Peel not far from Dr. Penfield Avenue.

On that very rainy day in May, I was walking home on the west side of Peel, heading north to Sherbrooke and beyond. I had just crossed de Maisonneuve Blvd when I spied a tall, blonde woman with a long-stride gait, walking up the east side and she didn't have an umbrella. As a result, her clothes clung to her and I could see she had long, shapely legs and a modest bosom. At Sherbrooke the light was against her, but the green light allowed me to cross over to where she was hovering under the Mayfair Shoe store sign, which was offering little protection. Since I figured she was going my way, I offered o share my large umbrella. She looked me over and said yes.

What struck me immediately was the freshness of her face and the apparent lack of makeup. A suggestion of Slavic features, perhaps. And her hair, it was natural, too, and if coloured, beautifully subtle. One could tell from her gait that she was a smart and determined young woman.

As we walked, we began an animated conversation and she asked my name. I replied, "Baron Dawe of Windsor-Peel" (the official name of the street). She said, "If you're the Baron, I'd like you to do something about the cockroaches in the flat I share with my friends from Vancouver."

Her name was Shirley Zitko and she was from Vancouver.

We talked all the way to her building, at which point I offered my card and suggested she come visit sometime. She told me later she'd accepted the umbrella, the card and the invitation only because she liked the way I was nattily dressed and that I carried a leather attaché case.

On another occasion she told me she thought I was gay because when she came to visit a few days later, I was entertaining a friend who, like me, was dressed in a tee shirt and jeans and lounging in rooms filled with antiques, carpets and paintings. It wasn't elaborate, but to an inexperienced young woman from Vancouver, it must have seemed so.

When my lady friend arrived from London, I introduced her to Shirley, who by now had become a friend, or pal, really. And I asked Shirley if she would be kind enough to take Mirella around the town on her day off while I was working. Shirley readily agreed because she liked Mirella very much.

Not long before she left to return home, Mirella and I were talking ,and she said categorically: "I think you're going to marry that girl." And I said: "Shirley? You must be joking; we're just friends." Mirella just smiled. I was serious, though. I was 27 years old and marriage or a commitment was the furthest thing from my mind as I was enjoying the fruits of my glamourous job and good salary.

Some ten weeks later, I saw my friend Shirley off on the train to Toronto, where she would meet up with my second oldest brother Larry and accompany him on the drive to Vancouver.

Larry had long planned to revisit Vancouver where he had lived for a number of years. And Shirley? Well, she didn't have the money to fly home so the offer of a drive by Larry was gladly accepted. Larry was a bachelor who had gone through a rough parting in his last relationship. Though it was never discussed, I hoped my friend Shirley and Larry might develop more than a friendship on that journey. They got along well but that was about it.

A few weeks later, I found myself in Vancouver on business and my world was about to change dramatically.

My company chairman, Sir Giles Guthrie, had gone to visit Boeing in Washington State to see the development of the new, high capacity 747 aircraft BOAC had ordered. He was then going to Vancouver for a meeting of business leaders. Word of his arrival had reached the press and I needed to be a buffer for him.

At the hotel, the chairman and I talked about a strategy for dealing with the press, but he soon felt tired and said, "John, I want you to sit beside me at this dinner tonight and we'll continue the conversation."

I was in a quandary because I wasn't invited to the dinner so I blurted out, "I'm sorry, Sir Giles, I won't be at the dinner tonight," thinking he would leave the conversation there.

Instead he demanded to know why not. I looked over at my

Canadian manager for help but he looked away. In what seemed like minutes but was only a nanosecond or two, and tryin,g to think fast on my feet, I replied, "Well, I'm getting engaged tonight."

My boss knew me well and said, "Now don't make any rash decisions, young man."

I said, "No, I've thought about it and I'm going to ask her tonight because she's invited me to her home for dinner."

Sir Giles said, "Well, okay, but I want to meet this young lady. Bring her along to the offices when we meet up tomorrow morning."

I left shortly after and when Shirley picked me up, I was quiet and preoccupied. As she was driving over the Granville Street Bridge, I told her what had happened, and she almost cracked up the car. By the time we got to her home, we had decided to get married and would do so the following year, after she finished the second year of her three-year university degree.

Dinner that night was a happy event even though we had decided not to mention our engagement to the family. We went out after dinner, but when Shirley got home, her mother, who always waited up for her kids to return, said to Shirley in her typically highly intuitive way that if she planned to get married any time soon, she had to know now because it would take time to order the grapes for the wedding wine she'd have to make. Shirley was taken aback but confirmed our plans to her Mother and asked that it be kept quiet for a while.

The next morning, she joined me at the BOAC Vancouver offices and made a big impression on the visiting brass who said all the right things to this blushing but confident young woman.

As for me, I was committed, but a potential hurdle loomed.

CHAPTER 23

Decisions, Decisions

I wasn't back in Montreal more than a few weeks when I got the word that would turn my world upside down. The London bosses wanted me to serve at head office for six months, starting in May 1967. It would be a secondment on a Canadian salary, something I could never refuse.

Suddenly I had what I considered a serious issue: I was committed to getting married in May. How, I thought, could I tell Shirley we had to put off the wedding? I struggled with this for a while before calling Shirley. I said there was no sense getting married and going together to London as that would be like "taking coals to Newcastle." That was the expression I used.

It was a moment of sheer stupidity and selfishness because what I was really saying was this: I didn't want to share my big opportunity as a bachelor in Swinging London with someone I had known for about 15 weeks.

Shirley's reaction was to pause for a moment then say, "Don't be so silly. Of course we'll get married and go to London. It'll be fun."

She should have called me a jerk. Instead, Shirley explained she wouldn't be able to stay the entire six months because she was committed to finishing her degree at McGill University, but she could stay for just under four months. Her calmness and maturity in responding to my nonsensical – no, stupid – comment convinced me even more I had made a brilliant decision.

The wedding and the move were still many months away, but lots had to be done. I had been watching the evolution of Expo 67 and playing a role when asked. I knew it was going to be the biggest event ever to be staged in Canada and that Montreal would become "the" tourist destination that year. Head office had indicated they wanted me in London to handle enquiries about Expo and other Canadian Centennial projects across the country. And it didn't take much analysis to realize BOAC wanted a British voice in Montreal to handle the world press, dignitaries, royalty and the like.

Frankly, too, the prospect of spending all that time in London on a Canadian salary was almost too amazing to bear. My London friends were happy I was coming ,and my Montreal friends were too involved in things Expo to comment one way or the other. I would be leaving my gorgeous flat and would have to find a home or homes for my stuff, but I had lots of time to prepare.

Shirley and I had known each other just a dozen weeks or so, had gotten engaged, then agreed to a May wedding, and I wouldn't see her for about eight months, unless we were able to organize a get-together. So I bit the bullet again and sent her an airline ticket to join me in Montreal for the holiday period between Christmas and New Year's.

This was a complicated exercise. There was no way a good Catholic girl could tell her family she was going to spend the holidays in Montreal with her fiancé and bunk in with him.

The story would be that Shirley would stay with my dear upstairs friends, the Gundys. Peter and Gayle were amenable to assisting with that subterfuge and the plan would be that anytime Shirley's mother called, either Gayle or Peter would run downstairs to get Shirley.

It worked well. The Gundys, by the way also hosted Shirley when she had to return early to Montreal from the posting in London to register and attend the first several weeks of classes. Peter and Gayle Gundy would become friends of ours for life. You couldn't ask for better friends and neighbours.

Prior to that pre-marriage trip, though, another significant matter arose for me. I realized that once married I would not be able to share my airline travel privileges with family and I had always wanted to take my mother on a trip. That's when she told me she wanted to go around the world, and that's what we did.

Other than a trip or two to the U.S., my mother hadn't been outside Canada, so getting a passport and health shots were the first priorities. She was living in Montreal at the time so the logistics would be straightforward.

Airline travel in those days was a big deal, especially long-range travel. Passengers dressed up rather than down as they do today, so looking your best was a key factor in getting the co-operation of airline staff wherever we travelled.

The first leg of the journey was Montreal to San Francisco, where we stayed the night. We then flew to Hawaii and spent one night. Except for the magnificent weather and Mother experiencing the sight of a banana plant, the Honolulu visit was uneventful.

The third leg was the long trip from Hawaii to Japan. There being no entertainment systems on board those Boeing 707s, we played gin rummy the whole time we were not sleeping. I was soundly beaten most of the time.

The air currents over the Pacific can play havoc with aviation. Airline crews had to be very vigilant because of the occurrence of CAT or "clear air turbulence." So it was that without warning our aircraft suddenly fell several hundred feet. As far as I could tell, everyone had followed the captain's admonition to be strapped in while seated so there were no injuries but it was scary nonetheless. Fortunately, the cabin crew were on a break at the time and were seated as well.

We were feeling quite okay when we arrived at our Tokyo hotel, so I suggested we go out for a bite to eat and maybe see the famous Ginza. Mother readily agreed so I went to the front desk and bought some Japanese currency. We went by cab to the Ginza and marvelled at the incredible crowds, lights and sounds of Tokyo. We both commented that there was no way we could live in such chaos.

Once inside the district, we got out of the cab and, when I went to pay, the driver, who spoke no English, indicated he couldn't break the bill I was offering him. I searched the pile I had been given and gave him a smaller note, leaving the balance as a tip.

We tried to walk the streets, but it was almost impossible. As luck would have it, we found a cabaret of sorts that offered some food and a show. We went in and got great seats for a show that highlighted a naked woman on a swing plus circus-type variety acts. Our food was simple and not very tasty. I paid and we left to get a taxi back to the hotel.

I commented to Mother what an interesting evening we'd had for a reasonable amount of money. I had given the front desk ten US dollars and they had given me this wad of bills. The whole evening had cost less than $10.

At about 3:30 in the morning, there was a pounding on the door, and when I opened it, there were two very anxious men standing there, including the one who had done the currency transaction. The older man explained a mistake had been made and I had been given exchange for $100 not $10.

I had to make up the difference from my limited funds. Our evening out had cost $87.50, not $8.75. That additional cost in 1966 was a lot but, in today's terms, and adjusted for inflation, it's the equivalent of $691.

Needless to say, we were happy to leave Japan the next day for Hong Kong, where we planned to stay for almost ten days. Costs in Hong Kong were a pittance compared to Tokyo. For example, my interline staff rate for a large suite at the Hilton Hotel was US$5 per night.

Flying into Hong Kong for me was an extraordinary adventure. The BOAC 707 captain found out I was on board and asked me to join him on the flight deck to sit in the jump seat. We talked about many things, including his love of Canada where he had spent some time working during the war. But he specifically wanted me to share with the flight crew the thrill of flying into Kai Tak International Airport.

As we approached the landing strip, we actually flew between apartment buildings and it was as if we could reach out and grab the laundry that hung on just about every balcony. The buildings appeared to be just a few feet away. I had never had a landing like it before and never since.

We had an absolutely amazing time in Hong Kong and loved every minute. We travelled by train to see the border in the New Territories and visited Shatin, the famous ancient walled city.

If you've ever experienced the smells of a giant seafood market, you'll know why my mother absolutely loved visiting one in Hong Kong. It was not only huge – it was a covered wharf that extended well over the water – it had hundreds of feet of ice-covered tables that were filled with every kind of sea creature you could imagine, and then many more. With her Newfoundland roots, Mother knew a lot about what lived in the oceans, but this was beyond her wildest dreams and imagination.

As you might expect, we ate many of these seafood delicacies at various restaurants, especially one magnificent Mongolian Hot Pot restaurant, the likes of which we had never experienced. Cooking our own seafood, meat and vegetables in broth boiling in a central hot pot while sitting at a large round table with strangers was a wonderful treat.

One night we did a very touristy thing; we went to a floating restaurant at Aberdeen where, for a modest sum, you could get a Chinese buffet and all the alcoholic drinks you could care to have. We had a terrific time, meeting people from all over the world but, near the end of the evening, we noticed a group of men who were not that happy and seemed quite sombre. I figured them to be military by their haircuts and I went up to one to start a conversation.

It turned out it was a bomber crew on R&R from making runs over Laos, an activity the U.S. had denied undertaking, even though it was widely thought they were trying to bomb supply routes into Vietnam, and some were in Laos. Analysts later claimed Laos was the most heavily bombed nation per capita on earth between 1964 and 1973.

These airmen knew what they were doing and knew the toll their activity was taking on Laotian civilians. They were in tears by the time the story ended.

It was a sobering experience, one that I couldn't share at the time, out of respect for the wishes of the crew, because it was America's Secret War and it stayed secret for decades. But it drove home to me that what we now know as PTSD is a very real condition and veterans who suffer from it need help, long-term help if necessary.

We reluctantly left Hong Kong with the most wonderful memories and some mementos. I still have an Omega watch that I bought there, though I haven't worn it for a while. But I also had two wedding rings made to my design. Shirley's, with a few small emeralds and rubies, is still with us, though it was replaced 20 years later. Mine rests somewhere in the wonderful bay that fronts the Greek village of Lindos on the island of Rhodes, having been lost on one of our many trips there.

Mother and I then travelled to London via New Delhi, Teheran and Tel Aviv. Bob Hughes and my other friends there were very kind to us and we spent a splendid week seeing what must be seen in London.

We were both thoroughly exhausted by the time we arrived at the staff travel facility at Heathrow to register for the flight home. But my luck ran out because there was only one seat for staff travel on the flight to Montreal. I insisted Mother take it and I would follow the next day.

We talked about that trip for years afterward. I still have all the 35mm transparencies I took on the trip but, sadly, they've faded over the years. Still, I don't need photos to remind me of that magical trip, as the best memories are firmly implanted in my brain.

CHAPTER 24

Preparing to Move and Say Goodbye

Christmas 1966: Shirley's visit was fast approaching, and I had things to do. One thing straight out of my personal playbook was to have a party for Shirley, where she would meet all of my Montreal friends, including girlfriends with whom I had stayed friendly.

There was a method in that seeming madness, namely, I was going to have to rely on a lot of friends to store my furniture and some valuables while I was away, and I didn't want to leave that chore to the last minute.

We had a terrific party, and everyone was genuinely pleased to have met Shirley. Not long after she left for home, I began to chat up my pals about storage possibilities.

At the same time, the city – indeed the whole country – was gearing up for Canada's centennial celebrations and Expo. The action at the Montreal Men's Press Club at the Mount Royal Hotel was non-stop, it seemed, with a regular stream of visitors from abroad to monitor the development of Expo.

The pace of life generally was frenetic. Down deep I was of two minds about leaving Montreal for six months. I knew I was going to miss all the parties that my public relations friends were planning for the opening of pavilions and the like, not to mention meeting people from all over the world in one location. But I was also going to the most exciting city in the world and it, too, would be a stepping-stone to places I'd always dreamed of visiting.

The 60s were one of the most dynamic decades in our history. It was not the best of times, necessarily, but it was game changing.

In Quebec there was a "Quiet Revolution" in which people supplanted the power of the Catholic church with the power of the individual. The political scene changed dramatically; Quebec culture blossomed and pride in that culture exploded. The success of Expo 67 showed the rest of Canada and the world that a new Quebec was very much making its presence felt.

While Quebec was creating a new beginning, the rest of North America was concentrating on the anti-war movement and civil unrest in the U.S. that spread elsewhere. Political assassinations and the civil rights battles characterized the decade in America. And it all culminated in a 1969 concert in a farmer's field in upstate New York at a place called Woodstock. It was close by, but my friends and I were too busy to attend. Besides, the Quiet Revolution had caused unprecedented problems at home.

For us in Montreal, in 1967, Expo allowed for a lull in the domestic terrorist bombings that had begun a few years before and had come to represent the new radical nationalism that some minority groups craved. Even the local revolutionaries realized there would be no sense causing trouble for Expo, which was helping them show the world what Quebec was capable of doing and becoming.

Since I would be missing most of Expo, I concentrated on getting to know as much about it as possible so I could converse authoritatively on the main elements of it should I be required to do so in London or elsewhere.

A colleague had come from London who would replace me for six months, but I left most of the handover briefing and important introductions to my able assistant Madeleine Pollock. My final chores involved finding homes for my stuff, selling what I wouldn't need, and preparing to go to Vancouver for the wedding.

My friends in Montreal threw me a stag party and my brothers came from Toronto. None of them was coming to the wedding and there has always been a difference of opinion as to why. My brothers claim (and Shirley backs them up) they weren't invited. I claim I told them I was getting married and they didn't believe me or showed little interest. I even suggested if they didn't want to go, then they could together fund a trip for my mother to be there, but she was hesitant to go alone.

The boys did come for the stag in Montreal, however, and it culminated in a significant poker game, always a trademark event when the brothers came together. I ended up losing almost all of my cash and, as they were driving me to the airport the next morning, I suggested the joke was over and could they return my money.

Needless to say, they did not and I arrived in Vancouver with a couple of suitcases and less than two hundred dollars to my name. I had no idea how it was going to work out. Thankfully, lady luck or an angel was on my side and my friends came to the rescue.

CHAPTER 25

The Wedding and Aftermath

Shirley had said she wanted me in Vancouver a week before the wedding because there were so many parties to attend. As it happened, I was not invited to any of them and I spent the whole week with my best man, David Nunn, whose family also put me up at their gorgeous home.

David and I had met in Montreal where he had lived in the fraternity house with me. I got to know David and his parents quite well on my frequent trips to Vancouver and his dad was very much a surrogate father for me.

It was through David that I met the young men who would be ushers at my wedding. What a crew they were. David had introduced me to them in Montreal where they lived for a time or visited often. David Graham was the youngest sibling of the well-known Graham family, whose roots began in Montreal but who eventually settled in Vancouver, where they lived in an enormous mansion on Point Grey near the University of British Columbia. Until his early death in his 50s, David was one of our closest friends.

Peter Brown became an iconic figure in Vancouver financial circles as the founder of Cannacord, the investment firm. We'd met in Montreal where he was training for a financial career with the firm Greenshields. He became one of the big movers and shakers on the Vancouver Stock Exchange, one of Canada's wealthiest people and a renowned art collector.

John Culter was the third usher. Another Vancouverite, he had also lived at the Zeta Psi house for a while. When we met, there was a family business in his future,but he was also entrepreneurial and, at one point, joined David Graham in a mining venture.

My best man, ushers, my father-in-law-to-be Ed Zitko and surrogate father, Ed Nunn, held a stag in my honour at the Vancouver Club on May 10, 1967. It was a subdued event, three days before the wedding, and I sometimes wish I had been as controlled at the reception following the wedding.

I don't remember much about the wedding: It was in a Catholic church on Cambie and 33rd Street, a lovely setting, really, and the wedding party was, well, beautiful.

I don't remember much about the reception, either. It was held at a hotel banquet hall near Burnaby. There were about 250 invitees and Shirley's dad Ed told me sometime later the bar bill was only $92, mainly because only my friends drank spirits, the rest of the guests had the wedding wine that Shirley's mom Anne had made when she heard we were engaged. It was powerful stuff and I stupidly had more than a few glasses, leading to a ridiculous groom's speech that I wish everyone would forget but they won't. I was fortunate to have some forgiving family and friends.

We spent the night at the Bayshore Hotel and then travelled the next morning to Toronto where we stayed at the Park Plaza and Mother held a reception at the house for family and friends.

The next night we were due to leave on BOAC for London but, in all the excitement, I had forgotten about the springtime change and we missed the flight. Instead we travelled on Air Canada who, for some reason I've never understood, refused to ask other passengers to move seats so we could sit together, and we crossed the Atlantic in separate economy compartments.

CHAPTER 26

Settling into Life in London

I'm not suggesting it was prophetic that we travelled to London separately but that tended to be a metaphor for much of our early life together – what Khalil Gibran referred to as "spaces in your togetherness." My airline job took me away quite a bit, and when Shirley eventually got into merchandising at The Bay, she travelled, too, sometimes a lot.

But that was later. Now we were in London, starting a new life together. Initially, we booked into a well-known short-term stay facility called Dolphin Square near the Thames in Pimlico. It housed a lot of politicians and was too far away from the action we desired. We eventually lucked out and got a wonderful, tiny flat on Chelsea Manor Street in Chelsea, also close to the Thames but, more importantly, in the heart of Swinging London – 61 Chesil Court was a delight.

Right above us was the actress Hayley Mills who was living with director Roy Boulting – never met either of them – and below us was an elderly man who was called Alexander James Gibson.

I spent many wonderful hours talking with this man who was nicknamed "Gibby" and who, into his 90s, still worked at translating Russian technological papers into English. He was the father of

Wing Commander Guy Gibson, of the Dam Busters raids, arguably the most famous RAF bomber pilot in the Second World War.

The BOAC offices were at Victoria, not a long bus ride away. I had an opportunity to visit aircraft manufacturing sites in Wales and England where the amazing VC10s were made. Of all the aircraft I had ever flown on, the VC10 and Super VC10 were the best. Just too well made and too expensive to compete with the likes of Boeing. And probably the safest commercial aircraft ever made. We also visited the early manufacturing facilities for the supersonic Concorde aircraft.

My role in the Press Office of BOAC was to handle requests that came in daily from media everywhere, directly or via our offices around the world. Most of them were routine but occasionally one came along that required some fine tuning, and I was involved in one of those, though no one ever formally confirmed it, including me.

A famous air correspondent from a widely circulated newspaper called about a story he had seen in the BOAC internal publication that was distributed to media for promotional purposes. The story involved an accident at the airport for which staff had been honoured for quick action to avert a disaster. The problem was there were no details about the accident.

Like any crown corporation, BOAC had bureaucratic ways of dealing with things and, when safety was involved, the best approach was always to say nothing or as little as possible. Well, that wasn't in my nature and as a former journalist I was curious to know about this accident, what had occurred and who had resolved it. So, I quietly investigated the details and was surprised that the Press Office briefing demanded nothing be said and that we offer no comment to questions about it.

I was on duty that weekend when the call came in from the

correspondent, and just hearing the chap's name sent a shiver up my spine, because in our industry these were very influential people. But I always felt I was a good judge of character and good journalism, and this fellow's work was always balanced and never alarmist. So, when he asked me questions about the accident, I told him and also explained why they had been kept classified. We ended up having a lengthy and very detailed conversation. I didn't want to think about what might happen as a result of it.

A few days later the office was all abuzz about an article this correspondent had written that put BOAC in the best possible light for training, safety and staff recognition, for everything, in fact, surrounding the accident (which, incidentally, was not aircraft related). The Chairman sent his congratulations and wanted to know who had briefed the correspondent on the story. They never did find out and it remained a mystery, though some of my colleagues had their theories.

When I wasn't working weekends and we didn't have social commitments, Shirley and I simply packed a bag and went somewhere. Flying, of course. The industry was booming, and London was one of the great commercial aviation hubs. BOAC was Britain's long-haul airline and our PR department had a good relationship with that of the domestic and European carrier, British European Airways (BEA). They gave me tickets anywhere on their system and, when possible, even upgraded us to first class. What a treat.

There weren't enough weekends available for travel to do every city we wanted to visit, but we chose carefully and ended up going to Copenhagen, Berlin, Paris and Rome. Each one has a memory, starting with Copenhagen. We chose it because we had heard so much about the friendly Danes and there was romance surrounding the Little Mermaid. Besides, we were assured of getting on that flight.

But from the moment we arrived at Copenhagen the disappointments started. First there were no friendly Danes. We learned later that the foul mood we experienced everywhere was the result of a days-earlier announcement that taxes were going up sharply. Danes were not happy campers.

Next, we had waited until arrival to book hotel accommodation and the only downtown room we could book was on a ship docked in the harbour. When we got there, we discovered it was a former ferry boat that had operated on Canada's St. Lawrence River and our beds were upper and lower berths.

The third and final disappointment was the Little Mermaid that sat on a rock overlooking the harbour. It was so small it was hardly visible.

The one big positive, though, was seeing many tributes to Hans Christian Andersen, author of so many classic children's fairy tales, among other writings.

Our trip to Berlin was even more educational. The city was still divided into sectors and was split between East and West by a wall that had only been finished a few years before. We saw what there was to see in West Berlin, including a terrific zoo, but were interested to see East Berlin, having heard so much about it. And everything we had heard was true. From the moment we entered via Checkpoint Charlie, the most famous crossing, we saw only dull, drab buildings and poorly dressed people who displayed attitude.

Some pundits claimed the Russians grabbed the best parts of Berlin when they entered the final phase of the Second World War, but even those buildings had not been maintained or cared for after all that Allied wartime bombing and strife.

We stayed in the East long enough to visit the huge Russian war memorial, our first glimpse of the kind of memorial I was to see in many places over the ensuing years. Someone characterized it as "brutalism design" and that's exactly what it was.

Our trip to Rome had a purpose. A few years before I had met in Montreal a Canadian photographer who'd found celebrity outside his country but little in Canada. (This would turn into a pattern of sorts and although I've seen it and heard about it often, I don't understand it.)

His name was Roloff Beny and he was originally from Alberta. His photographic studies of archaeology and shrines of faith, among many, became a dozen or more books of immense popularity among the establishment – intense, sumptuous coffee table books.

I had met Roloff very soon after joining BOAC because he was trying to curry favour with people in the airline industry who could facilitate his constant travels.

I had been invited to a private show and reception at the Royal Ontario Museum and later at the home of Lady Eaton. Eaton's had sponsored the creation of some wonderful fabrics employing Roloff's photographic designs and those fabrics were turned into clothes, which were worn by some of Canada's top models. It was quite a show but, at the after party, two memorable things occurred.

I wore my lucky three-piece blue pin-striped suit to the party and finished it off with a dark blue tie of extraordinary origins. It was created some 30 or 40 years earlier in silk and commemorated Imperial Airways, the British international airline that operated mainly to posts in the Empire and was to merge later with BOAC.

At some point in the evening, I was in conversation with the publisher Jack McClelland, when the artist Harold Town joined us and enquired about the tie. I told him about the origins. Later, after more drinks all around, I was surrounded by Jack and Harold, who proceeded to cut my tie with a pair of scissors.

I must have said something loudly because Lady Eaton came quickly by and chastised those two for their behaviour. I would interview Jack later in my television career but never raised the issue with him.

The other occurrence was more fun. I was, naturally, chatting up one of the models and, without my knowledge, a photographer caught the young woman, Olga Habbeshaw, with a look of "you've got to be kidding!" on her face. That photograph surfaced in a spectacular way two years later.

But back to Roloff.

He'd chosen Rome as his base and lived in a grandiose apartment on the banks of the Tiber River. Every year on what has become known as Canada Day, he held a party to which he invited friends, artists, politicians, ambassadors, the rich, everyone, in effect, who was able to influence his life somehow. Roloff found out we were in London from a friend at the (Toronto) *Telegram* newspaper, Stasia Evasuk, and invited us to this Centennial bash.

It was a spectacular party but I, as could often be expected in those days, overindulged and don't remember much detail, other than Shirley being one of the most talked about women there. On a trip to Scotland earlier that month I had bought Shirley a superb pantsuit and she was a sensation at the party. So much so that the story Stasia did for the paper featured Shirley doing what she does best on the dance floor.

That trip to Rome was with a purpose but we would return to see the sights and would, like others, fall in love with the city and Italy in general.

We also fell head over heels in love with Paris and France, but my second trip and Shirley's first would be in the company of my brother Larry who came to visit from Toronto.

In Paris I was able to guide Shirley and Larry to many of the places that had engaged me several years before. We had a wonderful time and it culminated with a dinner party at the home of Larry's

European colleague at Union Carbide, who had a gorgeous apartment overlooking magnificent gardens.

The hostess was serving artichokes and Shirley took a special interest in how she cooked them and, more importantly, how one ate them. Why? Well, to understand that I have to take you back to our first week in London.

Shirley and I both enjoyed the movie *Blowup* and I had learned one of the scenes was filmed in a restaurant just off Sloan Square in Chelsea, behind Peter Jones department store. As a surprise, I took her there for lunch. Acting as sophisticated as possible I asked the waiter for the day's specials and he said artichokes, so I ordered one as a starter. Truth be told, I had never seen one before, let alone eaten one.

It arrived and I took one of those delicious leaves and popped it into my mouth and began to chew. It was like shoe leather. I managed to swallow it and tried another one. It was the same. Shirley was watching me and asked if I was all right. I replied that I thought they were tough and called the waiter over to return the dish and order something else. He did so without comment, for which I was eternally grateful.

So now we're in Paris and the artichoke season is in full swing and my hostess places one in front of me along with a gravy bowl of melted butter. I poured the butter over the artichoke but waited to watch how they were eaten. Once I saw how, I dove in and enjoyed the leaves immensely. Artichokes have been a seasonal favourite in our home ever since.

Another important weekend trip for us was to the west of England, specifically the coastal town of Dawlish, Devonshire, where, I was told years before, our forefathers had lived before heading to Newfoundland.

That story had been investigated by one of my uncles who

had enlisted the help of Joey Smallwood, a lawyer who would later become Premier of Newfoundland and Labrador after Confederation in 1949.

According to the investigation, seven brothers with the name Daw had been fishing out of their port of Dawlish in 1594 and, on returning, were warned off and ended up sailing to what was then the first ever British crown colony called Newfoundland.

Settlement in Newfoundland was not encouraged in those days so, like others before them, they found worthy havens in what we now know as outports, mostly in the Port de Grave area of Conception Bay. As the story goes, four of the brothers were ne'er-do-wells and the other three decided to split the family by adding an "e" to the name. Both Daw and Dawe were common back in Devonshire and environs.

Shirley and I tried to verify that information by going to the parish church in Dawlish, where records of locals were normally kept. The local Church of England priest gave us access to the ancient records but, alas, they only dated back to 1620. He said that was probably the result of a fire or a tragedy.

What was interesting on studying the records from 1620 on, however, was we could not find one Daw or Dawe having been recorded as being born, married or died in that parish. We also visited several cemeteries to find the same thing, although in another county, we found some stones with the name Dawe and Daw, and the dates were a few centuries old.

All of this gave credence to the investigation and we were satisfied the story of the Daw(e) ancestors had merit. Besides, it was one of our favourite trips outside London.

CHAPTER 27

Meeting the Most Unforgettable Person

While our weekend jaunts to the continent were interesting, our life in London was extraordinary, thanks to a few people we spent quality time with and who introduced us to a lifestyle we thought to exist only in the movies. And it all began just a few weeks after we arrived.

I introduced you to Hal Shaper in a previous chapter as being someone with a wide circle of what you might call exotic friends. So, I really didn't know what to expect when Hal suggested we meet at a movie theatre to see *A Man For All Seasons*, a highly touted film that had just been released. There was specific seating for this performance and our tickets were in different sections. Hal introduced us to his date, Mariella, and then grabbed my ticket, giving me his. In other words ,he wanted to sit with Shirley while I was with Mariella.

This young woman was wearing the shortest mini skirt I had ever seen, and she was bountifully endowed with long slim legs and a full bosom. During the film, she told me later, she tried to get my attention, but I was enjoying the remarkable film too much to respond (hard to believe but true).

Afterwards, Hal took us to the five-star restaurant Monkey Island Estate, situated on an island in the Thames River and a favourite of families whose children attended Eton, the private school for boys. To be frank, I remember little about the lunch other than we talked a lot about the wonderful film we had just seen.

After lunch Hal drove us back to his flat in Chelsea (we lived close by). Shortly after arriving, Hal went into his bedroom and called for Shirley. I was sitting on the couch with Mariella and we both snickered when we heard Shirley say, "Hal, put your pants back on."

Mariella proceeded to tell me how randy (English for horny) she was, and I responded that I had been married only a few weeks and that we didn't have that kind of relationship. Mariella responded, "Well, do you mind?" to which I said "no" and she proceeded to pleasure herself.

It hit me immediately that all this was a set-up by Hal, a kind of test for me, really. I not only passed but it strengthened our relationship with Hal, and we began a friendship with Mariella about whom we knew little but were soon to learn a lot.

For starters, Mariella wasn't her legal name. Stella Marie Capes had been from Liverpool. On arriving in London, age 16, she performed as a topless dancer. A year later in 1957, she met and married a famous antique dealer and nightclub operator, Horace "Hod" Dibben who was 40 years her senior. Hod did what I call a "Higgins" on her, namely, he taught her to speak with a haughty English accent and to dress exquisitely but sexily.

They gave aristocratic dinner parties and one of them in 1961 was the infamous "Man in the Mask" Party at which the partygoers were mostly nude. Mariella was dressed in a corset and carried a whip, proclaiming she was the Government's Chief Whip.

Three of the participants that night were Stephen Ward, an osteopath and artist who threw lavish parties at his country estate, and two of Ward's "girls," Christine Keeler and Mandy Rice-Davies. Stephen Ward became one of the central figures in the 1963 Profumo affair that led to the resignation of John Profumo, the Secretary of State for War, and the defeat a year later of the Conservative government.

The press revealed the names of two women in that affair, Christine Keeler and Mandy Rice-Davies. The affair engulfed Keeler, who'd had intimate relations with both Profumo and the military attaché for the Russian Embassy.

The press did not, however, mention Mariella, who had taken the surname Novotny, which was the same as the then President of Czechoslovakia, a few years before she had made a scandalous visit to the United States.

One of her liaisons in 1960 New York, along with another woman of Chinese origin, was with the President-elect John F. Kennedy, and this caused serious consternation in government circles and the FBI.

Under questioning, Mariella once admitted she knew Christine Keeler and I replied I'd like to meet her. She took me to a pub in an exclusive part of London and there she was lunching at a table on her own. Christine seemed non-plussed by this greeting and meeting and said little. Years later when I interviewed her at Global News she denied having known Mariella, which I found curious, or having met me, which I understood.

Mariella once told me I was the only man who had ever refused her sexual advances, but I have no way of knowing if that was true. I do know we became friends and wrote to each other for several years.

She told me she was writing a book, a novel, that was a fictionalized account of her adventures in New York and London. She also said she would be using my name for a character in the book. It was called *King's Road* and when it was published, she promoted the release by posing nude in the back of a convertible car on a Saturday in King's Road, causing yet another scandal.

She half-jokingly said we should come over for the book launch party and we did. She couldn't believe someone would do that for her, but Shirley and I attended the party. I took no notes, but I remember that the party was attended by a wealth of aristocrats and business barons. I read the book and found it awful but, true to her word, one of the characters is called Dr. Dawe.

We drifted apart as Mariella's life took many twists and turns. She died in 1983, some say of an overdose, and that observation may have merit. Our friend Hal told me she died during a dinner party when she passed out and asphyxiated herself in a blancmange or pudding.

Rumour has it her apartment was burgled not long after, and all her diaries and personal papers were taken by a person or persons who wanted to conceal secrets.

It wouldn't surprise me one bit.

My long-time right hand at BOAC Madeleine Pollock at a Montreal medieval feast.

Shirley boogies with the host at Rollof Beny's famous Dominion
Day party at his exquisite River Tiber flat in Rome.

Allan Fotheringham, aka, "Dr. Foth". A couple of martinis in 1965 led to a long friendship.

Our first of 12 visits to Greece started on a ferry from Piraeus to Rhodes where we discovered Lindos.

*Our dear friends Jeannie and Nelson Saunders in their home at
Habitat 67 which set a new standard in urban living.*

1968 Weekend Magazine photo shoot for Keitha McLean's article on buying discarded treasures at Salvation Army. From left, Keitha, Ken Mallett (who many years later would be my executive producer at Global News), me, Bonnie Buxton, Shirley and Brian Philcox with unknown person in foreground.

Lifetime buddy Ian Henderson and his wife Mary.

Shirley in London with our great pal Joan Hughes and the kids.

My first ever cricket match in London.

My first Concorde flight at Mach 2, just over 1500 MPH or almost 2400 Km/H, from London to Beirut during a break in the Lebanese civil war, 1975.

Calgary Mayor Rod Sykes performs the White Hat Ceremony for crew of Concorde which British Airways flew from London to celebrate the opening of the new international airport.

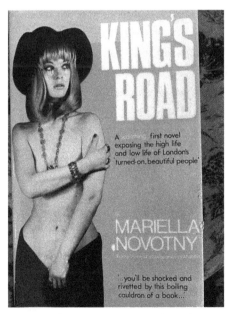

My friend Mariella Novotny's one and only novel was drawn from personal experiences. She promoted it by posing almost nude on a busy Saturday in Kings Road.

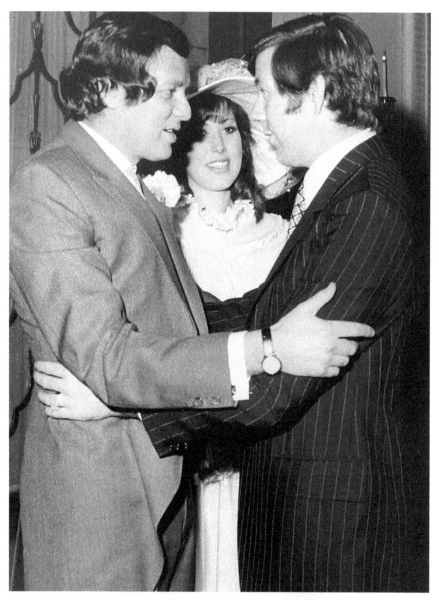

In the 70's renowned songwriter/music producer, Hal Shaper, was married to Suzy in a celebrity London wedding…and I was there.

CHAPTER 28

Beginning a New Life In Montreal

As the end of our stay in London loomed, I was bemoaning the fact to my colleagues when I got a surprise offer to stay on in London. It was very tempting, but the money was terrible, even though I would have been elevated to a senior staff list and would have made a good salary by British standards. Besides, Shirley had already left to return to Montreal where she was staying with friends and would find us an apartment and register to complete her arts degree at McGill University.

It didn't take long for Shirley to find us a lovely flat in a building on a cul de sac named Summerhill Avenue in the Montreal core. She then began travelling to various friends' homes to pick up the furniture, et al, that I had parked with them while living in London. There was no such thing as self-storage in those days.

By the time I got home, Shirley had done a magnificent job in setting up the apartment, which was small but perfect for our needs. And we were in good company; the great Canadian author and McGill professor, Hugh MacLennan, lived right below us. We stayed in that apartment for two years.

Coming back to Montreal was difficult in some ways but it was good to get home. Expo 67 was all but finished and everyone, it seemed, was exhausted. My successor for that period had made a big impression on staff and I had to work hard to re-establish myself in their eyes.

One interesting thing I learned later from my brother Frank, who had been in Montreal to visit Expo, was that my photograph had appeared on the famous "People Tree" in the Canadian Pavilion. This tree had, instead of leaves, photographs of one thousand Canadians in various places, poses, and the like, and visitors were able to walk through the "tree" to view them. My brother was shocked to find me in one of them and I was surprised he could recognize me because it's a shot from behind of me chatting up a woman who looks like she's saying, "Yeah, sure, I believe you…"

The photo was used because of the woman's look plus the fact that she was so obviously beautiful. And I knew right away who it was.

Her name was Olga Habbeshaw and she was one of the models who had worn the Roloff Beny-designed clothes at the Royal Ontario Museum launch two years earlier. I, of course, was chatting her up at Lady Eaton's launch after party. I didn't know if Olga was aware of the honour accorded her picture, so I made contact sometime later and she was appreciative.

Life as a married person in Montreal was certainly different than as a bachelor and I found it somewhat hard to adjust, making mistakes along the way. But overall, we had a lot of fun and maintained our love of travel while creating a home environment that met both our taste levels.

Before getting married I had got to know an art dealer on Greene Avenue in Westmount named Florence Millman. It was the West End Art Gallery and we became fast friends with Florence and spent hours with her both at the gallery and at auctions. She was our mentor on art and furniture. I often think if I had followed her advice more closely, we'd be very wealthy in art today. Instead, we have art we love but doesn't have the commercial values we expected. Much of this was my fault.

We'd go to auctions where Group of Seven sketches were selling for between $300 and $400 and we liked them. But instead of buying those, I bought work by newer artists, Quebec-based artists, a couple of whom were friends. There's no real market for much of the art I bought, but those Group sketches are worth 100 or more times what they sold for at those 60s and 70s auctions. Still, art would become one of our passions and we've continued to buy what we like.

In the following year, 1968, after Shirley had completed her degree, we began to travel in earnest at every opportunity. We made our first of 12 trips to Greece that year, along with an extension to Istanbul.

Friends will appreciate it when I tell them we never saw the most important historical sites in Istanbul such as Topkapi or the Hagia Sophia. We did, however, see the Spice Bazaar and Grand Bazaar. Shirley was deeply interested in merchandising, so the huge bazaar became our go-to place.

On our first day, we decided to have lunch in the Spice Bazaar at a restaurant with a neon sign that said, if I remember correctly, Bernini. It was the equivalent of a French zinc bar with marble and wrought-iron tables. We had a wonderful meal but were anxious for something sweet and couldn't understand that part of the menu.

Shirley caught the attention of a well-dressed man at a nearby table who had been patiently waiting for someone, regularly looking at his watch. In slow, deliberate English she said, "Ex-cuse me. Do you speak English?"

He replied, "Madame, may I help you?"

He turned out to be the Turkish appointee to the United Nations and he had been waiting for his wife, who never did show. We had a wonderful chat and he ended up treating us to lunch, insisting we were guests in his country and he wouldn't have it any other way.

That was the first of many meals we were treated to on that trip. In fact, since our small hotel came with breakfast, we never bought a meal the whole time we were there, thanks to the kindness of Turks we met. We left with a determination to go back to see the sights, but to this day we've never done so, I'm embarrassed to say.

But Greece was a different story. When we arrived in Athens on our first trip, we found it noisy and smelly (diesel fumes were shocking) so after one night at a hotel we went to the port of Piraeus where we could find a ferry to the islands. We purchased tickets for the furthest distance, which turned out to be Rhodes.

Our tickets gave us sleeping quarters for the night as it was a long journey. We met and befriended a group of young French students and I discovered ouzo, much to my chagrin.

I ended up celebrating too much, so Shirley left the deck and went below to our cabin. We shared that cabin with four others, and all were men. When they saw Shirley alone and looking pregnant in a loose-fitting empire style shift dress, they appeared confused and horrified. Their reaction worried Shirley so she retreated to find me on the deck and together we returned to the cabin. The rest of the night was uneventful.

The trip was glorious, and we enjoyed the stops at various islands whose names conjured up tales of romance and adventure. When we got to Rhodes, we had no idea what we were going to do, so we joined the French students in their trip to a tourist booth at the harbour.

They, and we for that matter, didn't want to be in another city, rather we wanted a quaint Greek village, ideally with a beach. We were told there was one such village about an hour and a half by bus up the coast, called Lindos. And that's where we headed.

As we pulled into the town square, it was obvious we'd made the right choice. The town of white low-rise buildings was spread below an acropolis, one that turned out to be the second most important archaeological site in Greece. As we alighted, we were met by townspeople who encouraged us to go to their homes to stay. We were attracted to a woman with the most unbelievable smile. Her name was Tzina Mingou and little did she or we know it, but we would be her guests for many visits to come, twelve in all.

One of the great joys in our life was going back to Greece in 2018, staying in Athens, which now was clean and welcoming, travelling into the interior on the routes of the Greek gods, and then back to Rhodes for a reunion with Tzina, if we could find her.

We did and spent four wonderful hours with our dear friend who was now 83, still single and a matriarch of the village. Lindos had become a significant tourist destination for cruise ships. When we began going there, it was an artist/author's colony. Still, it was a huge treat and the meal we had on the rooftop of Hermes restaurant with a view of the bay was spectacular.

Back in Montreal in those early days, I met a neighbour who was living in the ground floor walkdown of a magnificent old townhome across the street from us. He was in the advertising business and confided that he was moving to Vancouver. His flat would be available and we made arrangements to see it.

It was love at first sight for a number of reasons, including large public rooms, two bedrooms and a walkout to the garden. It also had lots of light. We were introduced to the owners who were happy to have new tenants without any hassle. We moved in and stayed for five years, paying little rent and allowing us to save for our own home.

Our landlord was a lawyer named George Allison who, along

with his wife Tula (both originally from Toronto), daughter Diane and son Jody, welcomed us as part of the family and we maintained that relationship long after leaving. The parents are gone but Diane is a widow living in Toronto and Jody ended up in New York where he founded a wealth management firm and remains a close friend.

The Allisons didn't need the income, hence the low rental cost, but they wanted the security of having someone living downstairs. And live we did. We did a terrific amount of entertaining and had family and friends regularly bunking in. We thought it would never end. And then one day it almost did.

BOAC in 1969 appointed a new general manager for Canada named John Gorman. My administrative boss up until then had been Geoff MacDougall, a former RCAF wing commander and member of the Montreal English establishment. We got along very well.

The first thing John Gorman did, however, was to tell me within a week or so of his arrival that I belonged in Toronto, that he could handle his own PR in Montreal. He was telling me bluntly that I had to move, shortly after Shirley had secured her long-awaited job at the Hudson's Bay Company.

There was no way I was going to move back to Toronto, so I refused. John had a military background and was taken aback at such insubordination but simply said that if I didn't move, I could commute to Toronto weekly, and I did so for many, many months.

In retrospect, these "spaces in our togetherness," as Khalil Gibran called them, were good for our marriage, but also beneficial for Shirley as she was able to devote more time to her new career as she started on a tear to the top of her profession.

And then, once again, fate entered the picture.

James "Jaspar " Cross, the British Consul in Montreal was kidnapped by a terrorist group known as the FLQ. Jaspar was a personal friend of John Gorman.

John had not only won the Military Cross and Croix de Guerre as a Captain in the Irish Guards during World War II, but after the war had joined the Royal Ulster Constabulary as a district inspector in the hotbed called Armagh, where he distinguished himself as a bold leader. He left that role in the early 1960s to join BOAC as head of security.

I mention this because John wanted badly to get involved in resolving his friend's kidnapping and was anxious to work with the anti-terrorist authorities, based on his experience with the RUC along with MI5 and MI6 against the IRA.

The BOAC management team steered him away from that personal involvement and I managed to get him some off-the-record deep background press interviews; thankfully, that alone seemed to change his attitude toward me and my office. John even helped me convince London of the need to hire someone to perform duties in Toronto and I was able to stop commuting.

John and I began to work very closely together. I realized I was working with someone who revelled in his business profile, so I worked extra hard to get him speaking engagements in some traditional business clubs and used every means to increase his profile. He really liked the speeches I wrote for him and rarely changed a word.

Unbeknownst to head office, we worked tirelessly but quietly to promote international aviation into Canada's western provinces, believing that BOAC would be the natural link between, say, Calgary and Vancouver and points in Britain. To show how much we wanted these routes and to win local support, we promoted heavily within BOAC to bring Concorde to Calgary for the opening of their new international terminal in 1977.

All the work paid off and about a year after the supersonic aircraft began scheduled services, we managed to get one to make the flight to Calgary for that opening. It was a huge success and held us in good stead politically for years.

All of the crew (along with yours truly) were given the traditional white Stetson cowboy hats and gold cufflinks in honour of the occasion by Mayor Rod Sykes. I still have mine. The crew loved it.

The aircraft left at early evening with a group of Calgary aviation lobbyists and some oilmen (and us) on board, heading for Washington. What happened on the runway that evening was extraordinary.

Without our knowledge, the airport authorities had arranged for the runway to be lined with RCMP vehicles whose security and headlights came on to salute a novel goodbye as we were taking off. It was thrilling.

It was some years after I left the airline that the newly merged British Airways achieved landing rights into Calgary and Vancouver. I just know that Concorde visit had something to do with the decision.

John Gorman left Canada a few years later for an airline posting in South Asia, but he departed the airline shortly afterward to return to Northern Ireland, where he worked for some government agencies before successfully entering politics and becoming deputy speaker of the Assembly.

With John Gorman gone, my duties resumed some normalcy.

Among the trips I took in those days was one to Majorca in Spain's Balaeric Islands. I was accompanying a small group of journalists, including a Toronto CBC personality, Alex Trebek. Alex had done his homework, and one place he took me was to a bar owned by a renegade American baseball player named Curt Flood. He had gone to Palma to escape the notoriety of the bankruptcy of his business and two lawsuits, not to mention the IRS lien on a house he had bought for his mother. The bar was decorated with his baseball memorabilia, but it didn't look out of place on this holiday island in the Mediterranean.

Later Alex took me to a shoemaker where we both ordered a pair of dress boots. The Majorcan craftsmen were renowned for the quality of their work and I wore those boots for many years before retiring them. Alex was one classy guy.

I decided while I was there to buy both my wife and my mother something I had heard women were very fond of, Majorcan pearls. They're actually manmade glass filled with wax and coated with a material to give them a real pearl look and lustre. They were renowned in the fashion world and they were not cheap.

The next day after buying the pearls, I got to thinking how I was going to get them back into Canada, because I was definitely over the all-too-modest limit of duty-free goods we were allowed to bring back after a certain time.

The biggest consideration was not lying to the customs guys back home. When you're in the airline business and frequently coming and going on international flights, there is a terrific temptation to buy things, but if you return and don't declare your purchases honestly, it could cost you your job and cause your company and colleagues serious trouble.

That day we were wandering in a market and I hit upon an idea. It was certainly worth a try, I figured, and if it didn't work well, I'd declare the pearls and pay the duty. So, I bought what in those days we called a "yard of garlic," a large number of garlic buds attached together and sold by the yard, or metre. I knew that those customs guys liked to confiscate food and plant items that were not allowed in on commercial flights. The garlic cost the equivalent of about $1.25.

When I got to customs at Montreal a few days later, I was asked what I had purchased on my trip. I replied immediately that I'd found this incredible bargain and held up the yard of garlic. I thought the customs guy was going to bust a gut laughing; and then he told his mates, "Look what John brought back" (they got to know most of the regular travellers in the airline industry). He confiscated it and said, "Off you go." He didn't ask any more questions, so I didn't have to pay duty on the pearls.

I never tried that again, and the only time customs ever pulled me over was when I brought back some honey on a trip to France (my favourite flavour, lavender). I declared it and the officer asked me to go to his supervisor's office. On the way, he told me there were international concerns about honey being used by terrorists to smuggle drugs and guns; I didn't have time to counter that this glass jar was transparent, so it was obvious there was nothing but honey in it.

Turns out it wasn't the honey; the officer knew me as a TV celebrity and his boss wanted to meet me. We had a good laugh over that.

I had a lot of time for people who interfaced with passengers at the airport. Not a day would pass that they weren't being challenged, yet somehow ,they managed to stay calm. That was back in the 60s and 70s. I have no idea how they handle the myriad complaints today that extra security has generated.

Over the years I've shared many of these stories with friends, and there was always one or two who would tell sad stories about their experiences with customs. They would always say, "You were lucky." But I think there's more to it than luck. Despite the "ploy" with the garlic, I've always been honest and answered questions forthrightly.

Shirley and I once went to California to celebrate my 50th birthday with a trip down Pacific Highway One. While in wine country I bought seven magnums of a local sparking wine to serve at my birthday party, which was a few weeks away.

On our return to Toronto and customs at Pearson, we were greeted by the customs person with this: "Welcome home, John, we missed you on 'The News At Noon.'" The officer beckoned us through, but I said I had seven bottles of wine to declare. "No problem, have a nice day, and Happy Birthday," she replied.

Believe it or not, I said, no, I've got to pay some duty. She looked at me, smiled and said, "OK, seven dollars." And that was that. And let me tell you, that wine tasted all the better at my party. I was one lucky devil.

Then again, maybe it wasn't luck.

I've always thought of myself as lucky, but I do believe good things happen to good people and, although I wouldn't characterize myself as good, I've tried to follow the Golden Rule my whole life and I think I'm enjoying the dividends of that.

CHAPTER 29

Lady Luck Likes to Hang Around

Losing a parent at an early age as I did my father and not having known him doesn't sound lucky and it wasn't. But I sure was lucky to have the mother I had and the brothers, too, for that matter. My mother once told Shirley something my wife never forgot nor believed, namely, that her sons never fought. Shirley always said there was no way four boys could grow in a confined space like a two-bedroom house with one bathroom and not fight. But the fact is, we didn't and for that I was lucky.

There were lots of what could be considered minor examples of good luck such as falling in an elevator shaft but only 20 feet because two weeks before the incident, a new regulation governing elevator safety had been introduced.

Meeting people I've already documented who had big impacts on my life, that's good luck, too. The most important of those, of course, is Shirley, but while you've met quite a few already, there are more to come.

There is, though, that other kind of luck, you know, the one that wins you card games or the one that is in play when things go awry.

During a documentary filming adventure in Sudan in the 80s, we were being driven from Khartoum to El Obeid by a former truck driver who had done the route for years. Problem was, desertification had removed all his landmarks (the drought was so bad the desert was taking over the land by eight kilometres a year) and we got lost for several hours. Thankfully, it turned to dusk, and we eventually saw a light and that led us to a person who was able to help.

On that same trip, we were returning to Khartoum by small aircraft and the pilot had expressed concern about the baggage we were carrying (17-plus pieces) – because it was so hot (almost 50°C) he didn't think we could take off on this country runway. We heard this awful noise, but as it happens, our wheels were scraping some bushes at the end of the runway and we were OK.

One year, Shirley and I decided to travel to her parents' homeland, Yugoslavia, for a visit. We began our journey in Zagreb, Croatia, then took a bus to the coast, travelling through the Dinaric mountain range.

It had to be the scariest trip I've ever undertaken. I had a window seat and when I looked out at the incredible views, I noticed there was no shoulder to be seen. In effect, the bus skirted along the edge of these mountain roads with only inches to spare – at night – and the drop into the valleys below was thousands of feet. We heard later that accidents were fairly common on these roads. We were lucky.

The best good luck story, though, happened on a trip to Las Vegas. I went there for a convention of the Society of American Travel Writers, of which I was an associate member, being an airline PR person. My group was staying at the Landmark Hotel but most of our activities were at Caesar's Palace.

I had budgeted to gamble no more than $20 a day. Doesn't sound like much but I was still in a recovery mode after living in London and getting re-established back in Montreal. Besides, I have always been a conservative gambler and knew my limits. I was in Vegas for five nights and, for the first four nights, I lost my $20 playing

Blackjack. On the fifth day, I had to go to a formal rental shop to get a tuxedo for a convention closing dinner with an intimate performance for our group by Frank Sinatra at the Palace.

When I paid for the suit in cash, they returned some coins, mainly silver dollars, and when I got back to the hotel at about 3 p.m., I dropped a few coins into a slot machine as I was heading up to my room. Lo and behold, I won maybe $20 or $30, I can't remember exactly. But for me it was an omen.

I quickly went upstairs and changed into the suit and went directly to the $1 Blackjack table. For the next two or more hours I couldn't lose, and I didn't want to leave. But my friends dragged me away for the dinner and concert.

No sooner was the dinner and concert finished (I was right beside the stage, about six feet from Frank Sinatra), I ran outside, got a cab and went back to the Landmark and the $1 Blackjack table, where I continued to win. A one-dollar table doesn't sound like much, but I was winning big, so much so, they increased the number of times the waitress came around with the free drinks.

And yes, I overindulged, and at times was grabbing chips, running to other tables and plopping them down and not even staying to see if they won. I was cautioned a few times, but I gave the security people chips to keep them at bay.

I don't remember when I went to bed or how much I cashed in, but someone said I was up a few thousand dollars at one point. I do know I paid for the entire week in cash and had more money in my pocket than I'd had on arrival.

I had an early flight to Chicago, so I expected I'd be sleeping on the plane, terribly hung over. The United Airlines 727 took off and we were heading to Chicago when an announcement came that Chicago was socked in by snowy weather and we had to divert to Omaha, Nebraska. By the time we got to Omaha, the situation had cleared at Chicago, so the plane was to land, re-fuel and get on our way.

We did that but, as we flew down the runway, an engine blew. Somehow the pilot brought us to a safe halt, and we were taken to the terminal, given hotel and food vouchers, and told we would be informed about the next flight.

Sure enough, the next morning we were called, and our flight was ready. As we were boarding, I noticed the registration and saw it was the same aircraft. I must say I was somewhat hesitant to stay on board but all's well that ends well. We got to Chicago where I got a flight to Montreal and arrived a day late, but I arrived. I kind of figured that Lady Luck was with me that whole trip.

The only other story about gambling luck occurred in London, during my tenure there in 1967. My friend Hal asked me once if I played poker and I told him yes, it was my family's main entertainment when we were young, since we didn't have TV. He wanted me to join him to play at his club one Saturday morning. It was at The Pheasantry Club on King's Road in Chelsea.

I readily agreed. There were a number of important literary and musical icons living and working there. I don't remember the names of the other players, but I do know I almost fainted when I heard there was a three-bump limit to a maximum of seven pounds sterling. That meant every bet could potentially cost seven pounds or, at the time, C$21. The biggest stakes I had ever played before this was nickel, dime, quarter, three-bump limit so the maximum bet could be 75 cents.

As you can imagine, I played with incredible caution, only staying in with cards that had optimum potential for winning. Occasionally I won, but at a point when I was down probably $50 or $60, a new player arrived. I cannot remember her name, but she was dressed in the trendiest fashion and was a fantastic looker, simply gorgeous. I figured actress or pop singer.

Well, this interloper, in about an hour, had won about five or six hundred pounds, which she simply grabbed from the table, said her goodbyes and walked out of the room. I was flabbergasted and protested but it fell on deaf ears. The other players didn't say anything, but their look told me it was not a big deal.

Well, it was to me. I was down to my last cash and only had traveller's cheques left, so my caution increased. As luck would have it, though, I started to win more often than not and, by the time the game wrapped up, I was ahead by about twenty pounds.

I couldn't believe my luck and I vowed there and then I'd never put myself in that position again. And I never did.

CHAPTER 30

Lucky In Friendships, Too

One of the books my friend Elizabeth McAulay introduced me to in 1961 was called *Mr. Blue* by Myles Connolly. It was an unusual little book that had a shaky start when first published in the 20s but went on to become a cult classic, albeit within the Catholic community, initially. I used to recommend it to young people along with Khalil Gibran's *The Prophet* as a book outlining a basic philosophy of life. If you can find a copy, I'd certainly recommend it even now.

One of the many people influenced by Myles Connolly was the famous film director Frank Capra, whose films *Mr. Smith Goes to Washington* and *It's a Wonderful Life* are American classics.

Myles Connolly uses the fictional Mr. Blue to expound on his ideas of living a good life. One of these resonated deeply with me and set me on a path that I've tried hard to maintain:

> "Life gives you pretty much what you give it. She gives beauty to those who try to add to her beauty. She gives happiness to those who share their happiness with her. She gives, even, love to those who love her. But these are very, very few. Almost all of us have a capacity for being loved. But few of us have a capacity for loving."

Many of the friendships I have made alone or with Shirley have reflected these words from Mr. Blue. Those friendships led us on many paths.

One such person was Florence Millman, owner of the West End Art Gallery on Greene Avenue in Westmount. I spent many, many Saturdays over many years sitting in the gallery, watching people and artists come and go and eavesdropping on their conversations about art. Florence had an eclectic customer base of friends as well.

Most were Jewish and it was from them I learned a lot about Jewish humour, knowledge that served me well in the years ahead. One of them was the architect and artist Harry Mayerovitch. He had an illustrious career and remained on McGill University's School of Architecture faculty until his death at age 94. At one point, Harry asked me if Shirley and I would pose for him; he wanted to do portraits of his family, but he also wanted to learn the portrait genre, since the majority of his work was not figurative. The acrylic painting of Shirley was not to our liking and I'm not certain what happened to it. Mine was much better and I still have it. In fact, it shows me with a moustache, something I tried to grow only once, and it was a failure.

Florence used to take us to art auctions to further our understanding of Canadian art and pricing. This became one of the highlights of our social scene in Montreal.

One interesting auction anecdote. We became close friends of a renowned Montreal restaurateur named George Mede. One night at an auction, he and I jointly bid on a small painting by the incredible Quebec artist, Jean Paul Lemieux, and we won it.

Two weeks later George called to say he'd had an offer for our painting of twice what we paid and what did I want him to do. Sell, I said, and he agreed. We doubled our money. In today's market, though, that painting would be worth 40 times or more than we paid.

George ran the Continental Restaurant on Mountain Street and offered some of the finest, modestly priced food in Montreal. He was a wonderful, classic individual.

I'll never forget another one of our auction pals, Irv Seltzer, who was also my dentist. Irv had a terrific eye for quality and a head for bargains. He created a huge wall in his home filled with Group of Seven sketches (those small 8" X 10" paintings that were done on location in the wild, then expanded to large works in studio), a kind of pension plan for the self-employed character. Irv was a lovely man who died much too young.

Unlike Irv I never bought any of those sketches, despite entreaties from Florence. Instead, for several years I came under the spell of a young modern painter who was either a genius or a con man, depending on your perspective.

His name was John Popovic, a Serbian with alarming good looks and a swagger that exuded confidence. We met at a vernissage of his work at a Sherbrooke Street gallery (getting a show on Sherbrooke Street was the ultimate). I found out about the show from a pamphlet that had been dropped off at the Montreal Men's Press Club.

His art really interested me. He labelled it "Celestial Art," which, he explained, depicted the power and explosive quality of nature. He refused to explain how he achieved the style, but it didn't take long for mimics to try to copy it, without success I might add.

I remember standing beside a man at the vernissage in front of a moderate-sized painting that had an NFS sticker beside it. He was as enthralled as I and insisted on meeting the artist to whom he made an offer on the spot of $15,000 for the painting. Popovic turned him down, expressing his indignation at the offer.

Later he would regret his rashness and, as it happens, I ended up owning that painting, which, like all of the others, has a value of zero.

Nobody to my knowledge ever visited Popovic in his studio and one can only speculate why. But every now and again he would load some work into his car and travel to towns throughout Quebec and Ontario, where he would track down doctors who were known to have money and who were always looking for investments. I don't know how successful Popovic was at this but, for the first few years of our relationship, he always seemed to have cash.

When he had his pockets full, he would invite us to the Troika restaurant on Crescent Street, where he would drink a lot of vodka. Later he would wave the violinist over to our table, give him whatever bill he pulled from his pocket (he only carried 20s, 50s and 100s) and ask him to play "Kalinka," the famous Russian folk song. Popovic would sing along, then invariably start to weep, in fact, we all did as the booze took hold.

It was rumoured that when he needed money, Popovic would go to places frequented by wealthy Montreal women, places such as the Ritz Carlton Maritime Bar. There, it was said, he would charm one of them and end up at their home where, among other things, he would choose a spot for the painting he had sold them.

This kind of behaviour couldn't last, of course, so he took other avenues, such as an auction. He publicized it widely at some expense but found he didn't have enough paintings to justify what the auctioneer indicated was strong interest. Would I, he pleaded, give him a few of mine to round out the offering, so to speak?

By this time, I had made far too many contributions to Popovic's lifestyle, so I was happy to unload a few. As luck would have it, the auction succeeded in selling only three paintings and all of them were mine. I did not, however, see any of the proceeds since Popovic said he needed the funds to pay for the auction and promotion. Instead he gave me two of his "important" works.

His final ploy was to open a Sherbrooke Street gallery with a partner to market his own work as well as other artists who were anxious to be showing on this prestigious street. They rented the street-level space at the bottom of Le Cartier, a fabulous high-rise at the corner of Peel and Sherbrooke and called it the Garner-Rothschild Gallery. The name reeked of wealth.

I can't remember how long the gallery remained in business, but it wasn't long, and I do remember one thing I did for which I may be grateful one day. I got the gallery to value my Popovic paintings for insurance and capital gains purposes and I still have that document.

John Popovic killed himself not long after the gallery closed. He drove his car into an abutment on Cote des Neiges. Despite the financial pain and consternation he brought me, I was sorry to hear how he ended his life.

Thanks to Florence and one of her friends, our art collection was to take a turn for the better.

CHAPTER 31

Long Friendships – Long Memories

I remember vividly how, for months, every Saturday I was in town I'd sit at Florence's gallery opposite a painting that I knew I just had to own. It was an oil of four young ladies in a scene that looked like it could be a confirmation of the youngest one. We never did know the name of the painting because the artist, Louise Scott, never named her work, leaving that to others, especially her patron Jack Greenwald.

I ended up buying that painting and eventually got to know Louise and Jack, remaining friends long after we left Montreal. Both are gone as of this writing, but they were two of the most unforgettable characters we'd ever meet. And that painting still holds a place of honour in our living room.

Jack was married to Constance Brown, who ran the foremost modelling agency in Montreal, if not Canada, for a time. One of her early finds was a young Yugoslav immigrant named Ivana who became better known as the wife of New York developer, now U.S. President, Donald Trump.

Jack helped run the agency but was an entrepreneur in his own right, as partner in an eastern Arctic company called Arctic Ventures in Iqaluit. He became a major source of fine Inuit carvings and paintings for his own collection and for galleries such as Waddington's. His business interests provided the capital to expand his art collection into fine European works along with antiques and silk carpets. A visit to his home at Habitat was always a treat and an education.

It was Jack who explained to me that something of accepted value will always hold that value, barring unforeseen or exceptional circumstances. He explained that quality diamonds, carpets, French furniture, sculpture, and the like, had the same value in Australia or Europe or the USA or Hong Kong, and any time a bargain was available, it had to be questioned whether it was genuine.

We had many long chats about the airline industry and art, among many things, but we never talked politics. Jack took pains to tell me the story of how Montreal Jews came to be in Montreal, from whence they had come and why. I was fascinated by all this because of their incredible successes in the arts and their wonderful sense of humour.

Jack was a patron to Louise Scott, whose work I came to admire and who we befriended not long afterwards. Jack's role as patron included managing Louise's output: working with galleries and generally promoting her work, which ended up in some of the finest collections in North American.

I remember once visiting Louise at her apartment in a working-class part of town. When we walked in, we saw she had been working on a huge canvas, and Shirley and I loved it. Jack eventually told us that he had named the painting "The Bar at the Orlofsky Hotel." There was no Orlofsky Hotel, only in Louise's imagination. This painting went into a show in 1987 and was bought by a man who, a few days later, had to walk away from the purchase and down payment, because he'd lost big in the stock market crash that year.

Now living in Toronto, I was told it was available and I managed to do a deal with Jack to pay for it over many months. I called it my pension plan painting and it hung in the dining room of our home in Rosedale and now our condo. It's always the most talked-about piece of art in our collection.

It never became a "pension plan" because its value is questionable. Louise had died and no arrangements had been made for a planned disbursement of her few assets, mainly paintings. In fact, it turns out she had warehoused paintings Jack had told her to dispose of and, after her death, these made it into the market, thus diluting her reputation. Jack had been powerless to completely control Louise; artists can be like that.

Jack was also a patron to a sculptor from Montreal named Jim Ritchie. Jim had been born into a fairly well-to-do family but wanted to be an artist, not a business person. He hung out in the core of Montreal, becoming a boulevardier along with the likes of Leonard Cohen, a friend for life.

In the late 50s, Jim left Montreal for France in the company of another sculptor named Robert Roussil. Ironically, they both died in France at age 87.

I believe Robert Roussil had a following and reputation in Quebec but for reasons I've not been able to fathom, Jim Ritchie never did. His work is in some important collections but, despite Jack's efforts, Jim never achieved the star reputation his work deserved.

I first saw his work at Jack's and was taken by one piece in particular, a bronze that was erotic in nature and typical of Jim's work at that time. Having expressed my love for it, Jack said he thought there might be a marble maquette of this one available. Besides, he said, Jim needed the money.

Not knowing the artist but respecting his patron, I sent off the money order and waited. Sure enough, about a month later I received a crated sculpture from Jim. It was in black marble and demanded to be touched, something our visitors are known to do; it became the first of many pieces I'd buy over the years.

Jim and I communicated for years and I have every one of his letters. In the years leading up to his death, we spoke on Skype, though he was always challenged by technology.

He came to Canada a few times and stayed with us. On one occasion in Toronto, we went to a well-known restaurant for lunch – Three Small Rooms – where we were joined by some other friends of his. We were having a terrific, boisterous time when, at one point, Jim said, "Listen, what do you hear." We said, "Nothing." "Exactly," he said, "we're the only ones enjoying ourselves in this whole place."

He obviously wasn't a fan of Toronto and the gallery he displayed in didn't work hard on his behalf, so he bailed. His main gallery was in New York, but he had others in Europe.

Jim lived a long life as a bachelor in the south of France – Provence – in a town called Vence, not far from the widely-known St. Paul de Vence, which is renowned for its modern and contemporary art galleries and museums such as the Maeght Foundation. Vence was a medieval town and home to the famous Matisse Chapel. It was quiet and suited him. Early in his life there he erected a huge sculpture for the town, something very modern and unlike his other work. Later, when he found his ultimate style, he created a remarkable piece called La Vençoise (The Vence Woman) and it stands some eight feet tall in a square in front of city hall. The city had insisted.

The Canadian filmmaker David Cronenberg did a documentary about Jim, but it never generated the expected interest in his work, although it gave him a lot of credibility. Jim found himself having to do his own promotional work with limited resources. On one of my visits, we did a video with me wandering through his home and filming him, answering my questions about his life and work. It was edited into a short backgrounder piece, but I'm not sure if it every got play.

Jim had many mistresses over the years, most of whom he met while sitting in his favourite spot in the main square of Vence. He never married, but one of his friends became pregnant and he found himself a father. The woman had the child, a boy, back in her hometown in Sweden, and Jim had a limited role in the child's upbringing. That child, though, turned into one clever person who made a great deal of money, but decided to give most of it back by forming a charity that, to this day, continues to develop schools around the world for children in need.

The man also bought his father a house partway up the mountain overlooking Vence. It had been owned by an aristocrat who had fallen on hard times. Jim's task in what turned into his retirement years was to a refurbish the house to its original grandeur and he did that.

The home had a pool and marvellous gardens, which at one point grew tens of thousands of roses, whose petals were sold to the perfumeries in the nearby centre of the industry, Grasse.

Jim organized the display of some of his significant marbles in that garden and around the pool, giving the gardens a museum-like feel.

We were lucky enough to visit Jim for a few days only months before he died. He looked frail but his mind was as sharp as ever. It was tough saying goodbye because we knew he didn't have long to live.

I was truly shocked that Jim's passing received no coverage in the Canadian media. He made a name for himself in France and is represented in art collections around the world. How Canadian that he became a forgotten treasure.

I often think of Jim when I'm dining out at one of Toronto's multitude of fine restaurants. I hear the buzz and feel the excitement in the room; I see the smiles on the faces of other patrons and delight at the quality of the offerings and professionalism of the staff. Jim would have been pleased to see how Toronto has been transformed, thanks mainly to the 300,000-plus Quebeckers who arrived in the late 70s and early 80s.

When you walk into our home, you're greeted by some of Jim's work and it's sprinkled throughout the main public rooms. They always draw wonderful comments. Jim's works share space with many Inuit sculptures we bought through Jack. Our walls are filled with paintings, a pastel and a lithograph by Louise Scott, and by paintings and a pencil drawing by another artist friend, Jérôme Couëlle.

CHAPTER 32

Our Friend, the Legend

Shirley met Jérôme Couëlle at work in Montreal where he was in charge of The Bay's visual store presentation. He had a slight lisp and was short in stature but Jérôme had a big personality.

We didn't socialize with Jérôme in those early days but we spent time with him at his summer residence in North Hero, Vermont, and fully re-connected when we moved to Toronto, where he lived first in a rambling house in South Rosedale and later in a tiny apartment near our home. Jerome loved our son Jonathan and treated him more like a grandson.

Jérôme was born in Aix en Provence, France, into an artistic family. Both his father and brother were architects, with the former being awarded the Legion of Honour for his extraordinary creations. It was to get out from under the cloak of his family that Jerome joined the French Foreign Legion and was posted to North Africa, where he developed a strong distaste for the military and went AWOL, ending up working in an iron mine where he fell victim to hemochromatosis, which ended up taking his life in 2015.

He immigrated to Montreal to work for a large materials corporation but soon gained a position at The Bay and remained there for the balance of his working life.

When I first saw Jérôme's art, I couldn't decide whether he was an artist or an illustrator. His work had a fantasy context showing, for example, birds holding umbrellas to protect them from pollution. It wasn't until I saw more of his work that I realized how prescient he was about climate change and its impact on living things. His work was intricate, and each painting took weeks to complete.

Jérôme was widely read and had a celestial mind. I wasn't surprised when he told a friend only months before his death, "I want to explore other planets, you see, I'm tired of this one."

He became a much-loved regular at our festive dinners and because of his love for our son, spent many a Sunday family dinner with us. I was always happy to have him at our table because, thanks to my cooking lessons, I was making a wide variety of soups. He ended up calling each a "museum soup" because, he said, they belonged in a museum. Quite an honour coming from someone who was a fabulous cook himself.

Jérôme and I had a mutual respect for each other, but I didn't get as close to him as Shirley (or Jonathan for that matter), because his celestial talk and interest in the planets and the spiritual world triggered Shirley's interest in the same things.

Where young people broke up sentences with "like" or "you know," Jérôme used "you see" as a way of making statements that you had to believe simply because he spoke them. On the last few days we spent with him at the hospital before he died, he spoke of going on another journey, and I never got the feeling he was concerned about the transition that was about to occur.

Jérôme's unique qualities and frankness often got him into disputes and, while I can't be certain, it had to be a difference of opinion that came between him and David Thomson that led the latter to break communication and contact.

David, now Lord Thomson, is one of Canada's foremost art

collectors, continuing the work of his father Kenneth, though breaking into new territory. He began to collect Jérôme's work in earnest, but I don't know the status of that collection today.

Ours is modest, just a few pieces, and the most important one we bought was sold because a family emergency brought an urgent need for cash. I regret that sale to this day. Still, we see his work every day and live happily having known him for so long and so well. When visiting the country, I never fail to think of Jérôme as I stare at the stars and try to decide to which one his journey has taken him.

Knowing Jérôme was just another measure of the luck that has accompanied me on my own journey.

CHAPTER 33

Competing with Nelson

Actually, that's a bit of a stretch. There's no way I could ever compete with Nelson Saunders. He was an entrepreneur, a salesman, a music aficionado, a gourmand, an oenophile, an art collector, and dilettante, generally, in many aspects of life.

We met through mutual friends. In the late 70s we spent a lot of time together and even after we moved to Toronto, the relationship continued effortlessly, even taking holidays together.

Nelson's wife was Jeanne, a pretty, very smart woman from Arvida, Quebec. Both had been married before, Nelson having had children, and together they raised two children of their own, Christopher and Tara Kathleen. They lived at the architectural wonder of Expo 67, Habitat, and were among the early adopters of that lifestyle outside the Montreal core.

Walking into their apartment was more like walking into an art gallery. The modern "boxes" that made up Habitat were ideal to show the depth and breadth of their art collection, which included Inuit and Jim Ritchie sculpture and Louise Scott paintings, among others. They, too, were influenced by Jack Greenwald, a long-time friend.

The first holiday we took together was to Jamaica where we rented a home on the beach in Ocho Rios that belonged to Sir Jack Lyons, the tea merchant in England. It was a nice home but had fallen into disrepair and the swimming pool was unusable.

We were in Jamaica at a time when the country was experiencing economic difficulties and the visit was not that pleasant. Knowing about food shortages in advance, we took some food on our trip, but it was confiscated at customs on arrival.

Having been in Jamaica some years before and remembering it fondly, I was saddened to see how the spirit had deteriorated. We also felt uncomfortable when, at any given time of day, locals would wander onto the property from the beach, some looking for food, which we, too, were lacking. Overall, not much fun.

Still, we enjoyed our time with the Saunders and subsequent holidays with them to Maine were superb. We spent many happy days at Kennebunkport in homes on or near the beach. We also spent many a night at the White Barn Inn and its piano bar where we regularly exercised our lungs. Nelson certainly knew his music, having been a manager of musicians in Ottawa, and I always considered music to be my life.

Jeanne was a school vice-principal, which meant she was riddled with work so her time away was vital. She was also a great cook, so we ate well and abundantly on these occasions.

The Saunders also had a unit in Manzanillo Mexico, Club Santiago, where they made some interesting friends, mainly Americans. We went to stay with them a few times and had a great time.

Nelson was a terrific tennis player and I hadn't taken it up seriously yet so couldn't play in his games. Eventually, though, I took up golf and we often played there with some friends.

At some point, an investment Nelson had made years before paid off in a big way and they ended up building a home at La Punta, a gorgeous gated community immediately beside the famous Las

Hades Hotel and on a point of land jutting into the Pacific. We spent many wonderful weeks there over the years.

I grew to like Mexico very much and later we would spend time in San Miguel de Allende in the mountains outside Mexico City and at Ajijic, on Lake Chapala, where there was a sizeable Canadian community, mainly Torontonians. We stopped going to Mexico because of the hassles with flying, which were all too common on those southern routes.

So we haven't been back to visit the Saunders in Manzanillo for many years. And that's too bad because my golf game has improved since we last played and my tennis skills are much better than when Nelson played against me in the day.

We keep in daily contact on social media, though.

CHAPTER 34

Our Days in Montreal Wind Down

When the Parti Québécois won the 1976 election and started to implement some of the policies that won them power, such as the French Language Bill 101, making French the only official language in the province, it triggered dramatic change in Quebec. And that, along with a pending referendum on separation, was the last straw for hundreds of thousands of English-speaking Quebeckers. The exodus began in earnest.

We had sold our house six months earlier in anticipation of this change. Ours was a row house in a community called Redpath Place, just in behind the Montreal Museum of Fine Arts. We loved it and the location.

But one day early that year, I told Shirley that all the talk of separation was getting more play and the politicians that were attracted to the cause had a lot of credibility, people such as René Lévesque. I felt we had no other choice but to sell because with a separatist government in power, real estate prices would plunge.

We sold and, according to our agent, we achieved the highest ever price per square foot for a house in downtown Montreal at that time. It was a paltry amount in relation to today's prices, but we experienced a handsome profit in less than two years.

The Canadian dollar was at a slight premium to the U.S. dollar, so we decided to put our capital into the U.S. for safekeeping. We chose Vermont because it was close and we loved that state, having visited it many times with friends.

We purchased a delightful 52-acre property. Ironically, a few years later, when we were forced to sell at least part of it, the most natural buyers were Quebeckers and that market became very tight. But that was still a few years away. Meantime, we were rental apartment dwellers in Montreal and owners of a fabulous weekend getaway under two hours south across the border.

It was a beautiful property that included the original farmhouse, a century-plus old schoolhouse that had been moved onto the property to become a recording studio, and a dilapidated barn that definitely needed to come down. All of that was on 12 acres on one side of the country road. On the 40-acre other side there was a tiny 18th-century cemetery, a beautiful meadow, a pond stocked with trout, a sugar bush and a river that served as a border to our best neighbour, the Chalifoux family.

We had bought the property from one of the management team of the U.S. musical group, Three Dog Night. The details are a bit vague, but he had secretly courted the wife of one of the singers and together they left California and ended up in the obscure Northern Vermont area, which had become a haven for draft dodgers and people wanting to opt out, generally. They were still concerned about possible trouble, though, because they slept with a handgun under the pillow of their master bedroom bed.

His name was Jonas and he established an interesting business buying up old Vermont barns and other structures to salvage the weathered barnwood and support beams for house construction in California, where rustic barnboard had become all the rage.

I had my first ever vehicle, a brand new 1976 bright red Jeep

Wagoneer Limited Edition, a comfortable apartment, a fabulous retreat in the U.S., and both Shirley and I were working in good jobs.

We waited a while before inviting friends down to the farm as we only had one spare room in the farmhouse. We decided to renovate the schoolhouse, but that project would wait for a while until we had the main house filled with furniture.

When the winter took hold, though, we decided it was time to share the place with friends Ian and Mary Henderson, and off we went in a blinding snowstorm. As we headed down the Eastern Townships autoroute, the driving snow intensified, and I was having trouble seeing out the window as it kept icing up. I stopped every so often and chipped the ice off, but it was a constant issue.

Ian said he was surprised at this because Jeeps had a reputation for performing in all conditions and was guessing that the defroster was faulty.

I said, "What's a defroster?"

Everyone was aghast that I didn't know, but they never stopped to think that this was my first car, even though I was 37 at the time. Anyway, I found it and we never had another problem.

One other time, I bought a chainsaw and used it for the first time when some friends were visiting. I had great plans to prune the sugar bush and other wooded areas, using the branches for firewood.

We gathered around one tree. I got the new machine operating quickly and held it against a target branch and started to push and pull it to cut the branch, but nothing was happening. My friend Danny said, "You might want to pull the trigger." It's good to have friends around when you're trying new toys.

Our garden the following year offered another fine example of that. My neighbour Andre Chalifoux had offered to till the soil on a piece of land about 70 feet by 70 feet between the schoolhouse and the barn. He kept saying, are you sure you want it this big? Of course, I replied.

With Andre's help and some seeds from a local store, we planted corn, summer squash, green beans, tomatoes, musk melons (cantaloupe) and broccoli. Andre also provided pig manure, which, while smelly, remained fresh the whole growing season and is truly the best fertilizer.

We ended up with the most prolific garden I have ever seen, from which we gave away bushels of produce. Andre was so right about the garden's size – we had developed a jungle-like environment that took hours to prune where we were able to do so.

Two things happened that made it all the more memorable. One Friday we set out from Montreal and I spoke on the way about the fresh corn we were going to have that weekend. When we got there, I rushed over to harvest the cobs, only to find not one left – the raccoons had feasted on all of it.

The other incident was also on a Friday night when, on arrival, I harvested enough broccoli for the entire weekend's meals. That night we had steamed broccoli with butter, and it was sensational, so fresh, so healthy.

The next day I told Andre and his wife how much we were enjoying the garden. His wife agreed but said wasn't it too bad about the broccoli. I replied, what do you mean, it was fantastic. She said her broccoli was devastated by little green caterpillars and she didn't want to eat it. When I said we didn't have any, she simply shrugged and changed the subject.

When we got home an hour later, I checked the balance of the broccoli I had picked to find it full of little green caterpillars. I simply washed them off and carried on.

When we renovated the schoolhouse, we used barnwood I had salvaged from our fallen structure. It became the wainscotting for our combined great room, kitchen and main bedroom. What I didn't know and what my general contractor didn't tell me, nor did

I bother to ask the property seller Jonas, was that barnwood needed to be treated to destroy the imbedded fly larvae and any other creatures that might be lingering. As a result, in the spring when the warm days burst forth, so did the pack flies, thousands of them, and it took quite a while to get them under control.

When the schoolhouse renovation was complete and the main farmhouse deck was finished, we decided to have a party to thank those who had worked on the project, neighbours and friends from Montreal. About 100 were invited and even more showed up.

It was to be a pig roast and we ordered from a local butcher a 90-pound pig, which he splayed (butterflied) so we could attach it in between two box springs and cook it over an earth oven. The springs made it easy to turn and cooking was guaranteed better than on a spit.

In preparation I had dug a deep pit and lined the bottom with rock salvaged by Andre from our garden site. Shirley's sister Carley came early and had a huge fresh salmon that she prepared, encased in aluminum foil and buried in the pit.

At some ungodly hour in the morning, at Shirley's insistence, my friend Ian Henderson and I built a tremendous fire of hardwood to make excellent coals. I wanted to wait until the noon hour before putting the pig over the pit, but Shirley insisted it be positioned earlier.

Our pit was obviously too good because the pig had thoroughly cooked by 2 p.m. and our guests would be starting to arrive at 6 p.m. Still, it was a huge success. I had bought ten local berry pies, thinking there would be enough for those who wanted dessert. They were gone in about five minutes flat.

It took most of the next day to clean up and bag all the garbage, and when I realized the dump was closed, I said, no problem, I'll take it back to Montreal because Monday morning was our pick-up day. When I tried to cross the border, the Canada Customs guy, who had known about the party, greeted me and asked if we'd had a good time. I said yes and pointed in the back of the Jeep where we had about ten bags of garbage.

I thought he was going to have a heart attack. He took pains to explain why we couldn't bring garbage across the border like that and I understood him completely. In the end, though, he looked the other way and we carried on, travelling nonstop to our apartment, where I loaded the bags into bins to lessen the opportunity for collateral infestation. I had learned a valuable lesson.

I was always learning lessons.

CHAPTER 35

Big Changes Take Over

In 1977 we decided to visit our friends the Houssers in Victoria. Barbara and Bruce were university pals of Shirley and we had a lot of fun times together in London and Montreal.

The Houssers ran a deli in Victoria, in fact, THE deli in Victoria, the world-renowned Sam's Deli that served soups and sandwiches that were loved by all, especially vegans. They had the best serving staff, too. For more than 25 years they excelled in this business.

They lived in a perfect house in Oak Bay, perfect for them and their three children. When we went to visit as a side trip to an annual Vancouver journey, we stayed in the library, sleeping on a shag rug. We figure it was there – well, it had to be – that our son Jonathan was conceived because almost to the day nine months later Shirley gave birth to this incredible baby at Royal Victoria Hospital. (Our son had to live with the reality that he was conceived after his parents shagged on a shag rug. Sorry, Jonathan, but that's how it happened.)

You never forget things like the moment the water breaks and you rush your wife to the hospital, and within minutes, it seems, she simply gives birth. It's all the stuff of Hollywood movies, right?

Wrong.

Shirley was on the phone that Friday night talking business when the water broke, and she insisted on completing a few projects before we got to the hospital. The labour lasted about 12 hours and I was with her the whole time, trying to be encouraging. Afterward, Shirley said the best-selling book by Burton White, *The First Three Years of Life*, was misleading when it said the birthing process was so natural and not painful.

Still, as if to prove Dr.White right, Shirley on Sunday was giving dictation and instructions to her assistant in her private hospital room, which she left the next day.

That happened in March 1978. A month or so later, we got the news my company was moving the Canadian headquarters to Toronto. And as it happened, The Bay was delighted Shirley would be moving there, too, because they had plans for her to take on a big new job. We were, however, faced with dilemmas.

For a start, we loved Montreal and our friends who resided there. It only takes a visit to Montreal and environs to realize what a special place it is culturally, topographically and architecturally. It reeks of age and history. It's far more European than any other North American city (well, maybe not more than Quebec City) and has a style that's unique thanks in part to the entrepreneurship of the expatriates that make up the dynamic immigrant population.

While Canadians generally had nothing good to say about Toronto, and still don't in some regions, the consensus was that everybody loved Montreal. There was a sense of style there that didn't exist elsewhere. Women and men both dressed with a flourish to attract attention.

As I walked to work every morning, I would pass some attractive women, and if our eyes met, I'd often say, "Bonjour" or "Good Morning" and more often than not I'd get a positive response. When I eventually moved to Toronto, I tried that and got glares.

One particular experience drove that home. I had been working in Toronto for just a few weeks when I went out for lunch on my own. I was often on my own because my co-workers brought their lunch from home and ate at their desks.

I was walking on Dundas west toward Bay and Spadina (where I hoped to find another great Chinese restaurant) when I spied a young woman struggling with baggage on the north side of Dundas, obviously heading to the nearby bus terminal. I jaywalked across the street and said to her, "Je m'appelle John. Puis je vous aider?" From the way she was dressed I knew she was Québécoise and she said, "S'il vous plait." And started to tear up.

She told me she had lived for seven months in Toronto and not once had a stranger been so kind to her. She had been part of that large exodus from Quebec after the Parti Québécois won power but was heading home because she didn't feel comfortable in Toronto.

I jokingly said, "I'd like to join you" because I wasn't all that happy either but, alas, that was a whim.

What was it about Montreal that gave it such character and spark? It certainly wasn't the English establishment that had run things since its founding. Most of them still thought they lived in England and saw no reason to learn French, denigrating the local language as a patois.

No, in my experience it was a combination of the expatriate community blending with the long-resident Jewish community. The expats brought a sophistication mainly from Europe and the Jews brought a sense of humour mainly from eastern Europe and Russia. Mordecai Richler was one of their heroes and his Duddy Kravitz character perfectly caught the essence of the Jewish people I came to know and love.

Jack Greenwald once explained the reality to me: Most of the Jews in Montreal came from Russia and environs. They came by ship and, on arrival in Nova Scotia, they boarded trains to the rest of Canada. The majority, Jack said, stayed in Montreal because they didn't have enough money to travel further inland. A large number went to Toronto and the balance travelled mainly to Winnipeg, with a small number of well-heeled travellers going as far as Vancouver.

There was always a lot of tension between the Jews and French-Canadians, but they also co-operated because both were looked down upon by the dominant English financiers and the WASP establishment.

I had a friend who worked at the Montreal office of the American securities firm, Bache & Company. I had met David Schwartz through his wife Leanne, who was working with my wife Shirley at The Bay. We had a lot of fun times with the Schwartzs and were so close that when we moved out of the ground level flat on Summerhill Street, they took it over.

All was not well in that marriage, though we didn't know it or feel it at the time, and one day not that long after moving in, Leanne arrived home to find David had packed up and left the flat. It was devastating and unexpected. David ended up moving to Toronto and remarrying. I saw him a few times but neither he nor we were interested in renewing the friendship.

Leanne, though, remained our very close friend until her early death from cancer. She was one great friend, so very smart and very attractive. After leaving The Bay she became entrepreneurial and mentored many people in the Montreal rag trade and entertainment industry. She also taught marketing at Concordia University for a few decades.

One of her first boyfriends after the marriage breakdown was a young man in the rag trade named Sam Caplan. Sammy introduced me to the breadth and depth of Jewish humour. He was incredibly fast with a witticism. In a pizza restaurant he'd try to order egg rolls and would hold up four fingers to order three; in a Chinese restaurant he'd try to order pizza. It went on and on and servers never got upset because he had a great smile.

The first time we had him to dinner at our house, I said to Sammy that he had to eat everything on his plate. "Remember the starving kids in Africa," I ventured, remembering what my Mother had said many years before. "Name two," he shot back. And that sealed our friendship.

Leaving the likes of Nelson and Jeannie Saunders, Leanne and Sam, Florence Millman and Harry Meyerovitch, Jack Greenwald and so many others was tough. I knew we'd stay in touch, but it would never be quite the same again.

As we drove away from our home in Montreal with the back of the Jeep loaded with valuables and Shirley holding in her arms the most valuable of all, our baby son, both of us were in tears by the time we hit the Decarie Expressway. It was a tough drive all the way to the 401 Highway.

But there was another issue, a practical, annoying one that had to be faced and we spent some time talking about that. We were moving to a high cost city and our capital was mainly tied up in Vermont. Really big decisions lay ahead.

CHAPTER 36

Life Begins in Toronto

Our first stop on arriving in Toronto was to see my mother who was thrilled beyond words to meet her grandson. But we wouldn't be staying in that tiny house. We had bought our own tiny house but hadn't sealed the deal, so we stayed close by with my dear friend Ian Henderson and his wife, Mary, on Inglewood Drive in Moore Park.

We had purchased a house in north Rosedale on Jean Street and ours was the first house at the end of the cul-de-sac that ended at the railway track that traversed Toronto, much to the chagrin of everyone who was within earshot.

But the house was all we could afford since our capital was tied up in the Vermont property. At the closing of our purchase I asked the seller, a lawyer named Rochester, how many trains went by each day. He looked me straight in the eye and said, "About 22 or 4." I responded, "Well, that's not as bad as I thought," having been worried because we could almost reach out from the side of our house and shake hands with a train's engineer.

We soon learned, though, that what Mr. Rochester meant was 22 to 4 during the day because there were another 20 or so at night. Another valuable lesson learned.

Once we had possession, though, I called upon my brother Larry to help and we gutted the kitchen, re-drywalled it and got it ready for new cabinets and appliances. It was a small house, but it was adequate for what furniture we'd brought from Montreal, though we had to use one room for storage.

We were in the house just a few weeks when a neighbour said he was getting a load of gravel and there'd be some left over, and would I want it for our dirt driveway? Absolutely, I said, and agreed I'd leave my car at the end of the cul de sac to allow access for the dump truck.

When I got home, I saw the mound of gravel and the bright yellow parking ticket on my car. All I could say was "Welcome to Toronto."

I rarely used the car during the week. Both Shirley and I took the bus from North Rosedale, she to her office and me to the subway and my office at the Eaton Centre. Every day we passed a house on Crescent Road that each of us mentioned how much we liked. It had great character.

We didn't stay in Rosedale very long, because of some drastic action we took at the Vermont property. Needing the capital but hoping to retain an interest there, we severed our 52 acres and then contracted to have the schoolhouse moved across the road to the 40-acre parcel. It was a real challenge for me, arranging it mostly from Toronto and then being there for the actual move.

We were successful, however, and when we put the 12 acres and farmhouse on the market, it sold rather more quickly than we expected to a well-known furniture manufacturer from Montreal, a man of European origin who knew the value of a property with views.

With the cash from the sale, we looked for a bigger house, away from the tracks but in the general area we were living in and we found it midway between Yonge Street and Avenue Road on Heath Street West. It was a charming house with a shared driveway and nice south-facing garden. And, in another lucky moment, we sold the house beside the tracks to a childless couple, one of whom loved trains.

We didn't do a whole lot to the house on Heath but Shirley orchestrated some changes, such as buying a Soleado print fabric to cover the walls of our master bedroom. It was fabulous.

It was a nice community with good neighbours, but changes were in the wind. Really big changes.

The first of these was accepting the reality that we couldn't keep the Vermont property. The running costs were high for the former schoolhouse and we learned that the buyer of the 12-acre property was treating the 40 acres across the road as part of his own domain.

But more importantly, an opportunity came along for me to change careers and I took it. That meant we wouldn't be going to Vermont for some time. We considered renting it but that wouldn't have been practical, so we listed the property and luckily it sold fairly quickly to a friend of the man who had bought the 12 acres. We didn't know it at the time, but the deal was clinched when the buyer agreed to sell much of the 40 acres to her friend who had been using it as his own anyway.

So, it was the end of our affair with Vermont. I would miss that fresh mountain air, our beaver pond stocked with trout, the sugar bush and the caves housing deer on the river that bordered our property, with our lovely neighbours the Chalifouxs.

We had only been there a few years but had partied with some fabulous people. Many of these were Montrealers who lived as far away as Stowe, people like Morty Pesner, who we'd met through Florence Millman many years before. Morty's family founded one of Montreal's renowned meat packers and his second wife was the great Montreal beauty and socialite Louise Pratt.

Other neighbours and friends included Don McGowan, the

iconic CFCF-TV weather person, who was an institution in Montreal television, and Pierre Desjardins, the insurance broker of renown who also happened to have sailed for Canada in the Olympics. Ray Heard, the Managing Editor of the *Montreal Star*, had a Vermont home nearby as did John Meyer, my boss at the *Gazette*. And there were many more.

And I can't forget the local tradesmen we got to know, some of whom had opted out of the American mainstream in favour of the solitude (at times madness) of Vermont. We used to meet up at Montgomery Center's Kilgore's Trout Saloon, named for the Kurt Vonnegut fictional character. The bar was right beside the Trout River.

Then there was the real estate broker with whom we did all of our deals and with whom we spent many quality times, Don Bordner. He was a central character in the area and must be missed since he moved his office to Stowe and set up shop in Florida as well.

So many memories …

CHAPTER 37

Really Big Changes in Homes and My Job

At about the same time we sold off our Vermont retreat, we sold our home on Heath Street and bought a house on Crescent Road and, yes, by sheer luck (or was it fate?) it was the same house that Shirley and I had admired during our bus ride to work every morning. That home at the top of the "T" of Crescent Road and Wrenthum Place had been owned by a variety of fascinating people.

First and foremost, in modern times, was Thomas Drew-Brook who had been adjutant to William Stephenson, the Master Spy whose career was chronicled in the book, *A Man Called Intrepid*, by William Stevenson. Stephenson had been chosen by Winston Churchill to form an elite spy faction during the Second World War and was to be trained in what became known as Camp X near Oshawa.

When those who came for training arrived in Toronto, they more often than not stayed at Tommy Drew-Brook's home at 119 Crescent Road. It was referred to as a "safe house."

After Drew-Brook, the house was owned by the daughter of the national *Weekend Magazine* outdoors columnist Gregory Clark. For years taxi drivers would regale us with stories about them bringing Greg Clark back home from his haunt at the King Edward Hotel.

Sometime later it changed hands again and this time the buyer was a cable television executive who, in turn, sold the house to a university professor and his wife and children. When we discovered it had been on the market for some time, we were a bit concerned, but it didn't sell at what should have been market value because of its location on the street and its condition – it needed some serious TLC.

We decided to make a low bid because of the need for renovations and we didn't know what our home would fetch in current conditions. Our low bid was accepted unconditionally, and we managed at the same time to sell the Heath Street home for a premium. The Crescent Road home was large, some 3500 square feet, and although we didn't have enough furniture for the three stories, we did have some useful furniture in Vermont.

Once again, as I had done many times before, I called on my friend Ian Henderson to help me. I rented a U-Haul for my Jeep and we drove down to Vermont and filled it with mostly antiques and useful things. Knowing we would have to go through Customs on route home, I listed everything we'd put in the box so that when we arrived at the border, it would be easy for the officer to check it.

Once again, as I'd learned when I had brought back that load of garbage following our pig roast two years before, the officer in change knew me and, after taking a cursory look at the box and my Jeep, let us go with a "sorry to see you go" farewell but a firm "don't put us in this situation again."

Most of the Vermont furniture we placed on the third floor, but some fine wicker was put into the beautiful sunroom that graced the front of the house. That room would become our main television viewing room, though, in reality, we didn't watch a lot of TV as I had become what they called an on-air personality at Global News. I have told the story many times and often people give me a quizzical look, but I swear this is how it all happened.

After some 15 years working for British Overseas Airways Corporation, which had merged with British European Airways to form British Airways, the glamour of working in what was an exciting industry was beginning to fade. We were operating huge aircraft, seating hundreds; there were ticket price wars and as the operating costs rose, customer service declined.

The politics inside the company were also fraught. There was job uncertainty after the merger and there was a constant threat from the U.S. headquarters in New York to convince London the Canadian operation could be managed from there. There were also people at PR headquarters who felt the Canadian operation would be better served by someone with a British accent.

I understood that completely. Years before I had hired a young man as my PR Officer in Toronto. His name was Douglas Port. He was smart and ambitious. He still had traces of a Scottish accent. London were impressed with him. The more responsibility I gave him the more he succeeded to win us the good, honest news coverage for which I had always striven.

One day Doug told me he'd had an offer he couldn't refuse to join Air Canada in a senior role. I had had a feeling he was anxious to get out from under me, as it appeared I was in no mood or position to move anywhere. He may have orchestrated his move, but it didn't matter; I was extremely proud of Doug and gave him my blessing, though London was a bit miffed, as I was led to believe.

Doug went on to achieve a number of important positions for the national carrier, ending his career as a senior vice-president.

All this happened at about the same time we were moving head office to Toronto, so there was no move to replace Doug, rather there would be a need for a French-speaking public relations person in Montreal. That person turned out to be Marie Bernier, a former runway model for Constance Brown's agency, who had a university degree and the strength of character to carry it off. Marie stayed with them through the airline merger but took a generous severance package that became available. She joined a small airline called Nordair, which, coincidentally, Jack Greenwald used regularly to send supplies to his store in Equaluit. The world she is very small …

Meanwhile, I was in Toronto and I wasn't a happy camper. The airline business was going through enormous change with the high occupancy 747 aircraft, which were originally supposed to have a comfortable seat pitch, but which changed into something akin to a sardine can. We still ran a terrific service, but it wasn't much fun.

My life outside work was not as energetic, and I was finding Torontonians somewhat anal. They also had their priorities wrong. I remember going to a party not long after arriving and one of the guests, a very social Toronto beauty, chatted us up. Her main interest was not in us, though, she wanted to know where we worked and how much money we made. That may have been her aberrant behaviour, but it was off-putting, if not downright rude.

A few months later another, much more interesting dinner party experience occurred at the home of fashion designer Marilyn Brooks. We became fast friends and have remained that way. I was also honoured to be the MC at her wedding to Kennedy Coles. But that was years off. I began to brood and that's never a good thing.

We made it through the rest of 1978 and all of 1979. In March of 1980 I received a telephone call from Ray Heard asking me if I wanted to play tennis. I was a real novice at tennis, but Ray had always tried to encourage me to play the game he considered great exercise and fun.

The *Montreal Star*, where Ray had been Managing Editor, had folded, leaving the *Gazette* the only English paper in Montreal. Ray had accepted a job from Bill Cunningham, the former foreign correspondent for CBC, who had been hired as Vice-President News at the Global Television Network, which had gone to air a few years before but was struggling financially. Ray loved a challenge, though, and readily accepted the job of News Director.

I met Ray at Global where he showed me around the facility and introduced me to Bill. To me it was a re-introduction because I was sure I had met Bill at the Foreign Correspondents Club in Hong Kong in 1966 when I had taken my Mother around the world. Then Ray and I went to the Parkview Club around the corner to play tennis.

Afterward Ray quizzed me at length about my views of Global News business coverage. He knew I watched his newscast because my sister-in-law Kate was a reporter there.

The next morning, I hadn't been in my office for half an hour when the phone rang. It was Ray and he asked me to join him and Bill for lunch at Barberian's Steak House, a block or so away. I said, "Sure, see you at noon."

I was on time, but they were about ten minutes late. It took all of a few minutes for Bill to offer me the job of Business Editor at Global News.

Obviously, I was taken aback. I had been looking for a change, but television news? I responded by describing TV news in a disparaging fashion. I called it superficial, alarmist and sensational. Bill looked me straight in the eye and said, simply, "Come and make it better." His retort disarmed me. I told him I'd think about and get back to him.

When I got back to the office, I called Shirley and detailed what had happened. She said: "Well, you've been wanting to get away from the airline. What have you got to lose? Try it for a year." I put the phone down, thought hard for what seemed an hour, then called Bill to accept his offer.

"When can you start?" he wanted to know then and there.

"In a few weeks," I responded.

"Good," was all I remember him saying. I put the phone down, stared at my typewriter for several minutes, then wrote a letter of resignation.

All of this happened in one day. I was giving up a most prestigious job, a good salary, wonderful staff, and travel perks to die for. This, for a job that paid less, working for a TV network that had yet to turn the corner financially, and with no guarantees I could pull it off.

A lot of people thought I was crazy; there may have been a touch of madness in the quick decision. But Shirley had a good job and could handle the mortgage and other expenses if things went wrong. In fact, the next few days were testy.

CHAPTER 38

A Ballpoint Pen, For God's Sake

It was really important I call London head office to tell them of my decision, over and above the teletype that had gone out earlier. My functional boss there, the PR Director, was a fellow named Alan Ponsford and we got along for the most part, but there had always been something about him that gave me a nagging feeling from time to time.

After asking for reassurance that this was real, he suggested I come over to London one last time to talk about the new job and my possible successors. "And don't make any plans while here," he insisted. He also asked me to bring Shirley along, but I told him she couldn't make it.

A few days later I flew to London and booked into the Selfridge Hotel. I spent a good day at the office, and that same night Alan hosted a dinner in my honour and invited his key personnel along. I was pleasantly surprised by this because it would give me an opportunity to personally say goodbye to colleagues.

The dinner was in a private room and fairly formal – stiff, and certainly not a fun occasion. All kinds of jokes were cracked about what I was letting myself in for as a business presenter on TV, and that sort of thing.

They also wanted to know if I had any successors in mind. I told them their best bet was a reporter in Ottawa named Sandy Gardner whose background fit the bill perfectly. (Sandy in fact got the job and never contacted or thanked me, ever.)

Anyway, about two hours later, Alan made a formal toast, presented me with a small wrapped box and wished me well, accompanied by several "hear, hears."

When I opened the present, it was all I could do to suppress the letdown. I had been gifted a gold-plated biro, or ballpoint pen. And as if that weren't enough, the dinner party immediately broke up, the couples all fled to their waiting cars and/or drivers, and I was left standing alone on the sidewalk, wondering what the hell had just happened.

I hailed a cab but instead of going straight back to my hotel, I asked him to take a long circuitous route because I knew it would be my last visit to London for a while. By the time we drove past King's Road, Chelsea Manor Street, Cheyne Walk and Albert Bridge, my eyes were moist with tears. I had come to love London and here I was giving it all up for the great unknown.

I flew home the next day and was determined to give the new job a great start. My final days at the Toronto office are vague but I do remember the staff gave me a rousing farewell party and I know for a fact many of them became fans of my TV work.

Global News V-P Bill Cunningham's exhortation to "come and make it better" convinced me instantly to change careers. Forever in his debt.

Long- time friend Ray Heard convinced Bill Cunningham to hire me at Global News.

Eccentric artist and dear friend Louise Scott.

West End Art Gallery owner Florence Millman was our art mentor and dear friend.

Sculptor Jim Ritchie creating in wax at his Vence studio-cum-apartments in France. We were avid collectors.

One summer ritual was a visit to artist friend Jerome Couelle's summer lodging on Lake Champlain in Vermont.

My first ever vehicle parked at our century farmhouse and schoolhouse in northern Vermont, The garden looks small but was 5,000 square feet and prolific.

Lugging the shooter's tripod on first overseas assignment to Europe in 1980.

Our Global crew for the documentary Children of the Nile with producer Larry Jackson in the middle and cameraperson Dan Laffey on the right.

Visit to the Great Wall at Badaling near Beijing 1988

I had a great crew for the arduous Soviet Union trip in 1989. L. to r. cameraperson Paul Freer, producer Heather Kelly and sound technician David Gebe.

220

Sitting in Winston Churchill's chair at the site of the 1945 Yalta Conference in Crimea. The chairs were wooden, basic and uncomfortable. The most important talks took place in the garden.

First Global Parade Broadcast
1985
Global
NEWS

First of nine Santa Claus Parade broadcasts co-hosted with the wonderful Fay Dance.

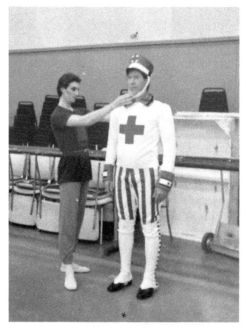

*

Getting ready to perform in The Nutcracker with the National Ballet.

Flying with the Snowbirds.

The Toronto Star had an article featuring my Mother's incredible apple crumble which Jonathan helped me prepare.

A Starweek cover in 1984 recognized Global's achievements but caused ill-will in the newsroom.

Simulating the Last Spike Ceremony at Craigellachie, B.C.

Heliskiing in the Purcell Mountains, B.C.

Cross country skiing in Mulmur Hills. Not as much fun as downhill.

Goofing off with Ronnie Hawkins at a charity event. I was always threatening to sing with his band.

Giving a major speech to the Women's Canadian Club.

Singer Julie Amato pies me in return for $800 in donations to Variety Club, my favourite charity.

Mila Mulroney invited me to an Ottawa luncheon for Nancy Reagan. She loved my firm handshake but said:" it might be a bit too strong."

Interviewing one of the stars of the Variety Club Telethon.

Shirley shares BBQ duty with our friend David Graham.

60th birthday fun with great family friend Trevor Allan, left, and Jonathan.

CHAPTER 39

Nothing Like a Fast Start but Oh My ...

I took no time off and reported to Global News almost immediately on leaving British Airways. I had negotiated a short period before starting at the studio so I could re-connect with some contacts in Ottawa and Montreal, with the hope they could be useful in my new career. Many of them wondered how I could make such a move, especially to Global News, which was widely known to be financially weak. What I tried to explain, though, was that Global had some of the best brains in journalism and to be associated with that crowd was an honour.

Back on Barber Greene Road and Global's studios, on my first day I was assigned a field producer to do a story for the newscast that night. I chose to interview someone I knew about the booming time share industry.

I cannot remember who the camera person was, but Bruce Cushing was my producer. We set up for the interview and I began asking a lot of questions. I should say right now I have an insatiable appetite for information. Curiosity is the key to good journalism.

The interview took some time, but we were able to wrap up quickly and make it onto the Don Valley Parkway before it started to get clogged; in those that days that was about 3:30 in the afternoon.

Bruce took the film in for processing (we were still many months away from moving to Beta video) and I started to prepare my script with Bruce's help on the clips.

Words fail me as I try to recount the tirade that followed when we handed over three cans of film for processing. I had no idea of the cost of film and processing and was unaware of an edict that had come down months before that no story could use more than a small amount of film. Going over the new limits could only happen with a scoop or a really big story.

Bruce took the brunt of the shouting, rightly so because he knew the policy and I didn't. But the camera person should have tipped me off, too. Anyway, it was day one and a big lesson was learned. The time share story was interesting but not great.

It took quite a while for me to win the respect of the general reporters because everyone thought business reporting was fluff. Still, they had plenty of time for Christina Pochmursky, who was running the unit after the former editor Raoul Engel had left. Christina became a huge help to me, too, and I remain eternally grateful for her guidance and friendship.

The biggest job I had was adapting my knowledge of business to finance, especially personal finance, which is what producers wanted to bring to their audience. Global had been the first network in Canada and maybe North American to have a dedicated business segment in their news line-up, so it was important it be done with respect to the needs of viewers.

Once a week there was a half-hour personal finance show called "Money Talks," which I also hosted, and it was through that program I was able to learn a great deal about personal finance from some of the best minds in the business.

Every weekday I was responsible for about three minutes in the evening show anchored by Peter Trueman and a shorter version in his 11 p.m. newscast. After a very shaky start on camera, I began to get comfortable, thanks to the operations staff, including floor directors and cameramen. Global's studio operations were in a word, fantastic, and I'm still friends with many of those I worked closely with in my 15 years there.

There isn't a lot to relate about those first few months, but with the summer came some serious challenges. Peter Trueman would have the summer off (as did Peter Desbarats, another journalism giant who hosted our Ottawa feed) and Ray Heard would need some of his people to stand in for Peter. Initially that meant the Noon News and weekend anchors got the chance to show their worth on the important 6 o'clock newscast.

That left holes at Noon News and I was asked to fill in from time to time. I was obviously very nervous but the audience, God bless 'em, were most supportive and I soon became comfortable. I substituted in other newscasts, too, but the Noon was my favourite since there was less pressure, knowing we had such a small audience.

Meanwhile, behind the scenes some big decisions were being made regarding the news department. Negotiations were being held with Toronto's top news anchor, Gord Martineau of CITY-TV, and Pierre Trudeau's former press secretary, Suzanne Perry (mother of *Friends* star Matthew Perry and wife of journalist Keith Morrison) to join Global, and the Noon and 6 o'clock newscasts were being revamped for them. Peter Trueman was party to this major change. He wasn't happy about it but went along.

The plan was to create a magazine-type one-hour newscast called the "News At Noon" and follow that with the flagship 6 p.m. newscast anchored by Gord and Suzanne, with Peter moving full time to the 11 p.m. time slot.

On the Noon show, Gord would invite specialists such as Bob McAdorey from Entertainment, Mike Anscombe from Sports, and me representing personal finance or business to join him for chats. The format was a bit loose, allowing Gord, for instance, to call me "Dr. Dawe." (Gord didn't know this but that's what my naughty friend Mariella Novotny from London had called a character in her racy book *King's Road* in a nod to our relationship.)

While the original Noon News was basically an update of news from 11 o'clock the previous night, along with whatever fresh material was available from the U.S. networks, the new programme produced by Wendy Dey had more resources and was completely fresh and lively.

Gord was the ultimate professional and helped Suzanne through her early days on air but, even then, she was never really that comfortable.

Late that summer, though, something happened that led to the proverbial you-know-what hitting the fan, and everybody got covered in it.

CHAPTER 40

What You See Is What You Get

There were forces within Global News that had no time for popular newscasters such as Gord Martineau. To them he didn't have the credentials; and despite Gord' success at CITY-TV and CFCF-TV in Montreal many years before, they felt he hadn't been in the trenches as a seasoned journalist, as Peter Trueman had.

I knew what Gord went through because I had suffered similarly at the hands of the then News Director Bruce Garvey and Executive Producer Ken Mallett. I once refused a story idea Bruce tried to foist on me and I was yanked off air for a day or two. Still, we ended up as friends.

Try as he might, Gord wasn't able to get them onside to him or his ideas and one day, after just 11 days on air and a few months of preparing for this new on-air gig, Gord quit. He told me he just found the news management too difficult to work with.

It happened so fast the news department had to scramble to get programs to air. But Heard was a mad genius (mostly mad, according to the majority of staff) and in what was supposed to be a stop-gap measure, he immediately put Mike, Mac and me on the desk to handle the hour as best we could.

Mac was a very well-known personality from CHUM Radio, in

fact, he was the first hugely popular Morning Man.

Mike was a well-known radio person, too, but he had made a mark in TV sports and had a wide following. As for me, I was the new kid on the block who had no broadcast experience and a limited journalism career, and who always claimed, "What you see is what you get."

A little digression is in order here. Mike was available because Global had hired Bob McCown to format and host a news sports program called Sportsline that ran after the 11 o'clock news and it became hugely popular. So, effectively, Mike moved into the news department, though he handled sports on the News At Noon when a sports reporter was unavailable.

Our producer was a woman named Wendy Dey, one tough customer. She had been a strong reporter and had great news sense, but she also had excellent insights and could read the possibilities of these three characters who had been thrown together.

Early on she had built into the program, after the news portion, time for the co-anchors to chat about stories or guests or whatever. This was a magazine format that was popular on morning television shows but never later. Martineau was the consummate professional with this format, his co-anchor Suzanne not so much so.

When we took over the program, this element became what many considered the most important part of the show, certainly the most talked about and, sometimes, most controversial. And we ran with it for the 14 years I was there.

Mac and Mike were known quantities, so I was the straight guy for much of the humour. For instance, Mac used to talk about my frugality and Mike would occasionally refer to the moths that flew out of my wallet when I opened it to pay for something. He also suggested I probably had the first dollar I ever made. Neither knew anything about my background, so this was the logical place to tell my story of the silver dollar.

I replied that, yes, I did have the first dollar I ever made and related to them and the audience how I had received the silver dollar from the Trevalyns of Hillhurst Avenue one Christmas about 24 years before, and that I still had that dollar.

They had a good laugh at that as did the studio crew, but in a surprising twist, the phone rang a few hours later. It was one of the Trevalyns who wanted me to know her father, now living in a home for seniors up in Sudbury, watched our newscast every day and had tears in his eyes when he realized I had been their paperboy for so many years. We had never met because they were what we called "Office Pays," subscribers who sent their money directly to the *Globe*.

I remember during another one of these chat times, neither Mac nor Mike had anything to say, so I tried to rescue the moment by making what was a truly inane comment.

I mentioned that I had recently switched to wearing boxer shorts instead of jockey shorts. I have no idea what prompted me to say that. I'll never forget the look on their faces and on the faces of the production crew and writers. It caused a lot of commotion, but Mac saved the day by steering the conversation back on track.

On another occasion, I drew their ire when, after they started talking about the music, they'd listened to back in the 60s, I asked, "Didn't you ever listen to Black music? All the groups you're talking about are white." Both got annoyed, Mike visibly, and I told them I was sorry off camera. But the fact is, in those days I listened mostly to rhythm and blues, Motown and modern jazz played mostly by Black musicians.

And one final tidbit, I once attended a Bruce Springsteen concert and the following day, while giving a review, I referred to the singer as Bruce Springstern. That caused a burst of laughter in the studio and the switchboard lit up.

The audience just loved these revelatory chats and we were encouraged to continue them.

As we progressed into the end of the year, you could tell how well things were going. Station management had figured a revamped News At Noon would see a growth in audience from, say, 60 or 70,000 to 100,000 and hopefully to 150,000 by the end of 1981. We were in fact well beyond that and were attracting so much audience that every other TV station in Ontario began planning a show to go up against us.

Eventually, strong competition and a change of anchors caused our growth to stall, but we had achieved many months of more than 300,000 viewers, unheard of in that time slot for a news program, and unheralded in the history of Canadian television broadcasting.

It needs to be said that what Global did with the reformat of the News At Noon reflected an audience reality that hadn't been fully recognized yet even by Global.

It was 1980 and the Canadian economy was weak as higher oil prices were being absorbed. There were large numbers of people on shift work who, aside from some morning variety show programming, didn't have a definitive news program to call their own. Most of the programming was aimed at children and was mainly American based.

What Wendy Dey and the News At Noon team did was to give this huge audience a first class news and sports broadcast along with live entertainment, relevant news interviews, book reviews and cooking segments with some of the best cooks in the business. Something to call their own.

Bryan Adams appeared on TV for the first time with Mac, KD Lang kicked up her heels for the first time in the east, and Celine Dion was a regular in her early career. And there were so many others. Perhaps the most significant person to grace our desk was

Jim Carrey, initially a struggling local comedian.

Bob McAdorey recognized his bizarre but extraordinary talent from the first time he paid us a visit. Every time Carrey had a stand-up routine to plug, he'd come on the News at Noon to banter with Bob. It was classic and I believe only Mac knew this young man was destined for greatness.

In fact, Carrey was at the dawning of a career that would explode in television and movies over the next two decades, and he's still a force though his broad appeal has declined.

As for me, I could only watch and listen to the two of them speak in a language I couldn't understand with contortions and mannerisms that dazzled the viewer.

At one point, Carrey was beginning to do impressions and Mac asked him for an example. Much to my surprise, Carrey began to mimic me, exaggerating my dulcet tones and finishing with my business report signoff: "And that's the bottom line. I'm John Dawe." It brought the house down, so to speak, and somewhere I have that performance on tape.

It was because the viewer never knew what to expect, other than a good news and sports broadcast, that we were told it wasn't possible to walk into an Ontario bar, restaurant, hotel, fire station or government office where their TVs were not tuned to Global's News At Noon.

And other stations took notice. One of the competitors was CBC, which we were to learn in 1985 was formatting a show for a national audience to be called "Midday." I hadn't realized I had some fans there and, out of the blue, I received a call asking if I wanted to audition for this show. I said, "Sure, but it has to be done very early in the morning when there's no one around who might recognize me."

The last thing I wanted was for Global to find out I was thinking of bailing, even though I was under huge stress, doing so much there, and the thought of working for the national broadcaster was just too tempting.

CBC set up the audition in the national newsroom at the old Jarvis Street location at 7 a.m. I drove down and parked in an empty lot, thanking my lucky stars there wasn't anyone around other than production staff.

As I walked into the building and was met by the security guard, he looked at me and said: "John, what are YOU doing here?" My heart sank. I knew we had lots of viewers at other stations but had no idea how popular we were among CBC staff.

I was taken to the Green Room where I met Barbara Frum, who was there preparing for an overseas interview. As you can imagine, my nerves were brittle. On the way to the studio I met other staff who also said "Hi, John" and I was done in.

We arrived at this huge, cold studio and I was seated behind The National anchor desk and given a script. I had no trouble with the paper script, but I had not yet had my eyes tested and I couldn't see the teleprompter on the camera clearly.

At one point I shifted legs and the cable for the lavalier microphone yanked the mic off my jacket. I reached down, picked it up and started to re-affix it when I heard this urgent voice shatter the studio's quiet: "Don't touch that mic." Seconds later a technician came running toward me and re-attached the mic himself. It all had to do with unions, and it scared the hell out of me.

After they moved the camera closer and I was able to read the teleprompter, the second part of the audition took over. I had to interview Andrea Martin. She was a well-known comedienne, charming and polite with a gorgeous smile, and her wit tore little pieces off little old nervous me.

My audition was a disaster but deep down I was happy about that. I just couldn't be myself in that atmosphere, under those circumstances. I would miss the camaraderie of the Three Nice Guys (as we were referred to at Global), and I felt a sense of loyalty to Global for giving me opportunities I would never have had otherwise.

On the other hand, there were many times we didn't feel appreciated for our contribution to the financial turnaround at Global Television, but none of us had the courage to start a fight with management over remuneration.

CHAPTER 41

So Much to Do, So Little Time

I did not have an employment contract with Global News, rather I was on staff. I was hired as business editor, but that primary role was supplanted within months by news anchoring and, eventually, feature reporting.

At one point I felt I was being exploited and I sought out the best media lawyer to prepare a contract for me. I was recommended to Michael Levine who turned me down: "John, I cannot represent you. I only represent superstars."

I knew this to be true because Gord Martineau was one of them. I didn't take umbrage at his comment and many years later we became friends through membership in the Toronto Lawn Tennis Club.

But I knew what Levine and so many others in the media didn't know, that was I was building a strong reputation among the most important people in our industry – the audience.

While some argued Global was exploiting me, I often felt I was exploiting THEM because everything they asked me to do I did, and willingly, because I relished the experience.

Six months after joining, I was co-anchoring the News At Noon, doing business hits into the 6 o'clock and 11 o'clock newscasts, hosting a half-hour finance program, as well as meeting the constant need for updates and promotional hits. And that was all in studio.

Outside, there were telethons such as the Variety Club and Muscular Dystrophy fundraisers and other promotional appearances. The best outside work, though, was going to Ottawa for budgets and international travel.

In October 1980 I covered my first federal budget lock-up in Ottawa. For the uninitiated, a budget lock-up is organized by the government to introduce sensitive material to the media so they can study it and be prepared to report it once the material is made public in the House of Commons, usually at 4 p.m. after the stock market has closed.

This budget by Pierre Trudeau's finance minister Allan MacEachen was one that some Canadians still believe to be one of the most sinister ever, because it introduced the National Energy Program or NEP, which, among other things, was aimed at redistributing Alberta's oil wealth to the rest of Canada, especially Quebec.

I was in the lock-up and relied on non-partisan experts who were also there to be briefed on the budget and the NEP proposal. At the end of my budget story, I did what's called a "piece to camera," which is meant to supplement the main material and show that the reporter is on location where the news is happening. In my closer, I used the word "sinister" to describe the NEP. What I didn't do was attribute that description to an expert.

My video story was relayed to Toronto and was seen by the executive producer and anchor Peter Trueman before it went to air. Peter was livid that I would use that word sinister without attribution, and ordered the ending edited from the item.

It was a learning experience for me and I vowed to be as objective as is humanly possible in my reporting going forward. Sadly, reporters, anchors and hosts today haven't learned the same lesson. But I don't mind saying that my negative assessment of the NEP and its impact on the west turned out to be prescient.

Also, in the fall of 1980, I did my first significant foreign reporting when I travelled to Europe with a cameraman to cover some crucial meetings of the General Agreement on Tariffs and Trade, or GATT. Those meetings were held in Geneva but, while overseas, we did some work at NATO's Brussels headquarters and in Paris.

We had just purchased video cameras for our cameramen and were not totally familiar with them, so my guy, Don Pursur, and I travelled with camera/lighting kits for both video and film. The number of pieces of luggage we travelled with was ridiculous. Part of our trip was under the auspices of NATO and we travelled in coaches. Every time we moved, it took so long to load the bags, other journalists on the trip pitched in to make sure we all got to the function on time. I can remember some very high-profile journalists doing so.

Our first stop was Geneva. I had been to Zurich years before but never Geneva, so this was a treat. A treat, that is, until I discovered the cost of meals and transportation. Our per diems were gone by lunchtime.

One memorable moment there occurred when we were approached on the street by this remarkably tall, beautiful woman who spoke to us with an Australian accent. She wanted to know where David Bowie's house was because she had met him at a concert in Australia and he'd told her to look him up anytime she was in Geneva.

We had a great laugh over that. In fact, we laughed a lot because all of this was so new to Don, who had never before been to Europe. Even after a long day of filming, he'd slip off on his own at night because he had to see everything. He did that everywhere we went.

While most of the stories we did were related to trade and finance, we did some softer features just for fun. The one I remember best, because of the terrific response we got back home, developed one day as we were walking in one of the wealthier sections of Paris, the 6ᵗʰ arrondissment. I spied this beautiful shop with an outdoor display of gorgeous fruits, vegetables and what we now call pulses and legumes. It was so cleverly displayed I told Don we had to video it.

I went inside to gain permission and to learn the origin of the bulk of the dried foods. "Canada," came the reply and the beans (navy beans) were from Ontario. I knew we had farms producing beans in the Zurich area; in fact, they hold an annual Bean Festival after the harvest.

We did some pieces to camera and put the story together when we got back home. Viewers in Zurich and nearby Bayfield, among others, got a big kick out of it as did the provincial ministry of agriculture.

That trip was only eight days or so, but it seemed twice that long. And as always, we were under pressure to prepare the stories as soon as we returned, plus I was required to anchor the news and business report.

I remember one trip almost too well. It was not my greatest hour, but I have to tell the story. Global News had strong audiences outside urban areas, which was only right because that was our mandate. We often got requests to travel to far flung parts in the province for one reason or another and, whenever we could, we did.

On one occasion, the Board of Trade in Cochrane, Ontario, invited me to speak to an audience of regional boards and chambers of commerce, about 400 or 500 people, which my news director thought it would be good to do.

It was to happen in January. My flight to Timmins and drive to Cochrane were without incident. My speech went over really well as it combined some business, economic and political observations, with some humour. What I failed to notice was every time I picked up my water glass it was never empty and tasted more like Scotch.

Well, it was Scotch, and by the time the speech was over, and the audience had begun to disperse, a couple of local characters came to thank me and invite me to become a member of their club. I was honoured and readily agreed. About ten minutes later, we were about 10 or 12 people in cars heading out of Cochrane to a local lake where they had built this "clubhouse."

I was escorted inside where there was a huge sauna. The whole gang (guys only, obviously) disrobed and we went in. But only for a few minutes because we were soon heading out the door into the cold night and down to the dock, where someone had chipped a hole in the ice, and we were required to immerse ourselves while holding onto the ladder.

We did this then rushed back to the sauna, outside of which there were glasses of whiskey waiting. But not long after, we headed back out for the same routine. It's a bit of a blur but I think we did it three or four times.

By now I was really inebriated, it was very late, and I had to get up early enough to catch a 7 a.m. flight out of Timmins. I don't remember getting back to the guest house where my bag was but, the next thing I do remember was being awakened by flashlights held by two towering men who turned out to be Mounties. The group realized there was no way I would make the trip without an escort. Those fellas helped me dress and pack my small overnight bag and got me to the plane on time. There was just one problem. I was still hungover, having had only two hours of sleep.

When I got back to Toronto, I went straight to Global and they insisted I go on air. Somehow, I managed to do it, but some viewers did call to ask why I was having some trouble verbalizing and reading my script, but I also got several calls from Cochrane to say, "Well done."

I've got the certificate of membership bestowed on me as a "Knight of the Sauna at Green Pastures by the frozen shores of Poole's Lake having observed the Ritual of Ordeal by Steam and Duly been Boiled Alive in all modesty and honour." How can you not just love those folks in northern Ontario!

Unfortunately, demands on my airtime were such that I couldn't often get away from the studio except for some special assignments.

One of those was the first visit to Washington of Prince Charles and Lady Diana, who by now had become a global media sensation. I believe I was chosen to fly to Washington to cover that visit because I had co-hosted with the wonderful Deborah Burgess the Global broadcast of the marriage of Charles and Diana.

Now that I think of it, that wedding coverage was a remarkable feat, given that we went up against all the other networks who had teams over in London for the St. Paul's Cathedral Wedding of the Century. Global didn't have that kind of money, so we took our regular network feeds, employed people with an eye for detail, and ran video that we voiced over, at times using guests.

One of those was a friend of mine named Marina Sturdza who claimed to be a member of Romanian royalty. On her death in New York, it was confirmed that indeed she was, and she was accorded a funeral fit for royalty. We became friends because she married an old friend named Denis Harvey, whom I had known from his days at the *Hamilton Spectator* but who also worked in senior executive positions at the *Gazette*, *Toronto Star* and CBC before passing at a fairly young age.

I mention Marina because here we were in the Don Mills studio, describing in detail the protocol, fashions and personalities that only an expert could provide. We were on the air for about eight hours, Deborah reminds me, and Marina was with us for much of that. And she did it out of friendship as there was no budget for an honorarium.

From having covered the wedding, I was now going to be in Washington to cover this royal visit. I had only had a few days to prepare (while still performing all those other duties, of course) and in the material collected I found a notice that the couple would be guests of the British Ambassador to the United States at a reception for the top American and foreign press. But we'd made our decision very late and had not received an invitation.

My one and only idea to try to correct this potential catastrophe was to call upon an old friend from my days in the airline business. Lewis Roberts had been the Canadian marketing manager of the British Tourist Authority and we worked very closely on joint promotions for many years. When he left the Canadian head office in Toronto, he was given a big promotion and headed to New York where he oversaw the U.S. marketing efforts.

The day before leaving for Washington, I made an urgent call to Lewis and he came through for me. Waiting at my Washington hotel the next day was a formal invitation to the reception. I can't tell you how important it was that I be there, especially since there were only about 20 invitees in all from the British media and key American journalists. I appeared to be the only Canadian.

I took my best dark blue suit and decided on an unusual tie, for no other reason than it fit with the suit perfectly. It was a tie given to me in thanks for work I had done with the Empire Club in Toronto, and I liked it a lot because it reminded me of the Imperial Airways tie I had lost to the tom-foolery of the artist Harold Town and publisher Jack MacLelland many years before.

In the reception line, I was introduced to Charles, who looked at my tie and said, "You're not one of the American press. I know that tie. That's the Empire Club tie. Are you Canadian?"

I was floored by this and responded briefly. Had I had more time, I might have reminded him of our cursory meeting on the tarmac of

Vancouver Airport so many years before.

But if I was floored by Charles's insight, looking into the eyes of Diana, Princess of Wales, was one of the most disarming moments of my life. She was everything they said about her, and more. She had overheard the conversation about the tie and had a smile that could melt Antarctica. But it was those eyes. The few seconds we shook hands lasted a lifetime.

I moved on and made a conscious decision not to get involved later in the couple's casual conversations in small groups, mainly because the American media were so anxious to chat with them and this was their show. But I did overhear some bits and pieces and decided it was just as well. Enough said.

I was doing live hits into all the newscasts, and the next day my co-anchor Mike Anscombe asked me, after I told my story about meeting the royal couple at the reception, "Well, did you fall in love with her?"

He could have phrased it better but, not wanting to debate it, I replied, "Yes, I couldn't help myself."

That led Ross McLean, a former CBC personality and now television columnist for a newspaper, to write that that exchange exemplified the coverage that Global accorded the royal visit, while Wendy Mesley of the CBC "did some credible journalism" in Washington.

I was really offended by that comment, as were some viewers, one of which, a former McLean co-worker, wrote to say: "Don't let his words bother you. He's a bitter person."

It still bothered me at the time because I knew how much pressure I'd been under during that visit and how we'd filed for every newscast. After all, we were three people, me, a cameraman and a field producer. While the CBC probably had a dozen or so people at a minimum.

In fact, that reminds me of my trip to Vancouver for the opening of Expo 86. Once again, we were a small crew but this time we were joined by a reporter, Jeffrey Kofman, who subsequently went to the CBC and later CBS in the U.S.

We did fresh stories, interviews and live hits into every Global news show. That entailed very long hours of work, given the three-hour time difference between Vancouver and Toronto.

CBC, meanwhile, had TV and radio crews from Toronto, Ottawa, Montreal, Vancouver and Victoria, along with Knowlton Nash from The National. By coincidence, Knowlton and I were on the same plane flying to Vancouver. Same plane, except Knowlton was up in the pointy end of the plane and I was in the back, and not far from me sat his teleprompter operator.

That was the kind of big budget competition that we, as a regional network, faced daily. But although flat-out working for Global took its toll physically and emotionally, I somehow found time for a life with the family.

CHAPTER 42

The Hills Are Alive ... In Mulmur

Giving up our farm in Vermont was a tough decision, albeit a necessary one. But I longed for somewhere to go to get away from the city and the studio whenever possible.

On planned holidays we invariably headed back to Maine with our friends the Saunders. We simply couldn't let those Montreal and northeast U.S. roots go. We did that for many years, settling on Kennebunkport as our most favourite destination, even at the time of the first Bush presidency.

We were flush with money, having sold Vermont and with both of us having well-paying jobs. Being two very busy people, we had to have help with our son, and when our first nanny left, we lucked out finding a lovely woman from Guyana to live in and help us for five years. Her name was Violet, and we helped her get landed resident status in Canada. She left us after five years for broader duties with more responsibility, but we were very happy for her and still stay in touch.

For a short while we had Christine Juste, a lovely young French woman from Marseille, live with us, but she went back to France, became a lawyer and political activist ... and is still doing that. Our final nanny, though, was a remarkable young woman from Quebec named Marise Blanchard, whom we supported to get a liberal arts degree from York University. She stayed five years then went back to Quebec, became a teacher, then settled into family life.

Not long after joining Global, I got the itch to get a country retreat. Shirley supported my plan but was far too busy to spend too much time traipsing through the countryside looking at properties.

One weekend while Shirley was on an overseas buying trip to China, I did something naughty. I found what I considered an ideal country place, a solid small house with a great room, just two bedrooms, but a really nice view and 13 acres of land. It was in the Hills of Mulmur, specifically the Pine River Valley. It was the retirement home of a Toronto doctor who, with his wife, had decided a warmer clime was more important.

I made an offer and it was accepted. Shirley was not amused when she returned. She did like it and saw the possibilities, but the thought of having this kind of responsibility didn't sit well for a while.

The day we moved in our next-door neighbour came running toward us as we were out looking at the property. "John?" she said. "It is Johnny Dawe!"

The woman was indeed an old friend from high school days with whom I had double-dated. Her name was Sandy Hoseason then, now Sandy Spencer, and she was a dynamo in the investment industry, working in sales for Wood Gundy. She was married to a lawyer, had two gorgeous daughters and they owned most of the property around us, with much of their land bordering the Bruce Trail.

With help from the Spencers, we met a lot of weekenders and local people and were lucky enough to join the Mulmur Hills Racquet Club with its two tennis courts and tiny clubhouse. Among the other people we connected with were Bob Farquharson, one of the best-known gurus of mutual funds in Canada, and his wife Gail, who had gone to St. Clement's School and dated a friend of mine.

This, I figured, was going to be a lot of fun. And it was for about seven years, during the latter part of which both Shirley and Jonathan tired of the requirement to go every weekend. I ended up often going alone because it was necessary to keep the lawns cut and the house needed maintenance from time to time. We also had raspberry bushes to harvest, among other things. In winter it was extremely important to ensure all was well because we were in a snow belt.

During those years, though, I learned to ski, as did Jonathan and Shirley, first at Mansfield, then later at Talisman and Mount St. Louis Moonstone. We enjoyed it and took a few trips to ski, including Whistler and, of course, Jay Peak in Vermont.

On one occasion we skied at Panorama Ski Resort in B.C. and Shirley's sister Carley joined us. One day Carley asked, "Who wants to go heli-skiing?" I stupidly agreed to accompany her. I say "stupidly" because I wasn't a strong enough skier to handle the punishing powder of the Purcell Mountains. Still, off we went. We got a lengthy briefing and we were given our tracking devices (which the searchers would need to find us in the event of an avalanche).

On the first run, I trailed the group because I had fallen and found getting up in deep powder extremely difficult. You have to try to use your poles for leverage, but they can't find bottom because the powder is so deep. It's actually quite scary.

I could see the group had turned to the left and were a long distance in front of me, but now were skiing straight on. So, I decided to take a short cut by going straight instead of turning. I fell again and this time I ended up about six feet from the edge of a cliff. The group had turned left because of this one- or two-hundred-foot drop that couldn't be seen because of the snow. So, my fall was a godsend. Lucky me.

I took my time getting up, then went to the left and followed their tracks to where the helicopter was waiting to go to another run. We had purchased a half-day package and I ended up doing it, but my old muscles felt that strain for many days after. I was in my 50s at the time and only skied for a few more years.

One of the highlights of our years in Mulmur was spending time with Al and Pauline Orr. Al, an engineer from Queens, was the retired head of Atlas Steel, one of the great manufacturing companies in the St. Catharines area. He was widowed and Pauline, his second wife, had worked for Air Canada in Montreal. We had mutual friends and stories to tell so we became fast friends.

The Orrs had a big property not far from Creemore. A golfer, Al had developed three golf holes on the property to keep his game honed and to entertain his friends. He was a good tennis player, too, despite sore legs that he'd acquired when he played football for Queens.

Al and Pauline's greatest gift to the community, though, was The Orr Olympics, an annual event in which a large number of friends would compete for crazy prizes in a variety of sports.

My first time at the games I teamed up with Al's neighbour to play horseshoes and we won. I did well at a golf exercise, too, and shooting hoops in basketball. It was a day of huge fun and it ended with a fabulous dinner.

Truth be told, one great draw for the games was the participation of John Wiggins, a marketing man who had the good sense to create the most successful microbrewery in Ontario called Creemore Springs, right in the town of Creemore. No Orr Olympics was complete without a keg or two or ...

We met and socialized with a large number of wonderful people in the Mulmur area, including Lieutenant General Richard Rohmer (Retired) and his wife Mary-O. The General, a lawyer and author, was an advisor to the Chief of the Defence Staff in Ottawa. A decade ago, the General was described as one of Canada's most colourful characters of the second half of the past century. We were saddened by Mary-O's passing at the beginning of 2020.

There were judges, lawyers, bankers, business owners, artists, entrepreneurs – a great variety of interesting people who loved country living.

As our seventh year rolled in and with the it the market crash of 1987, it was made plain to me that neither Shirley nor Jonathan were keen to go to Mulmur every weekend. What I should have done was rent the place for a few years, but instead, I put it on the market. It sold quickly and my neighbours were not happy at the change. We got back what money we'd put into it, so there was no financial loss, but I left pieces of my heart up in those hills. Moreover, three years later the property had tripled in value.

Not having the country home gave us time and resources for travel. Shirley had the left The Bay and started her own consulting firm at home, and getting away, especially to the west coast to see family in the good weather, was a good thing.

It was around that time that our friends the Houssers in Victoria purchased a cottage on a lake on Salt Spring Island. We started going there on a regular basis and I must say, it was love at first sight.

I remember once I mentioned on air during one of our chat times that I felt Salt Spring Island was the best kept secret in Canada. The iconic Vancouver newsman Jack Webster heard about this and let me know in no uncertain terms that he didn't want me to say another word about it publicly because the last thing they wanted was hordes of easterners buying up island property.

Salt Spring also figured large in our relationship with David Wood, whose specialty food shop on Yonge Street in the Rosedale area launched a prepared food revolution in Toronto and probably

Canada. He appeared regularly on our News At Noon program, preparing dishes that he always claimed were "dead easy" to make. He also wrote cookbooks. So successful was he that some investors suggested he expand and open a very large shop in what used to be called North Toronto (as it happens, a stone's throw from my family home).

It was an emporium like no other but a number of factors, including start-up costs, lack of parking, and a poor economy forced it to close.

David and his wife were over for dinner one night when our Salt Spring friends, the Houssers, were there. The talk was all about the beauty of living on Salt Spring. The rest is history. David and the family went to Salt Spring, bought a small farm on a lake and opened a cheese factory. His products are among the most sought after in gourmet shops in Canada.

We ourselves came close to buying some property there and I have kicked myself many times for not having done so. One of life's great mistakes, but sometimes I blame Jack Webster, whose wrath I didn't wish to invoke by buying there.

CHAPTER 43

World Travel Awaits

In the early 80s there was a civil war in the African nation of Sudan. At the same time the country was being devastated by drought, a condition shared by neighbouring countries, as well. Unless you were alive in what are referred to as the "Dirty Thirties" when parts of North America experienced drought, it is difficult to imagine what a drought could be like, Canada being such a lush country. I was about to find out.

Global News decided to do a documentary on the conditions in Sudan, concentrating on how Canadian aid was helping to alleviate the hardship and illness. The crew would be three people: producer Larry Jackson, cameraman Dan Laffey and host/reporter, me.

We were well briefed on how bad the conditions were there and took all the necessary precautions. What you can't prepare for, of course, was seeing the devastation first-hand.

The crew plus 17 pieces of luggage flew first to Cairo to check in with the Canadian Embassy, which also handled affairs for Sudan. Cairo was in the midst of building a subway and there was dust everywhere. It got into our hair, our clothes, and our eyes and nose and mouth, and it was not pleasant.

But our arrival at the airport there was even worse. As we were

were about to check with customs and immigration at the airport, it was made clear that we would have to pay baksheesh (basically, a bribe) to get our equipment and ourselves into the country. The junior officials wanted a lot of money, several hundred dollars, but we were determined not to play that game. They held us up for about four hours, but after a crew change, we were allowed in.

That left a bad taste in my mouth, as did the dust.

The next day we flew to Khartoum with all of our papers in order and there was no repeat of the Cairo airport experience, but the trip from the airport into town was an eye opener.

I had only seen refugee camps and temporary shelters in newscasts, but here and now, before even settling into the country, we saw thousands of people living in squalid conditions along the road from the airport. It was horrific and heartbreaking.

We settled into our hotel and Larry immediately contacted an official of UNICEF, which was assisting us with our logistics. The country director for the UN agency invited us to his home for dinner and a chat.

As I was getting ready to go, I looked in the bathroom mirror and started to panic. My tongue had turned black and all sorts of scary things popped into my confused and very tired head. I called Larry and told him I couldn't go, and I needed to get to bed.

I slept well and the next morning joined the crew for breakfast. My tongue was still discoloured but less so than the previous night and I was having no ill effects.

Someone asked me if I had been taking any medicine for constipation after the lengthy flights and I responded yes. I can't recall the product name but apparently it was well known to leave the tongue black after sucking on the tablet. So instead of contracting one of the horrible diseases that we were about to see too much of, my condition was self-inflicted and unreal. Naturally I felt foolish.

We began our work that first day. Some of what we did has been lost to memory but early on, we had to go to the Sudan interior city of El Obeid where there was a huge refugee camp and deplorable living conditions. We had a local driver and an old Land Rover.

By the time we were outside the city, we could see what the drought had caused. It's called "desertification" and occurs when there's no vegetation to hold the soil, which turns to sand and is blown by winds to create more desert. It would take many hours to get to our destination and, as we drove, I couldn't imagine how the driver could tell where we were. The road had disappeared and the landmarks he used when driving lorries (trucks) on this route had disappeared. It was just sand everywhere. And it was soon obvious we were lost, and we were about to lose daylight.

As luck would have it, a few hours later he spied a light and drove toward it. In the middle of what was now desert was a house with some light coming through a tiny window. The driver knocked on the door and spoke to someone.

The next thing we saw was a man in flowing robes coming toward us holding a tray, and on it were cups of sweetened tea. It was a gesture toward strangers that I knew to be common in Greece, but not here. How wrong I was. It was Ramadan, the holiest period of the Muslim calendar, and our host was simply following the teachings of the Quran by welcoming us with refreshment.

What we found out later was that the sugar he used for our tea was his last. That experience has never left me and I think of it to this day as we witness a world in which Islamophobia is rampant.

Our driver was able to get help with directions using the stars, and we did make it to El Obeid unscathed but dead tired. We had picked up a case of Pepsi-Cola in Khartoum, a gift from the local bottler who happened to be a friend of someone I knew in Toronto. That case of soda came in handy because there was very little water to drink in El Obeid.

When we saw the huge main square the next day, Larry described it as a giant Swiss cheese. This significant area was grassless and spotted with holes that locals had dug to find water, and what little they found was hardly potable.

We next went to a huge refugee camp. It held some 75,000 people, mostly from Nigeria. They had left years before on a pilgrimage, walking to Mecca to perform the Hajj, something every Muslim is required to do once in their lifetime. They arrived in El Obeid at the height of the drought and were forced to halt their journey. They were in very rough shape.

Just outside the camp there was a small medical clinic. During our filming we saw parents carrying young, crying children into the clinic through one door, and an hour or so later leaving by another door with their dead child. That sight and others like it often caused tears to well up but I forced myself not to weep because of something I had been told before this trip by a renowned Ontario doctor of Armenian descent, Dr. John Basmajian. He warned me never to let the tears start to flow because "if you do, they'll never stop." It took me years to get over that scene, if in fact I ever did.

Another scene generated the exact opposite emotion. While we were there, it rained powerfully one day but only for a few minutes. The ground was so dry and hard the rain didn't penetrate, rather it pooled and, for a short time, turned the soil contaminated by animal and people feces and urine into a dangerous, smelly sludge. But it was wet, and the children played in it, sporting wide smiles and expressing a joy that was totally uplifting.

Sadly, I cannot remember his name, but one of the great characters who would have a role in our documentary was a man from Alberta whose job was to drive from one village to another with a truck and drill rig to create wells for the people. What was amazing was how basic his efforts were. Once a spot was dowsed, it was drilled, collared, then topped with a pump. He developed a good sense of where he'd find water and had a terrific success record. It was efficient and cost-effective.

Water obviously was the key for Sudan and other affected nations to survive this latest drought. But food was needed, too, and one of the projects we reported on was an experimental sorghum farm that was developed by the Canadian International Development Agency (CIDA). Sorghum is a cereal grain that grows well in drought conditions. Canada, during the Dirty Thirties drought had developed ways of growing grains that required shallow tilling of the soil so as to protect more of the soil from being lost to winds.

To get a complete picture of the operation, Dan and I climbed a very tall tower. One of the reasons I was there was to help Dan with the shooting because one of our helpers had dropped the camera, damaging the viewfinder beyond repair. The only way Dan could shoot after that was to have one of us hold a small monitor that allowed him to frame his shots.

One of our side trips took us to Port Sudan on the Red Sea. This was where the ships docked laden with relief for the famine that had stricken Sudan. There was one ship with its cargo intact that had been there for a long time, so long that according to locals the cargo had begun to rot. It was the first shipment, apparently, that had been financed by the Bob Geldof "Do They Know It's Christmas" song campaign and later Live Aid Concert. We were told the reason the ship was still there was because no security arrangements had been made to guard the lorries (trucks) that would distribute the food and drivers were concerned they would be intercepted by black market gangs. Other non-governmental agencies offering aid, such as World Vision, had made arrangements and their shipments got to those in need.

We were in Sudan for some three weeks working in temperatures that were 40° Celsius or more. But it was a very dry heat and any sweat immediately evaporated so there was no discomfort. The only real issue the weather prompted was its effect on our equipment. The Sony cameras were rated for 40 or 45 degrees and we were in constant fear they would stop working.

On the trip we ate what we could and drank a lot of Pepsi, especially when there was no water available. After that trip I never had another Pepsi.

On our final day, our producer told Dan and me that we would be heading back to Canada without him. He was going on a holiday to Greece and he had arranged this beforehand without telling us. We were miffed because it meant Dan and I had to return home with about 15 pieces of luggage, and we had two stops. Moreover, it meant we couldn't work on the documentary until Larry returned to base.

Dan and I flew to Rome with a very long stopover in Riyadh, Saudi Arabia. That prospect didn't bother us too much because we believed the airport had a lot of amenities. What we didn't expect, though, was on our arrival we were effectively incarcerated in a holding room filled with deportees and other dicey characters and guarded by soldiers with machine guns. This was common practice apparently for film crews in transit.

After several hours in the room with nothing to do, I pleaded with the guards to let us stroll for a bit and they eventually relented, but after a few minutes of wandering we found nothing of interest, so we returned to our room empty-handed.

By the time we got home we were both exhausted but Dan, knowing I'd have to be on air the next day, insisted on taking care of the equipment and our tapes.

The next morning, I arrived at the studio and we did some editing for the news that day. It took several days to recover fully from that trip and, as I write this, I recall the constant dust we ingested in Sudan, even in Khartoum, which is situated at the confluence of the White Nile, beginning in Lake Victoria, and the Blue Nile flowing from Ethiopia.

Drought causes desertification of arable land at an alarming rate, as evidenced by the inability of our driver to find his landmarks during our trip to El Obeid. That city is about 360 kilometres from Khartoum and the drive should have taken us close to six hours. Instead it was more than ten hours, and we were lucky to have found help when we got off-track.

Before the producer made it home from Greece, I did a number of feature stories, but work on the documentary didn't start until his return since he had full control. What went to air was not what some of us expected, and it was a lesson I never forgot, namely, if I'm fronting something, I've got to have some control over it.

CHAPTER 44

Witness to History

In the television news business, most days are routine and unfold pretty much as you'd expect. The news flows in, decisions are made about what will be covered, stories are packaged, intros, voiceovers and briefs are written, and then it's lights, action, camera on the news anchor or team to promote what's ahead that hour.

Events such as wars initially created more than normal stress on the operation, but even that coverage would settle into a type of routine. What caused more excitement and stress for the newsroom was the sudden tragedy or significant event that demanded full attention and coverage.

The first event on our News at Noon watch was the assassination attempt on U.S. President Ronald Reagan on March 30, 1981. After making a midday speech in Washington, Reagan was shot and wounded by a deranged young man named John Hinkley, Jr. The attempt occurred at around 2:30 p.m., well after our news programme had finished, but the hours before the start of the prime-time news programme at 6 p.m. were our responsibility, so we did the updates until Peter Trueman and his team took over. My main role later that day was reporting on the stock market impact of the assassination attempt.

I wasn't on the air for the death of John Lennon that occurred around 10:30 on the night of December 8, 1980. The world-famous member of the Beatles music group was gunned down outside his home at The Dakota in New York City by Mark David Chapman. But we knew that event would be extremely important for our audience and, from early the next morning and for several days afterward, we covered every aspect of that death and its implications and ramifications.

In doing so we established a bond with our audience – an intimate relationship – that was unique, and we knew who those viewers were. The audience wasn't made up of just those people who didn't work for one reason or another; we had tens of thousands of shift workers who saw our program as their definitive news show. But thanks to Mac, we also had live entertainment, and that broadened our appeal to include restaurants and hotels across the province. For a number of years, you couldn't walk into a sports bar with TV sets around the perimeter that were not tuned into the News At Noon. And woe to me if I forgot the thousands of firefighters for whom our program was their midday treat, as they hung out on duty hoping their talent and expertise were never needed.

There were times, though, when events happened when we were on the air or about to go to air.

For me the most profound of those events was the Challenger disaster of January 28, 1986. We were a few minutes from taking the desk for a newscast and were watching a live feed of the latest space shuttle launch from Cape Canaveral, Florida. There was a lot of interest in this flight because among the crew was a teacher named Christa MacAuliffe, who was the first civilian to join a shuttle flight.

Some 73 seconds into the flight the shuttle disintegrated after an external fuel tank exploded. Seeing this and being the closest, I ran to the news desk, put on my microphone and within seconds we were on the air announcing the tragedy. Speed is everything in TV. My moment wasn't the smoothest, but we beat our main competitor CTV by an estimated eight seconds and that pleased us.

The rest of the day was a blur for me. I remained on the desk until 3:30 when my co-anchor returned from a scheduled lunch and took over the live hits. I was mentally and physically exhausted, but I still had my business report to do.

On top of that, the News Director asked me to voice the famous poem "High Flight" written by an Anglo-American Royal Canadian Air Force fighter pilot, John Magee, Jr., in 1941 during the Second World War. It was emotionally tough to do. Our chief editor took that voice and married it to video of the Challenger pre-flight preparations and the disaster, and the resultant piece was extremely well received and unique at the time. (And if you don't know the poem, I strongly recommend you read it.)

The sudden pressure I was under that day manifested itself in some breathlessness from hyperventilating. I had seen this happen to others, but it was the first and not the only time I experienced it.

CHAPTER 45

Another Really Big Trip

I never had that hyperventilating experience during the nine years I co-hosted the Santa Claus Parade, during which there were always moments of panic for one reason or another.

Among all my other duties, management wanted me to host the parade with Faye Dance, a personality well known to Global audiences for her role as host of the lottery draws. Faye was the consummate pro at these live events, and we seemed to hit it off.

Global had won the right for exclusive coverage of the Toronto parade after previous broadcasters either lost interest or found it too demanding. Global decided to contract for it, and they did an amazing job promoting it, to the delight of the parade directors and sponsors.

One year, long before the parade operations began to take shape, I was called to a meeting to discuss something extraordinary. The Toronto parade was going to be shown in the Soviet Union and a broadcast crew was coming from the state-run television network Gosteleradio in Moscow to cover the parade from a booth right next to Global's.

As well, Faye and I would be going to the Soviet Union to do some feature filming to promote this important event. For the first time ever, Soviet television was going to carry commercials and the revenue from those would go to support a hospital treating mainly child victims of the Chernobyl nuclear disaster.

Western commercials on Soviet Television! If such an event were being done by the Americans or the British, it would have received global coverage. As it happens, it was barely noticed in the media outside Toronto. It says so much about how poorly Canada promotes itself on the world stage but that's another sad story.

The reason it didn't get international publicity could be because of the relationship that George Cohon, the head of McDonald's in Canada, had with the Soviet government in the era of *glasnost* and *perestroika* under leader Mikhail Gorbachev. Mr. Cohon's fast food empire was expanding into the Soviet Union, starting with a huge venue in Moscow. Maybe it was all too commercial. I don't know, but I do know it was a very big deal culturally and politically and the story was given short-shrift from the outset.

Just imagine, all that children's fantasy in the form of themed floats was being transmitted to hundreds of millions of people in the Soviet Union, who doubtless had little or no idea what it was all about, aside from what they were told by the Russian TV hosts. All this before the dissolution of the Soviet Union two years later.

A few months before the parade in 1989, Faye and I along with a three-person crew went to the Soviet Union. We stayed at the Hotel Ukraina, well known for its architecture, being one of seven structures by the same architect in Moscow commissioned by Stalin. We were also close to Red Square and the Kremlin.

We naturally thought we were being taped in the hotel, so we didn't spend much time talking shop there. But every time we left the hotel with our driver to go filming, we were stopped by the police and had to give them a carton of American cigarettes bought at the tourist's store and a small amount of cash. It was another case of paying baksheesh but one we couldn't argue with because it was so small an amount. Mind you, it happened every day.

We filmed in and around Moscow for several days, including going to the children's hospital that would benefit from the parade advertising revenue. That was a shock for me and one I guess I should have expected.

The hospital was only five years old at the time, and as we walked through the halls, we could see the cracked concrete, water and other damage. Russia was joked about for its shoddy construction, but this was not funny. The rooms and operating theatres were sparsely furnished and it was obvious it needed a lot of help and equipment. There was also a strong odour of mildew. I have no idea if the parade commercial advertising revenues ever made it there, but I hope so.

Since McDonald's would be the first fast food company to open in Moscow, and since the initiative was Canadian, we decided to do a business story tying it to the new economic openness in the country. The story I prepared, though, got me into trouble with George Cohon because, in my investigation of the new venue, I found that the price of a Big Mac was going to be the equivalent of a week's salary for the average Muscovite. That was something they didn't want publicly talked about before the opening.

At one point, Faye and I went to a Georgian restaurant to have dinner with our Soviet broadcast partner and his wife. The food and wine were fantastic, but it was a toast by our hostess, who worked for Intourist, the government tourist agency, that was most memorable. It's a Georgian traditional toast and I want to share it with you:

> "Here's to your death ... but I wish that the oak tree
> from which your coffin will be made has not been
> planted yet."

The speaker paused after uttering "death" and I was worried, not knowing what was coming next. A little weird, this toast, but poignant, too.

A number of things about that trip were a bit offbeat. It started the first night when we went to the hotel dining room for dinner. The tables were long, bringing the guests together. In the middle of the table were alternately a bottle of vodka, a plate of oily charcuterie, and a bowl of black caviar on ice. The special that night was roast chicken, my favourite, so I was happy.

Happy, that is, until the dinner came. The roast chicken was some skin attached to bone. There was little if any meat. When I enquired about the "chicken," I was told it was fairly normal for the best cuts – breasts and legs with thighs – to be reserved for important guests and/or political cronies.

Also, that first night, I noticed the waiters carrying large amounts of currency under a napkin but clearly visible. Turns out the waiters did a thriving black market in currency exchange. Their rate was 14 roubles to one U.S. dollar some seven times the official rate. This was risky, but by now everyone was doing it so I deemed the risk was minimal, non-existent, even. I decided to get some just in case we needed to pay more baksheesh and who knows what?

As it happens, there was nothing to buy in Moscow. I went to a music department store and was told the wait for a musical instrument was nine months. The stores we saw were empty. I managed to buy some tea and some art off a street vendor to bring home, but that was about it.

From Moscow we travelled to Yalta to visit a camp where Young Pioneers trained. The organization was founded by Lenin to promote communist ideals among the elite youth and operated between 1922 and 1991. We were there to meet some of the youngsters who would be going to Toronto to participate in the parade on the Russian float.

That visit gave us an opportunity to see where the famous (some say infamous) Yalta Conference took place in 1945 between the Allies to discuss postwar reorganization of Germany and Europe. I was surprised at how sparse the furnishings were, including chairs that would be uncomfortable after sitting in them for a time. Of course, I had to sit in Churchill's chair and was given permission to do so.

Our last stop on this trip would be to Yerevan, Armenia. We were there one year after the 1988 earthquake devastated the country, with some communities completely wiped out because of poor construction materials and methods.

If you look up that earthquake, the death toll is always figured at around 25,000 but there was a reason for that, or so I was told. In a catastrophe where the death toll is above 25,000, other nations do not need the approval of the country to send aid, and the Soviet Union did not want a lot of western nations arriving in Armenia to help out. Some estimates had the actual death rate at closer to 60,000 or more, and I could understand why when we travelled to the countryside. The damage was extreme and widespread to all structures of recent build.

In one community, we were filming close to what looked like a trailer park. It was actually portable housing that had been donated to the people by the government of Norway. We were interrupted by an Armenian woman, dressed in black, with a weathered face that looked like it had seen the devil. She was carrying a tray of plums and wanted to share her meagre ration with us. Such kindness under such circumstances was heartwarming.

We found the Armenians to be generous with their time, understanding and their humanity. We visited a display of children's art and ended up doing a story on the transition of the colour and subject matter of the art from the early days of the earthquake to what the children remembered one year later as they were adjusting to life, often without family and friends. It was a remarkable movement from blacks to muted colours to bright colours. They were adjusting and it was wonderful to see and hear their stories.

We did a feature report on those orphaned children and the report somehow made it to Boston. Some weeks later I was approached by an academic in child psychology there who wanted access to our video, and we of course let them have it.

That children's art feature garnered a lot of positive viewer comment but the most important reaction for me came from another journalist, the venerable Lawrence Martin. If you'll indulge me, I'll quote from his letter, dated November 2, 1989:

> "This is superior work. I think you really managed
> to capture the sense of the story, without resorting
> to the sensational. It was a very original idea to
> visit an art school after the earthquake in Armenia
> and see the changes in the kids' view of life. As a
> westerner going in there, I was especially taken by
> the fact that you weren't carrying any ideological
> baggage. No prejudice came through, only a sense
> of feeling and understanding."

I worked with an amazing crew on that trip. The producer was Heather Kelly, the cameraman was Paul Freer, and we had a sound technician on this occasion, Dave Gebe. It was a luxury having such a great crew because a year earlier I had done a week-long trip to China with just a cameraman, and that was one of the toughest trips ever for a number of reasons.

CHAPTER 46

China Was Slowly Opening Up

Hardcore journalists could argue that I should never have accepted the offer by my producer to do this trip to China in 1988. Air China had opened a new route from Toronto to Beijing and had run a promotional contest on Global News, for which our producer accepted the offer to have a two-person crew on that inaugural flight. She asked me if I was interested in going.

I was for a number of reasons, foremost among them was that I wanted to see first-hand how the changes to the government's policies on capitalism were affecting its people. China had quietly begun to develop their own "openness" policy, much like the one on which the Soviet Union had embarked. Also, it was only for a week, and when you're working the kind of hours I was working, breaks are hard to find. So, when one comes along, you grab it.

My cameraman was Vince Robinette who had been a former video editor, so I trusted his eye. It was going to be a grind because I had a few stories I wanted to do, and we also had to do some promotional filming for the producer.

On the flight over, I got to know the contest winner, Sandra Hutchison of Barrie, and her mother, along with a few other westerners on the flight. One of them was Doris Giller, wife of Jack

Rabinovitch, and the person for whom Jack named Canada's foremost literary award, the Giller Prize, after Doris's death in 1993. Doris, too, was anxious to get a taste of the "new" China.

Having been in the airline business, I should have known better but, no, I tucked right into the airline meal that included shrimp. I simply disregarded the fact that shrimp is kept "fresh" by spraying some preservative on it. I reacted badly to that, developing an allergy that stayed with me for a few years, but, thankfully, it wasn't bad enough to spoil the trip.

From the moment we arrived until the day we left, Vincent and I were busy. We were booked into a new American chain hotel on the outskirts of Beijing that offered American cuisine. That turned out to be a godsend for Vince because it didn't take long for him to get tired of Chinese food. As for me, I couldn't get enough.

We had a car and driver along with a student guide/translator because there was no way we could have done what we did on our own.

Outside Beijing we visited one of the most comprehensive industrial/agricultural co-operatives whose name translated into "Evergreen." It was managed by a charming woman who took great pride in showing us many but not all of its features. It was a huge tract of acreage and at one point I looked miles away on the horizon to see what appeared to be an airport complex. When I enquired what it was, I was met with the Chinese equivalent of a "no comment." I assumed it was a military base.

Still, we were there to see the essence of the "new" economy and sure enough we happened on the best possible example. We saw a house being built beside an existing row of houses close by a large field of crops. These workers seemed tp be enjoying the hard labour creating this home and I asked our guide to get their story.

It turned out these houses were owned by the workers. Once

they met their quota for their work in the fields, they were allowed to take any of their extra product to Beijing and sell it into the free market. The monies earned went into homes like the ones we were seeing, and extras such as satellite dishes for TV reception. This encapsulated what the new "free" economy was all about in 1988.

On another trip outside Beijing we went to Badaling, one of the main tourist entrances to the Great Wall. They chose this location for the long view accorded the wall and its condition, which had been improved over the years, because much of the wall had been in various stages of deterioration along its 21,000-plus kilometre route.

I must admit I was a bit shocked to find our entrance to the wall blocked by a security person who wanted baksheesh – $100 U.S. – to film on the wall. It took a while, but our guide finally convinced the guard he was making a mistake and we made it onto the Wall. It was busy but well worth seeing. It's alleged to be the only man-made structure that can be seen from space. I'm sure that's true.

Back in Beijing we were introduced to a young academic couple, as we had expressed an interest in seeing how people lived. Their apartment was on the eighth floor of a 15-story high rise. These two were tenured professors but we also met a retired limousine driver who had a larger unit on the penthouse floor.

The young academics talked at length about their life and we had a good look at their apartment. Their furniture was very nice, but the look of the unit was spoiled by the appearance of electricity wires that were not embedded in the walls.

The meal the young woman created for us, though, was spectacular. Like the luncheon we'd had at the Evergreen cooperative, this one had about 12 courses. Poor Vince had a rough time but was able to miss some courses in order to film the setting.

That night we had arranged to meet some officials at the very first discotheque nightclub in Beijing (perhaps in all of China) that had opened only a few weeks before. This was a big deal for them and something about which I was anxious to report.

Unfortunately, Vince retired to bed with a sour stomach as soon as we got back from the luncheon and couldn't make the disco. Reluctantly, I went on my own to find two government ministers, their aides and wives waiting for us. When I arrived alone (with my translator) they were most gracious but, after introductions and greetings, they quickly left, obviously disappointed I wasn't filming them boogying on the dance floor.

The other occurrence worth mentioning was our visit to a world-renowned shrine on the outskirts of Beijing whose name escapes me as I write this. We were filming the extraordinary buildings when a large cadre of Chinese soldiers marched into view from around a building. I asked Vince to capture this on video because it was an unusual site at a shrine. No sooner did he start to film when an army officer intervened, waving and telling us no, no, no (at least that's what I was told). I smiled and said OK and we stopped. Luckily, they didn't demand our tape and that was that.

Several months later I realized what we had seen. The government had positioned army units all around Beijing as a precaution for what they feared would be unrest by students in what became the Tiananmen Square Protests and Massacre in June 1989. But we could not have known that.

(Thirty years later, in the summer of 2019, the Chinese government positioned Chinese troops on the outskirts of Hong Kong as the student protests there became more violent. Thankfully, unlike the Tiananmen Square tragedy, the troops around Hong Kong were not deployed.)

Back home I managed to get five or six feature stories to air and the reaction to them was positive.

I also made an immediate appointment with an allergist because my reaction to the airline food preservative was giving me problems. It turned out I had to forego eating shellfish for a long time, but I also had to give up drinking beer, most of which also has preservatives. Thankfully it didn't apply to Scotch ...

CHAPTER 47

It Takes All Kinds

In my heyday at Global I was often asked who my favourite interview was, and it was always difficult to answer because I enjoyed almost all of my interviewees, granted, some more than others. It will come as no surprise to learn the ones I remember most were with women. I have always enjoyed the company of women and I found generally there was a high degree of integrity among women interviewees.

It's been said that I was a soft interviewer, that I wasn't confrontational with my subjects, especially politicians. My response was always the same: If a politician or business person wishes to lie or mislead in response to a question, that is his or her problem and the audience will certainly pick up on it. I never felt the need to display some macho "gotcha" approach to interviews.

There was one, though, that I remember along those lines. The person's name is gone but he was running in the Oshawa region for federal politics. He was a well-known union organizer. In response to a question that had to do with workers' rights, he made the case for Canada's adopting policies that existed, he said, in Britain at the time. It just so happened I knew what he was saying was false and I confronted him on it and asked him, rather cheekily I might add, why he would want to lie about something like that.

Getting caught out on TV didn't sit well with him and a few weeks later he bowed out of politics, which really was a good thing.

Some politicians such as Ontario Premier David Peterson were always elusive and full of the blarney. You knew it and the audience knew it so it wasn't important to try to confront them.

And then there were politicians such as Premier Bill Davis who you could always rely on for an honest answer. Having interviewed her a few times, I always felt his wife Kathy was behind Bill's public integrity.

The former federal minister from Newfoundland John Crosbie was another who displayed integrity in his interviews. And it's certain his wife Jane insisted on that. Another straight shooter for me was former Prime Minister John Turner who, coincidentally, was the first person I ever voted for when he ran in the Montreal riding of St. Lawrence-St. George in 1962.

Elinor Caplan was both an MPP and an MP. I knew her better when she was a provincial politician for the NDP and she was among the best of the bunch in terms of integrity.

My favourite politician interview, though, was with René Lévesque, granted, after he left politics. He came to our studio to talk about his book, *Memoir*. Talking about his party's goal to break up Canada, I said I couldn't like him for that. He replied that he understood and was not in the least put off by the remark. His dedication in the book reinforced that. But more importantly, I ended the interview asking how he wanted to be remembered. Without missing a beat, he said he wanted to be remembered as someone who led an "honest government void of corruption." And that's exactly what he did. And while I don't know for sure, it had to be a first in Quebec.

Political interviews were fairly common on magazine-type shows. Producers liked to get politicians on camera, but I personally didn't think our audiences gave two hoots about them. In fact, I think too much time is spent talking politics in television news because it fills a lot of time and is easy to do. If we spent as much time discussing matters such as personal finance management or family legal issues, we'd all be better off in so many ways.

Interviews were given about three to three and half minutes in news programmes. Politicians knew this and were well trained in how to take lots of time saying nothing or diverting the questions away from anything controversial. They all get media training, which entails developing key messages and sticking with them.

I recently heard a federal minister, Bill Blair, use the word "safe" about 20 times in an interview about gun control. He never once answered a question and always returned to mentioning that the role of government and the police was to keep citizens "safe." Gun violence is on a frightening upward curve, in Toronto especially, and little concerted action has been taken to stem it.

While not an interview, per se, an interface with Prime Minister Brian Mulroney proved most telling. Several months after taking office in 1984, the Mulroneys planned a series of intimate dinner parties at 24 Sussex Drive with a broad spectrum of Canadians, in order to get a better understanding of the issues facing the country and how his government was handling their new power.

I was lucky enough to be invited, joining Knowlton Nash of the CBC and Lloyd Robertson of CTV and their wives, along with a handful of others, including the Richardsons from Winnipeg. My inclusion in this illustrious group was probably due to Shirley. Mila Mulroney pointed out that she had followed Shirley's wonderful career and had been anxious to meet her.

During the pre-dinner cocktails, I found himself talking to Brian and, after a few niceties about the times we'd spent at "The Swamp," as we called the bar in the concourse of Montreal's Place Ville Marie complex, I commented on how some of his cabinet ministers were using the media for their personal gain and not necessarily to the advantage of the new government.

This observation seemed to anger Mulroney and he abruptly walked away. Seeing this, Mila came over and asked what had happened. When I explained the nature of my comment she replied, in effect, that those circumstances would change. And sure enough, some three or four months later, cabinet ministers were discouraged from holding impromptu media scrums and the ministers towed the party line in all matters.

Mulroney's reaction to my comments bothered me because I had a lot of respect for him. I felt strongly he was on the right track in dealing with Quebec and the economy. I supported the Meech Lake Accord and said so publicly, though I later apologized because I was a stickler on remaining non-partisan, which I am to this day.

Occasionally I was lucky enough to do interviews with senior celebrities such as actor Peter Ustinov.

He enjoyed coming to Toronto and while it would normally have been Mac doing the interview, Mac wasn't available, so I drew the short straw.

We had a terrific interview at a downtown hotel. At one stage I referred to his work as a UNICEF ambassador and sought his views on why the west had not intervened yet in the horrible events taking place in the Balkans at the time where it was clear genocidal events were unfolding.

"Watermelons," he said, "there's not much more than watermelons produced there so the west has little interest."

I was taken aback by his candour and the entire interview was like that along with some dry wit. I came away with a greater understanding of his stature in the industry and as a citizen of the world.

I was fortunate enough to do many of the cooking segments on the News At Noon and met some of the best chefs in the business such as David Wood and Rose Reisman. But there were many more from across Canada.

Canada was in the throes of a food revolution, centred on Toronto, where diversity was the key to an extraordinary number of new products. Included in this were fresh products that once were available only seasonally but now were available year-round.

And by the way, by this time Toronto had benefitted from the arrival of some three hundred thousand creative minds and food junkies from Montreal, compelled out of Quebec by the separatist movement.

David Wood, a Scottish immigrant, borrowed from gourmet food shops in New York to usher in a new era of pre-prepared foods from a tiny shop on Yonge Street. His ideas were later copied and expanded upon by the most prestigious purveyors of fine foods such as Pusateri's and Summerhill Market.

To cook your own the diversity was even greater thanks mainly to a brash new marketing whiz with the grocery chain, Loblaw.

It was a fateful day that I met Loblaw's brilliant Dave Nichol who appeared during the launch of his President's Choice line of groceries. I say "fateful" because Nichol created a revolution in the packaged food industry, albeit borrowing ideas from the innovative Trader Joe's chain in the U.S. Over many appearances, our audience had the benefit of first-hand exposure to new products and serving ideas.

Private branding of quality grocery products was in its infancy when Nichol drove it to extraordinary heights and all of the chains jumped into the fray. The PC lines are still strong, but in my opinion, they've been surpassed by the Kirkland brand from Costco, although that brand has a very limited range of product.

I don't mind boasting that the News at Noon, headed by

producers Wendy Dey and her successor Calla Farn, was instrumental in contributing to the food revolution through food segments that, literally, brought the world of good taste and nutrition to our viewers.

We had other segment experts, too, such as Jane Harvey, who handled our family law discussions for many years. Jane not only broke ground in Canada as the first storefront lawyer who had rates posted on the wall, but she also became a good friend off camera, and our families in later years travelled together to the Middle East and Argentina, among other places.

Book interviews were one of my specialties, too. Except in rare circumstances, I would never agree to an interview if I hadn't read the book. A number of authors would comment off camera that they were shocked I had read their book because their experience with TV interviewers was that reading the book didn't seem to be a priority.

The author James Clavell, for one, expressed his amazement that I had read his book *Whirlwind*, a tome of almost 1200 pages. He told me most interviewers simply asked him questions that had been prepared by publishers' publicists.

One author who wished I had stuck to the publicist's questions was Peter Arnett, the correspondent from CNN who had been in Baghdad at the outset of the Gulf War and had become a huge celebrity. I asked him a number of questions about his personal life, relying solely on material from his book, and he took umbrage at that. Within my earshot he blasted the publicist for having brought him to Global.

I enjoyed interviewing Timothy Findlay a lot but one of my favourite authors was Farley Mowat. Both men were great characters, one a fiction writer, the other non-fiction.

Among women writers, Gloria Steinem forced me to think far

outside the box and I really liked her books. I'll share with you an amusing moment with her.

She came to Toronto on a promotional tour and I had just read an interesting article about her in a New York based magazine. The picture of her in the article had her in what I assumed was her bedroom having tea while lounging on the bed. I noticed the teapot didn't have a cozy, but I also knew Americans didn't use tea cozies.

The next day on my way to the interview at a hotel, I went to Eaton's and bought a tea cozy with a lovely paisley design that matched her bedroom décor. She viewed the gift with the most quizzical look and said not a word, though she sought help from the publicist who said nothing. I said nothing and we did the interview.

One of my most poignant interviews was with Margaret Trudeau. I was a bit taken aback when I learned after the interview that Ms. Trudeau had told the publicist that in Toronto the only TV interview she would do was with me. I had never met her before but found her life story compelling.

The producer liked the interview so much (she could talk to me in my earpiece at any time) she told me to keep going and it lasted some 15 minutes, three times longer than normal. I found Margaret's comments about mental health, family pressures, and so on, most compelling. The interview was really animated and natural. I thought she was terrific.

My co-host Bob McAdorey did the entertainment interviews but when he was away or when it was someone special to one of us, we were given the nod.

On one such occasion I interviewed the wonderful cabaret singer Dinah Christie. We were at North Toronto Collegiate at the same time (though I'm older, I also managed to fail a grade, so she caught up, so to speak) and were friendly, although we didn't hang out. I followed her career with interest, especially when she became one of the hosts for the CBC program, "This Hour Has Seven Days." Dinah would sing these parodies and was a delightful addition to the usual display of gravitas.

After that TV show ended its long run, Dinah did a lot of cabaret with the late, great Tom Kneebone, and to promote one of these she came on the News At Noon. After she got her message across and sang a song, she asked me if I'd like to sing something. This was not staged but when I suggested the Canadian classic "Four Strong Winds," she was delighted.

Well, you had to see the tape to believe it. I kept my eyes shut almost the entire time because I was afraid to look at the camera or the crew who were obviously having a giggle about this turn of events. That wasn't the only time I sang on camera, either.

Another singer, well, poet, singer, author, renaissance man, Leonard Cohen, agreed to do an interview with me in the Global garden one fine summer's day. It would be a long interview for use on a "Local Hero" series I was developing. My producer wanted to extend the normal interview time of two and a half to three and a half minutes to five or more, depending on the subject matter, for use on weekends when news was often in short supply.

Off camera, I raised the event I had witnessed so many years before when he had given the concert at the asylum in London. He gave me a strange look and said not a word. I never pursued it, not wishing to embarrass him. He was a difficult interview but charming.

One time I got carried away with what I thought was the power of celebrity. Someone I respected got into a lot of trouble over what were unquestionably derisive comments about Toronto's Black community in 1982. I thought I could help him out.

DJ Phil MacKellar had been hosting his morning jazz program on CKFM when he took a telephone call from a friend, forgetting his microphone was hot. It was July 31, the start of the August long weekend and his friend wanted to meet downtown. MacKellar mentioned that the Caribana Parade, an annual summer event performed by Toronto's predominant Caribbean islands Black community, was going to be diverting traffic and, in doing so, he used a racist description which I won't repeat here.

The Black community was outraged, and it caused huge waves in the media for weeks. MacKellar was fired and was never able to get work again.

I saw a lot of irony in the whole story because I knew MacKellar was the foremost authority on jazz in Toronto with a 34-year association with the community, which, by the way, was among the top ten in North America. He counted among his friends many of the best jazz musicians, Black and white, in Toronto.

Not only did MacKellar have his radio show, he also did live broadcasts from the famous Queen Street jazz emporium, the Town Tavern, where, when I was 18, I used to sneak in using my oldest brother's birth certificate, because the legal drinking age back then was 21. Almost always after those shows I would head to the First Floor Jazz Club on Asquith Street where so often groups would come to jam after their club gigs.

It was through MacKellar that I got to know a lot about jazz and I even met some of the greats such as Jackie and Roy Kral, as well as the terrific local talent like pianists Wray Downes and Norm Amadio and drummer Archie Alleyne.

Feeling strongly that even the worst offenders deserve a second chance, I spoke to our News at Noon producer and requested we ask MacKellar on the program to explain what had happened and to show our huge audience how contrite he was. I knew we had a sizeable Black audience and it was growing. I felt it was the least we could do to have the full story aired instead of hearsay and rumour, which frankly clouded the issue even more.

MacKellar agreed to come on and we had a terrific interview, touching all the bases and repeating his apologies. That was in August. Sadly, it didn't seem to help. The station didn't receive one telephone call complaining about the interview but MacKellar never worked again, and a few months later he died of a heart attack.

I bumped into his wife a few years later. She told me how much Phil had appreciated my attempts to help him regain his reputation. She also offered me the opportunity to borrow anything from his extensive record collection.

Coincidentally, back in the 50s I got to know Sharon Glover, daughter of Elwood Glover, the celebrated host of CBC radio and later TV with a program called Luncheon Date. Elwood was a huge fan of jazz and did much to promote Canadian musical talent. Sharon allowed me to borrow some of Elwood's extensive collection of jazz albums and I did, treating them with kid gloves and a new phonograph needle.

This talk of jazz albums brings to mind one of the stupidest things I've ever done, and that was to give away my fabulous collection of at least 250 jazz records. The music industry convinced us that albums were out and tape was in. I spent hours converting my records to cassette tapes, then gave my records and top-of-the-line electronics away in favour of a tape deck. What a mistake. Those tapes I made were soon useless as CDs became all the rage then music streaming, and quietly, ever so quietly, vinyl came back and the reproduction equipment is superb.

I won't get fooled again.

CHAPTER 48

Working with the Best

During my first year at Global I experienced my first ever (and let's hope only) cracked bone, the collarbone, damaged when I tried to emulate a great baseball player and make a diving catch at third base during a charity baseball game. Such collarbone cracks are not treated; you simply wear a sling, keeping the bone at rest until it heals naturally.

The next day I did the News at Noon, wearing a sling that was colour coordinated with my suit. Unbeknownst to me, the audience reacted negatively. I got some help preparing my copy for the evening broadcast and arrived on set wearing the sling. The News Director was livid and during the lead-in commercial he insisted I lose the sling. I had no choice.

At about the two-minute mark, halfway through my segment, I was doing a voiceover and the news anchor beside me turned to gesture for something. The back of his chair hit my chair and that jolted the bone, igniting a very sharp pain while I was presenting my story. Somehow, I managed to get through my segment. The news anchor never knew what happened and I never said a word.

Truth be told, what could I say to Peter Trueman? He's a big guy, 6' 5" for sure and solidly built. When his chair hit mine, it was like a tank hitting a grocery cart. But he was our leader; a solid journalist who anchored a news team overflowing with strong talent.

When Bill Cunningham, the vice-president of news, many years before was asked to create a first-class news team for Global, he did just that, hiring some print journalists with broad experience and, with the help of Peter, turning them into broadcast journalists.

Peter himself was the face of Global News. He brought to the screen gravitas, field experience and credibility, something news readers at other networks didn't have. And he mentored those of us who didn't have the background.

My first and biggest lesson occurred when I went to Ottawa to cover my first federal budget – the one that introduced the National Energy Program, the policy I had called sinister. Thankfully, Peter had caught my editorializing slip before it got to air and later explained what he had done. It was a valuable lesson.

The *Toronto Star* had a weekly TV insert and one week they featured a readers' poll of TV personalities. I was honoured to place second to Peter as the most trustworthy news anchor in the newspaper's market. We were strong then, but Peter knew it wouldn't last.

One thing that Peter did in 1980 was write a book called *Smoke and Mirrors* that contained the most prescient look at television news ever at the time. He was worried where TV news was heading. He saw how marketing and sales people were influencing news presentation. But most importantly, he foresaw how something he called "infotainment" was creeping into commercial TV newscasts. I'm not certain if he coined that description but it was the first time most of us had heard of it.

Ironically, I was party to that creeping change as part of the News at Noon, which evolved into a news magazine, albeit with a hard news beginning. Peter could accept that during the day but he didn't want to see it on his broadcasts. In writing the book, Peter did what he had to do and, even though it didn't prevent the steamrolling of infotainment, while he was in charge of content on his newscasts, it was thwarted.

Peter Trueman also developed for his newscasts what he called an "Endall" which was an opinion piece he would write, giving his opinion on issues of the day. Because it was so labelled it was perfectly acceptable and viewers respected him because they were mostly balanced.

Peter's role at Global News diminished in the early 80s and by the time he left Global in 1988, it was, according to some reports, out of disgust for the way newscasts were formatted and produced. But he didn't stop producing quality journalism. Among projects he fronted was a series on Canada's national parks that was a big success on cable television.

Behind the celebrity, though, Peter Trueman was involved in something more satisfying. Peter in the past four decades or so has worked quietly, tirelessly and anonymously, giving speeches, mentoring and sponsoring, or whatever was required to help people in need. I know this because in my travels, some of these people have opened up about their respect for Peter.

This was our leader when I joined Global News. And in retrospect, Peter represents many of the bosses or colleagues I've been lucky to work with over the years, including those wonderful tradesmen I worked with as an apprentice in construction – the carpenters, the bricklayers and the high steel riggers. My first serious job in journalism was being a gofer for the *Gazette* financial editor, John Meyer. I was in his employ when a significant change was about to create havoc in his world.

Montreal was the financial capital of Canada up until the 60s but with the Quiet Revolution in Quebec society, the shift to Toronto had begun. John Meyer's column was still the most widely read and respected in the country ,but *The Globe and Mail* in Toronto was about to strike a blow.

It was to be announced in an advertisement the *Gazette* sales staff had received and approved for a new publication called "Report On Business" and it would be available daily in *The Globe*, which by now had started circulating in many parts of the country.

John saw the ad that was going to appear in his financial news pages, and he turned red, smashed out his ever-present cigarette and stormed out of the office. He returned still fuming because the general manager wasn't there.

The manager eventually came to our office and the two argued over the merits of allowing the ad to run in the *Gazette*. John lost the argument and it was only a matter of time before *The Globe and Mail* Report On Business became the journal of record for business and financial news. Just as it was only a matter of time before the financial engine of Canada re-positioned itself in Toronto where it remains to this day.

My tenure at the Canadian Dow Jones News Service was too brief to establish a strong relationship with my boss, Doug Colvey, but I admired the man greatly for his expertise and fatherly advice.

When I was working for the Canadian Pacific Railway Company, the second in command of the public relations department was a fellow named I.B. "Barry" Scott. He respected my hard work and tenacity and gave me some interesting projects, which I handled well enough to get an early promotion. I ended up not taking the promotion because it meant moving to Toronto and I was destined to stay in Montreal. That's when I got the great job at BOAC.

As for Barry, he eventually ended up running the railway, rare for an internal PR person, but Barry was that rare person.

In retrospect, though, the best boss I ever had was the one who gave me and my colleagues the most headaches. Ray Heard immigrated to Canada from South Africa and later London to work for the *Montreal Star*, becoming that paper's White House correspondent while working as well for *The Observer* newspaper of London. Ten years later he was named managing editor of the *Montreal Star*.

When that paper folded in 1979, following a lengthy printer's strike, Heard joined Global News as news director under Bill Cunningham and later succeeded Bill as Vice-President, News. Bill, a renowned Vietnam War correspondent, had created a news team that he dubbed "the Viet Cong of TV news reporting." Heard was the perfect commander to take it into battle.

It was under Heard's tutelage that Global News surged in its viewership while controlling costs, an element that was extremely important in those years when Global was still struggling. As an example, when we covered the Royal Tour of Prince Charles and Diana, we were three people: A field producer, a camera person and me. We did feature reports and live hits into all the newscasts for a few days, competing with the likes of CBC-TV who had at least a dozen staff on hand.

Heard's antics oftentimes were akin to those of a madman and staff were bitterly divided in their opinion of him. I had known him for many years from my days in Montreal and knew that behind the "mad" façade there was a genius at work. He demanded loyalty, hard work and long hours, and since I was new to the business, that suited me just fine.

Heard was also innovative. Global's Christmas Day newscasts were pretty bland, highlighting the Queen's message. Our News at Noon had begun to draw large numbers so he asked me to anchor the Christmas newscast and I agreed, provided I could have my two-year-old-son with me at the end of the broadcast to help me wish everyone a Merry Christmas.

He agreed and that broadcast attracted a huge audience. The impact was so strong, the following year the Lieutenant Governor of Ontario, John Black Aird, asked if he could be part of the program, along with his grandchildren. We readily agreed and His Honour and I shared many good times during his tenure at Queen's Park.

Heard was also responsible for some of my most prolific feature reporting assignments and I'm sure he had a hand in my becoming a co-host of the Santa Clause parade broadcast. He always told me I didn't disappoint.

When he left in 1987, there was joy in the newsroom, but those that followed lacked his tenacity and vision. Worse still, changes in on-air personnel were made that badly affected audience numbers.

CHAPTER 49

The Studio Lights Begin to Fade

Just as I have worked with some great people, I've also worked with some jerks, but until I got to Global TV those were few and far between. At Global the whole concept of family seemed to be accepted … by everyone except management, of course, and every family has its nuts and ne'er-do-wells. With the odd exception, I could accept those with egos, after all, it's an ego-driven industry. But bad decisions on staffing and content used to get me down.

There's something about the news business that has always disturbed me and that's wrapped up in the old maxim: "Never let the facts get in the way of a good story."

That hit home to me in April 1989 during what became known as The Great Federal Budget leak. The story that the public heard was that Global News Ottawa bureau chief Doug Small got a call from a John Appleby, a disgruntled federal government employee, whom he later met in a parking lot. Appleby gave him a document describing the budget highlights. Small then went on air declaring, "I've got the budget" and proceeded to mention some of those highlights.

I'm not sure if Small ever knew or cared about the full story, but Appleby had earlier tried to sell the budget details to an Ottawa news outlet who had refused to deal. The man then called us at

Global News in Toronto. The call was answered by a junior in the news department, Tina Gladstone, who transferred it to as assignment desk person, Sharon Murphy, who then transferred the called to me. I was in an editing booth at the time so my competent right-hand person, Paul French, took the call.

The caller wanted to know if Global bought stories. Paul assured him we did not but kept him on the line to get an understanding of what he was selling. On hearing it was the federal budget details that were to be released the next day, Paul motioned to a colleague to get me out of the editing suite.

On hearing what was transpiring, I immediately contacted Howard Bernstein, our News Director, who agreed I should call a contact in the Finance Department whom I had known for years, named Ben Ward. To me, calling Finance was the ethical thing to do, but it would also ideally authenticate the leak and establish whether Global had the budget details on an exclusive basis. Mr. Ward appeared nonplused but didn't enquire about any details of the alleged leak.

Paul French had asked the caller to call back, which he did. At that time Paul had a pre-determined response and asked the man to call our Ottawa Bureau Chief Doug Small and make arrangements to get the document to him.

I then tried to contact Ben Ward to advise him we were getting the document and to seek comment. Mr. Ward was not available at either his office or home telephone numbers.

Doug Small met with the caller and received what turned out to be a copy of the Budget In Brief, an executive summary providing details of the main elements of the budget. Later in our newscast he revealed the contents on air in a manner that disturbed me because of its disingenuousness.

Many viewers were livid about the budget leak and called in

to complain, using language such as "dishonourable," "reprehensible," "disgusting," "opportunistic" and "disrespectful." Those who had cared to acknowledge that we had contacted the Finance Department to inform them of the leak agreed we had done the right thing in reporting it.

It was a sensational story and one that led to Doug Small (and Mr. Appleby) being charged by the Mulroney government, charges that were withdrawn the following year, but which allegedly cost Global some $100,000 in legal fees.

In the immediate aftermath of the scoop, I took a call from a writer for *Maclean's* magazine and related the story, but all of the Toronto detail was left out of his subsequent report. Paul himself gave a terrific interview (with management's blessing) to Barbara Frum, of the CBC's flagship show, "The Journal," that had much of the story though not all.

Paul French was also contacted at home at 4 a.m. by the Royal Canadian Mounted Police, who by now were investigating the leak as a possible criminal act.

There was a strong argument to be made – as Small did – to disclose those budget details and I agreed with it. I personally wouldn't have done it the way he did. I had told the man who hired me at the outset that I didn't like television news for its alarmist and sensationalist approach to news reporting.

Among the papers I looked at for this memoir, I found a letter from Howard Bernstein commending me for the way I handled the Great Budget Leak.

My motto was always "What you see is what you get" and I didn't profess to be a hard-nosed journalist like Claude Adams or George Wolfe, and I didn't have the camera presence of news anchor Richard Brown. I also came into the industry cold and had to work with long-time radio/TV personalities.

What I had in spades, though, was the support of the operations staff, the floor directors and camera operators, who were always ready to help and encourage me when necessary, and I've aways been grateful for that.

But some further background is necessary. I joined Global in 1980 and the network had not yet turned the corner financially. In fact, it had only been operating six years and was rumoured to still be in financial trouble. They gambled by hiring me and improving their news content. Somewhere along the way, things began to happen, and as someone who was front and centre in this, I could feel it and it was great. We were doing some interesting things, thanks to people like Ray Heard, and some of them bothered Peter Trueman, but we were in survival mode in a highly competitive industry.

Our audiences were building nicely. And we were rapidly losing our reputation as the "Love Boat Network," which was a reference to the re-runs of that sitcom that helped the network to create a foundation of revenue.

At one point it was decided to expand the news. There was a hole to fill between the end of the highly successful "The Young and the Restless" soap opera and the 6 o'clock prime time newscast. It was decided to fill it with "First News" at 5:30, which would bridge the daytime drama and Peter Trueman's classic supper-hour newscast. The entire 90 minutes would be revised and I was asked to co-anchor the start of the new programming.

I readily agreed, especially because the producer would be Wendy Dey with whom I had worked so well on the hugely successful News at Noon.

We gave audiences this package to transition from the soap time slots to the evening sitcoms. It would start with First News, which had everything you needed to know in a truncated format plus an interview and feature reports. Some elements of this newscast included material that Peter Trueman had warned about years before. Promoting upcoming shows, for instance.

To give you a sense of what "infotainment" was, I was once given some copy to read during a program a few years after our launch. I was on air doing the hard news portion of First News and had no time to study the script. The copy told of the death of one Harris Glenn Milstead, a.k.a., Divine, at age 42. After the program I protested the inclusion of that brief because it made no sense to me. "Who the hell is Divine?" I shouted. Turns out it was a transvestite actor and the young producer thought the news important because "it may have been a drug overdose." The rationale drove me crazy with frustration.

"The Young and the Restless" had huge numbers and First News held on to a large share of that, which we then handed to 6 o'clock, for the best audience it ever had. This format was highly successful for a few years, during which there were on-air personnel changes. Nevertheless, it turned into a growth product.

And then in 1987 something happened. The Vice-President of News, Ray Heard, was gone and a producer from the CBC, Rudi Carter, was hired to replace him. He brought new, trendy management ideas, such as "quality circles" in which journalists and producers would sit around and discuss ways to improve the product. The process might work well in a widget factory, but in a newsroom it was ludicrous.

What happened next was even more so. Carter made wholesale changes to those anchoring our most successful programs and, sadly, management bought into the changes. I truly believe they allowed it to happen because they were preoccupied with an internal ownership battle.

The Three Nice Guys on the News at Noon were split up, with Mike going to anchor the 11 o'clock news. I cannot recall the specifics of the other changes, but they were dramatic. The bottom line, though, was that we were letting down the audiences we had worked so hard to build under difficult circumstances.

Some six months later, Carter was fired and shown the door but, sadly, the changes he made were not reversed.

For us on the News at Noon it was devastating, because by this time we might still have been number one in the time slot, but the competition was widespread and aggressive. We didn't have access to the top-notch guests we'd once had nor the musical talent that had daily graced our stage. Bryan Adams had appeared on TV with his band for the first time with us and KD Lang did her thing with Mac, not to forget live performances from Celine Dion, Jim Carrey and many others.

Later, something even more traumatic occurred when one of the network owners bought out his two partners for what was said to be a large premium over analysts' forecasts.

As with any takeover, the buyer has to find ways to recover the costs and Global's answer was to bring in a new president with a reputation for ruthlessness. This person held staff meetings and told these groups they could be forthright about their views on programming and the like. I, of course, had some strong views and expressed them, only to watch this person write them down in a little black book. I could see what was happening and knew it was only a matter of time. And sure enough, within weeks I was accused of sexual harassment.

I was called into a meeting room with the new vice-president of news and the head of human resources and told a verbal complaint had been made about me that amounted to sexual harassment. I was not told what I had allegedly said, nor to whom or when. The V-P said I had a reputation for "lechery." He actually said lechery.

At that point I jumped up to leave and said I'd talk to a lawyer, but I also said, "You don't know what lechery means, do you? What I think you meant is flirt and, yes, I'm the worst flirt in this building. But lechery, that's something else."

He backtracked and said there was no written complaint, only verbal, and it wouldn't be on my record. But the damage had been done. I realized then and there that all those good times, the hard work and the successes meant nothing. I was just a number, and it was a big number, so they had to get rid of me.

The so-called sexual harassment claim was the beginning of a "paper trail" of the sort that managements use to develop a case for employee dismissal. The next thing that happened was I was removed as co-host of the Santa Claus Parade broadcast after nine years working with Faye Dance, in what can only be described as hugely successful programming.

I was tired of it all and of what I saw happening to Global News. My departure would be a blessing.

When I think back on those years at Global, I realize how lucky I was to have been a part of something, a recovery of sorts from what appeared to be a sure death to a significant force in the market. But I realize, too, it could have been so much better.

When we were busting our butts to produce fine programming that the audience liked, the rewards were going mainly to the owners and management.

I couldn't believe it when I learned that after the two owners were bought out, they purchased gold watches and prepaid gift cards for certain members of management. I personally would have distributed some of the goodies, however small, to the operations and production staff who performed so well over such a long time under difficult conditions.

Further, I used to wonder why it was we were never nominated for television awards when we had done so much innovative news programming. It was eventually pointed out to me that in order to be eligible for industry awards, a programme had to be nominated, and that came with a fee of $25, which management was reluctant to pay.

Sour grapes? You can be sure of that and it has nothing to do with ego. I believe that awards are an excellent way of recognizing hard work and dedication by the news teams that make the programmes happen. Besides, seeing our competitors regularly reap those awards was always a blow.

(And by the way, Global management wasn't alone in not nominating their programmes. CITY-TV never did, either, claiming the awards schemes were rigged to favour the CBC, which always took home the majority of awards.)

Under subsequent managements, though, Global has won many awards and I'm delighted for them.

CHAPTER 50

New Challenges, Sort Of

Although I knew my time at Global was up, I also knew it was going to be difficult. I had made a lot of sacrifices in my nearly 15 years at Global News and had suffered family issues because of that. I was also old, 55, too old to think of gaining an on-air slot in an industry that had become so youth oriented. And how do you explain going from a highly trusted face on Global to an outcast overnight?

As it happens, you don't need to explain. People in the industry knew what was going on and the audiences generally didn't care, despite the fact they were always displaying devotion and loyalty.

So it was that I wrote a letter to management suggesting we talk about my future, because they obviously didn't want me around. A few months later I was asked to join the vice-president of news and his human resources colleague at a nearby hotel. The writing was now on the wall. I knew what it would be like because I had taken the precaution of contacting a lawyer friend who guided me through some typical scenarios. He also gave me some numbers to think about when the offer was tabled.

What happened next was almost laughable. As I read the offer, I verbally noted some things that weren't in it and every item was greeted with, "Well, you can have that" or words to that effect. Most importantly, though, I could not argue with the basic offer because it met my lawyer friend's highest standards. I couldn't see any reason to have the agreement lawyered, but I didn't say so then and there. I was also told I could leave immediately.

"No way," I replied. "My News at Noon co-anchor herself is away and the show needs continuity. Besides, I want to say a proper goodbye to my audience." They agreed and I was able to have a two or three-week period before leaving.

This is important to understand because I was not being let go with cause, so management was amenable to my requests for a quiet, smooth transition.

It also gave time for my pals to organize a farewell party. It was held at a restaurant on the Danforth and it was terrific, and remarkable also for the people who didn't attend, including my very longtime co-anchor. It was very telling and drove home the reality that such relationships can be quite superficial.

I had a great laugh at the parting gift. It was a gorgeous cardigan sweater, because the staff knew how much I enjoyed wearing mine around the shop and they wanted a new look.

I never told them,but the sweater was far too large and I didn't have the heart to return it, so I gifted it to my oldest brother. He loved it, too.

When I eventually told other colleagues that their time would be coming up, some smiled, suggesting, "Not likely, mate." Eventually, all of them except Bob McAdorey would be shown the door by security. At least my departure had some grace and style.

Still, it was tough. Later that day my old buddy Bob McCown called and asked me to appear on his radio program the next morning. I would do so after a night of partying with colleagues, which was not a good idea.

Bob and I went back to the days when he launched Sportsline

and often we talked about the business of sports, even on the air occasionally. He was smart that way.

On his programme, we had a good chat about those early Global days. Later his boss called and offered me a job doing business reporting on the radio. I was honoured but the remuneration wouldn't have made up for the loss in continuance of salary I would be getting, even though I probably could have been getting both. What I really needed was time to think about my future.

After appearing on Bob's show, I was at home around nine o'clock in the morning, resting on a sofa in our family room and just about falling asleep when I heard this: "What number do you want?" It was Shirley, explaining I had my choice of numbers for the new business phone she was ordering for me. No rest for the wicked.

I needed a new telephone contact and I needed to promote my availability for hosting what are known as "industrials" in the trade, videos that sponsoring companies used for training or promotional purposes. It wasn't long before I got some of those. The two most memorable were a video explaining the training and regulation of Ontario trucking and drivers, because the industry had been coming under criticism and scrutiny.

The other was a video explaining the benefits to men with prostate cancer of the radical prostatectomy or total prostate removal in which there could be awkward side effects such as incontinence and impotence. And to explain how those effects could be avoided or minimized, the producer, urologist John Trachtenberg, managed to get General Norman Schwarzkopf of Gulf War fame to comment for the film, because he had had a radical procedure and managed to avoid the side effects through hard work and determination.

When I hosted that film, I also brought along for an important educational segment a long-time friend from my days at Global, Fred Ketchen. For many years Fred and I had held an interview on the news about the daily stock market activity. He was well liked, and I knew his presence would benefit the film immensely.

I don't keep in touch with a lot of former Global colleagues, including Fred, only the ones with whom I'd had a relationship that transitioned the business. We didn't have social media in those days and it's the social media today that allows me to maintain these contacts and watch developments.

Aside from hosting industrials, I also did some media training after leaving Global. I'm not going to go into that experience because I'm probably the best example of someone who shouldn't try to do something with which they're not 100% in sync. I really tried and I know I did some good with a few clients, but it wasn't my bag. I think I was too much into full disclosure and up-front comment.

Something else happened in 1994 that set my mind wandering into different ideas for future work. I was asked to play a role in a movie with some high-powered actors such as Nicholas Cage, John Lovitz and Dana Carvey.

It was called *Trapped in Paradise* and it was shot in the winter of 1993/94 in Toronto and Niagara-on-the-Lake. I was to be a news announcer (of course) who described a crime that had been committed and warned that the criminals were still at large. My scene was the first filmed and that occurred, ironically, at Global's studios.

For purposes of full disclosure, I will admit I was told the producers first wanted Gord Martineau to do the part, but he refused.

I also re-wrote my script and performed well, quickly and efficiently. The rest of the filming was done elsewhere, including Niagara-on-the-Lake, with most of the outside shots performed in what turned out to be the coldest and snowiest winter in decades.

When the movie was screened for the crew, I came away from seeing it with a smile and thinking, that's a nice, fun Christmas movie. It should be a success. Well, it was not. It was a bust, lasting only a week at the box office. It's not even mentioned among some of the actors' filmographies.

I was given a five-year buy-out contract for the movie, after which I would get residuals. The cheques still come in every year. The last one was for 81 cents if I remember correctly.

That experience got me going about film, though, and I wrote a film treatment, which I presented to the *Trapped in Paradise* director George Gallo. He never mentioned it nor did I hear from him again.

I wrote the treatment in 1994 and the theme was collusion between the government and big pharma over drugs being developed to treat AIDS. It had an investigative journalist as heroine. In 2001 the wonderful thriller writer John Le Carré published *The Constant Gardener* and its theme was so similar as to be scary: collusion between government and big pharma on a tuberculosis drug with a journalist hero. It encouraged me to try to write another screen story years later. That screenplay never sold but I'm thinking about revising it.

Another project that came my way in 1994 was the opportunity to return to Africa and do some feature reporting for World Vision. This led to one of my favourite journalistic endeavours. Together with the high-profile media personality, Catherine Swing, our film crew travelled to Uganda to report on World Vision's field work to mitigate the devastating effects of the AIDS epidemic.

One of the main projects was a microloan program in which women only applied for small loans to start small businesses. Most loans were less than $100. This project was fashioned on a successful system operating in Bangladash that had turned into a major force there.

The program was very successful in Uganda where women had been forced into unfamiliar roles because the AIDS epidemic had taken a heavy toll on the male population. And when I say heavy, I mean it. We visited villages where there were no males above the age of 14 to be found.

One day when we were filming on the banks of Lake Victoria, I asked some local people why there were so many fishing boats on land and not out on the lake, which was Africa's largest inland fishery with abundant perch and tilapia.

Their faces saddened as they explained fishing had been banned several months before by the government because of atrocities committed during the genocide in neighbouring Rwanda. The bodies of thousands of murdered Tutsis had been thrown into rivers that flowed into Lake Victoria and rendered the bounty there unpalatable if not diseased. Some 15,000 bodies had been recovered from the lake by Ugandans under a government program and buried in a consecrated mass grave. The majority of them were children and some of their body parts were still clothed in school uniforms. This was devastating but I knew it to be true.

Uganda itself had been struggling to recover from the strife of the despot Idi Amin's presidency that ended late in 1979, but whose effects were still felt in parts of the country in the 90s. The Rwandan tragedy simply compounded the region's many problems.

Our filming there was to illustrate how funds raised by World Vision were making an impact in some parts of the country, and the stories were used back home on the organization's annual telethon, which Catherine and I co-hosted.

I must share with you one moment of levity on that trip. We were filming on the highway, the main road that linked Uganda with Rwanda. That road had constant traffic of trucks taking food, medicines and other supplies to Rwanda in the wake of the genocide. Along the route were rest areas with vegetable and fruit stands, restaurants, and so on. We were there because the country had built a very modest structure to indicate where the Equator was, and we wanted to film it.

At one point my curiosity about the offering at the fruit stands got the better of me and I wandered over to enquire about a specific object, a huge pod-like tree fruit with a light green, nobbily skin. It was something called jackfruit and I learned later it's part of the breadfruit family. I bought one. It was really big, about 40 pounds, and I intended to take it back to the hotel where we would enjoy it with our dinner that night. Having put it in the back of our vehicle, I forgot about it. But the others didn't.

Without my knowledge, they concealed it with the equipment, took it into the hotel and dressed it up like a person wearing a Tilley hat. It was presented at dinner and we had a good laugh before asking the staff to prepare it for our dessert. The flesh tastes sweet with pineapple or banana flavours and is subtle, almost savoury, so we all enjoyed it.

That night in my room I wrote a poem about the experience and here it is:

JACK'S STORY

UNDER SUNNY UGANDAN SKIES
I GREW TO ENORMOUS SIZE.
THEN CAME THAT FATEFUL DAY
(IT WAS NOON OR LATER)
I WAS RESTING, AT BAY
VERY CLOSE TO THE EQUATOR.

(AM I IN THE NORTH OR SOUTH?)

SALES WERE SLOW, THE TOURISTS
WERE FEW
WHEN SUDDENLY THERE APPEARED A
CANADIAN TV CREW.
THEY WERE TRYING TO WORK WITH ALL
THAT NOISE

OF TRUCKS HEADING WEST WITH FOOD
FOR THE BOYS.
(THE GIRLS IN THE CAMPS DIDN'T
REALLY MATTER;
AND IT WASN'T IN THEIR NATURE TO
RAISE A CLATTER.)

(AM I IN THE NORTH OR THE SOUTH?)

ONE OF THE CREW WAS A WOMAN
OF BEAUTY
AND I HOPED SHE WAS LOOKING FOR
SOMETHING FRUITY.
BUT HER DEDICATION TO THE JOB
AT HAND
KEPT HER AWAY FROM MY SIMPLE
FRUIT STAND.
ALL BUT ONE WERE TALK, TALK, TALKING
AND HE PAID NO ATTENTION (YET
WHISPERED WHILE WALKING).

(AM I IN THE NORTH OR THE SOUTH?)

JUST BEFORE THEY WRAPPED UP
THEIR SHOOT
(IN DESPARATION BECAUSE VEHICLES
WOULD ONLY HOOT)
THE MAN WITH THE MIC LOOKED IN
MY DIRECTION
AND SMILED A SMILE THAT WAS FULL
OF AFFECTION.
HE APPROACHED, CASH IN HAND, AS A
MAN ON A MISSION

IT WAS ONLY LATER I LEARNED THEY
WERE FROM WORLD VISION.

(AM I IN THE NORTH OR THE SOUTH?)

HE CARRIED ME CONFIDENTLY TO THE
BACK OF A TRUCK
(IT HAD RAINED AND I WORRIED ABOUT
ALL THAT MUCK)
BUT IT TURNED INTO A PLEASANT
RESTING PLACE
IMMEDIATELY BESIDE A YOUNG MAN
WITH A RADIANT FACE.
THE DRIVER WAS FAST AND I FEARED
THE WORST;
WHEN WE STOPPED AT A MARKET I
THOUGHT I WAS CURSED.

(AM I IN THE NORTH OR THE SOUTH?)

THE DELAY WAS SHORT AND WE WERE
SOON AWAY
STRAIGHT TO A HOTEL, IT HAD BEEN A
LONG DAY.
THE MAN WITH THE MIC HAD
COMPLETELY FORGOT ME
SO THE ONE WITH THE CAMERA SHOWED
GREAT PITY
AND CARRIED ME GENTLY TO HIS AIR
CONDITIONED SUITE
WHERE HE SPOKE TO HIS MATES ABOUT A
RARE TREAT.

(AM I IN THE NORTH OR THE SOUTH?)

WOULDN'T YOU KNOW IT I'M COVERED
WITH STUFF
AND I WANTED TO SHOUT: ENOUGH
IS ENOUGH.
I WAS CARRIED TO A DOOR THEN PLACED
ON A BED.
A PHONE CALL BROUGHT FOUR MEN,
THOUGHT I WAS DEAD.

WHAT NEXT I WONDERED AS I DREAMED
OF MY TREE
SURELY SOMEONE, SOMEWHERE WAS
THINKING OF ME.

(AM I IN THE NORTH OR THE SOUTH?)

THE NEXT THING I KNEW I'M SITTING IN
A CHAIR
STILL WEARING THE HAT THAT COVERED
MY HAIR.
AND EVERYONE'S LAUGHING, TAKING
PHOTOS, TELLING JOKES;
THESE CANADIAN TV PEOPLE ARE SURE
STRANGE FOLKS.
BUT THE JOKE WAS ON ME AS I LEARNED
OF MY FATE.
I ENDED MY SWEET LIFE AS DESSERT ON
A PLATE.

Maybe you had to be there ...

Before going on that World Vision trip, I had often questioned
the plethora of appeals by organizations who were helping children

in far-flung parts of the world, but mainly Africa. I had been asked by many charities, domestic and international in scope, to help them in their appeals, but when I asked to see their financial statements to understand how much of their fundraising actually got into the field, they were usually not forthcoming. World Vision, however, complied and I was pleasantly surprised to see first-hand how much productivity and good came from their fundraising. The entire experience was very moving and educational.

Among other organizations that I was happy to assist in their fundraising efforts were The Variety Club, Children's Wish Foundation and TV Ontario.

I especially liked the Variety Club, mainly because in those days more than 90% of the funds raised went into programmes for the kids. One year, the day after co-hosting the Variety Club Telethon, I was anchoring the News at Noon when the renowned singer/actress/comedienne Julie Amato came on the programme to discuss the results of the Telethon and thank our audience. She also hit me in the face with a coconut cream pie, a prank that I had agreed to because it led to a significant donation of money by some people in Kingston. The pie filling ruined my suit and my co-anchor was quite annoyed, but for me it was worth it.

When I returned home from the World Vision filming in Africa, there was a period when I was doing little. But it didn't last long because I got the call I had secretly hoped would come: The CBC was looking for someone to do some back-up business reporting and would I be interested. Would I? It was a golden opportunity and I grabbed it.

It wasn't the money initially that attracted me, although that did come in handy when my Global benefits ran out. And I would be freelance, part time, not a staffer, which meant I didn't get benefits at CBC. But I didn't mind; the chance to work there meant everything to me.

CHAPTER 51

Life at the CBC

Back in the 50s I heard a song sung by Anita O'Day called "Pick Yourself Up." I loved it then and love it now. It became my theme song and, through thick and thin, it has helped me adjust to change. It's been said that change is a good thing and I believe that, but only if you can adjust quickly and efficiently.

I was working from home and the business phone rarely rang. When it finally did ring with a friendly voice at the other end, that was a red-letter day.

Old friends were working for CBC doing business hits from the offices of Reuters, the worldwide news agency and data provider. Fred Langan had been a top news correspondent for CBC and Patrick Bolland had been Fred Ketchen's back-up as my daily stock market news provider during my latter days at Global. I was offered an opportunity to do some back-up and it was the sort of work I could do with my eyes closed.

I readily agreed and for an indeterminate time I worked in the Reuters offices before the operation moved to the new CBC head-quarters on Wellington Street. Working at CBC was more demand-ing in terms of security, channels of command, and so on, but it didn't take long for me to fit in because most of the people I worked with knew me from Global and we got along fine.

We did business news hits into CBC Newsworld, CBC Radio and, occasionally, the main television network. Eventually there was a nightly business program that brought all of the day's business and financial news together, and for a while I hosted that. But it wasn't meant to be. I don't know for sure, but I believe certain people didn't think it was appropriate to have a part-time casual person doing such an important job when there were full-time staff available. Being part time gave me a lot of freedom of movement, and personal circumstances were such that I needed that.

One of the most comical things in my early days there occurred when I went for a smoke in a designated smoking room the CBC had assigned on a couple of floors, making it convenient for those who were addicted and would otherwise have been forced outside.

Including Peter Gzowski. I was told the room I frequented was created for him, but I didn't know that when I walked in one day and headed straight to the only empty table and chair. I noticed there was a package of DuMauriers there and a full ashtray, but it was vacant, so I sat down.

I was getting strange looks, and several minutes later I knew why. Peter came in and headed straight to my table, which was really his table, and I got the glare. I noticed others in the room smiling but everyone realized I had made a mistake and would learn from it. I did. I didn't smoke a lot in those days; it was a filthy habit and it took a few more years to kick it. Another of my favourite smoking buddies was Michael Enright and he was smart enough to kick the habit as well.

For a number of years, the work was fairly routine and I felt that I fit right into the Corps, as it was affectionately called. That was about to change in a dramatic way, however, during the summer of 1999 when Gerry Schwartz, the founder and CEO of Onex Corp. made a bid to buy both Canadian Airlines and Air Canada.

It was an earth-shattering story on many levels, and I won't take the time to go into the details and the controversy. But on the day the story broke, I was able to give the overview a lot of context because of my experience working in the airline industry. My shift that day was over at 4 p.m. but the producer of an evening show hosted by Ben Chin asked me to participate in an analysis of the story they would do with me and a former *Globe and Mail* reporter in Ottawa named Christopher Waddell.

I had done two or three hits an hour as this story unfolded and was quite tired, but the producer convinced me to go home, have a rest and come back a few hours later, which I did. They set me up in a small studio so it would appear Ben was speaking to a remote location for me and for Waddell. I was very familiar and comfortable with this format.

As we got into the story, I tried to explain that merging the two airlines would be extremely difficult since they seriously loathed each other and would bring such different baggage to the table. There had been rumours that Air Canada, still a crown corpora- tion, was going to use its political clout to prevent the Onex bid and would itself try to take over its rival.

I cautioned this would never work because of the bad blood between the two airlines that went back decades. But, I insisted, Onex Corporation had a lot of expertise in working through these kinds of issues and could do it.

Waddell suggested Gerry Schwartz didn't have the political clout to pull it off and I countered by saying that Schwartz had been a "bag man" in Ontario for the Liberals and was very well connected. I ended by saying that if Air Canada did succeed in taking over Canadian Airlines, it would be akin to committing hara kiri because it wouldn't survive the myriad challenges. Please cover your eyes and ears, because there's no other way of saying it, but the shit hit the proverbial fan after that news hit.

The next day before my shift, I was told I had been pulled from working for CBC Newsworld and Radio for what was described as "cronyism," which apparently translated into some form of relationship I had with Schwartz. And that note came from the top, Tony Burman, the vice-president of news.

I did have a relationship of sorts with Schwartz since we lived on the same street and I used to see him a few times a year as he went jogging through Rosedale. I had interviewed him during my Global days, and he had been a partner of the new owner of Global, Izzy Asper. But other than that, nothing.

What I was able to surmise later was that there were two possibilities for being yanked off air: One, I had embarrassed Waddell by pointing out he was wrong in his assessment (Waddell was a go-to guy at CBC for just about everything involving Ottawa). Or two, Air Canada heard what I had said and took umbrage by calling CBC, its partner in a number of endeavours, and complaining about its treatment. Whatever happened, I was gone.

Air Canada did take over Canadian Airlines International only to subsequently file for bankruptcy protection when high labour costs and heavy debts from that takeover dragged it into financial trouble. To this day there is still bad blood between the staffs of the two airlines.

I could have declared "I told you so" but didn't. Burman was still the editor-in-chief and the ultimate power, but I still had much expertise to offer. I didn't have to wait long after being pulled off Newsworld, less than a day, in fact, before being recruited.

I had been working as well for an independent CBC channel called Newsworld International (NWI), which had been formed by CBC and Power Corporation to provide a 24-hour news cycle on Direct TV being aired in the U.S.A., northern Mexico and parts of the Caribbean.

The executive producer with whom I worked closely wrote the day after Burman fired me, asking if I would consider working for them full time (still as a part-time employee, mind you) doing mainly business reporting and news anchoring.

It took me a nanosecond to say yes and I was soon on a team that included some of the finest journalists this country has ever produced, including Bill Cunningham, who had hired me at Global, Doreen Kayes, former Middle East Bureau Chief for the U.S. network ABC, Jim Reid of W5 fame, Sandra Lewis, Lorne Saxberg, and many others, under the wing of executive producer David Nayman and General Manager Arnold Amber, a CBC iconic producer.

It was a thinly staffed organization, meaning everyone had to work longer hours than, say, their CBC network counterparts. But what we turned out drew more and more audience as Americans in particular got fed up with their biased networks and cable news operations. We didn't have any marketing clout and had to rely on quality production and word of mouth to build an audience.

I was never party to numbers as I had been at Global in the early days, but I do know when we ceased operations five years later, there was a flood of comment from our regular viewers. As I understand it, the channel actually made money, but both CBC and Power Corporation wanted to cash out, so it was put up for sale.

It was bought initially by USA Networks, leaving the operations under the control of CBC. Some five years later, in 2004, it was purchased by an investment group headed by Al Gore, former Vice President of the U.S. He turned NWI into a channel with a perspective on national issues geared to the youth market, called Current TV.

Current TV lasted about nine years. Gore then sold the channel for a huge amount to the Al Jazeera Media Network, which created the Al Jazeera America network focusing on international news. That network failed in 2016.

The year I joined NWI full time, 1999, was also the year my mother died and that coupled with other issues on the home front made life trying.

Global's Christina Pochmursky, with Jonathan, was my friend and mentor in TV business reporting.

Loblaw's Dave Nichol, marketing guru and foodie.

Designer Marilyn Brooks and I mimicked Eydie Gorme and Steve Lawrence at a charity lip sync contest. We were runners up to a young man from The Toronto Sun, John McDermott.

Preparing to read A Christmas Carol at a Rosseau charity event.

Reworking the script with the World Vision features crew at the Equator marker on the highway linking Uganda and Rwanda, 1994.

The World Vision crew dressed "Jack" for dinner. The restarant staff at our Kampala hotel loved it, too.

Many of my tennis buddies gathered at The Lawn to wish Bernie Kaufman a happy 97th birthday in January 2020.

Many CBC colleagues met to give me a rousing send off in 2004. Great bunch and talented.

Our 13th trip to Greece took us to important mainland sites such as
Epidaurus where Asklepios created the art of holistic healing.

One of my favourite travel photos: This is a homage to Mother Earth in Tashkent, Uzbekistan.

Perfecting my form at Myrtle Beach.

Dining with David Wood at Salt Spring Island, B.C.

CHAPTER 52

An Era Ends

There comes a time in everyone's life when they have to grapple with the loss of a parent. I didn't know my father because of his hospital incarceration when I was a baby, but his loss still affected me. My mother's passing was something else. She knew it was time and planned for it accordingly.

All her life she had dedicated herself to others, from the time she accompanied her Mother on her duties in Newfoundland helping outport families deal with the death of loved ones – and that meant helping to wash dead bodies as a young teenager – to caring for her second husband who took many years to succumb to illness. But especially to her boys and their families along with those in the community who needed her healing hands.

When she decided it was time, she also decided she wouldn't be a bother to anyone.

One Thursday about two weeks before her 90th birthday, Mother went to have her hair done. On the Sunday night, as had become routine, she prepared a dinner for Shirley, Jonathan and I. That night she seemed to be moving a tad slower than normal, but she responded to my concern in a typical manner: "Oh, it's okay. Steve (our family doctor Steve Meda) told me to use the heating pad when I go to bed. It'll be okay."

We had a lovely dinner and, as usual, Mother refused our offer to clean up. As we drove home, I mentioned her changed manner to Shirley, and when we got home, I telephoned Mother to see if she wanted me to take her to the hospital or anything. "No," she said, "I'm going to bed now. Love you."

When I got to the CBC early the next morning, the first thing I did was call to see how she was doing. There was no response, so I knew something was amiss because she was always an early riser. I tried a few times more over the course of an hour or so and finally the phone was answered by my brother Larry, who had been mother's caregiver for many years and lived close by.

Larry told me Mother had died. It was a shock that was only somewhat allayed by my knowing that something had not been right the night before. My colleagues Karen Percy and Harry Forestell said they'd cover my shifts and I drove to the family home on Craighurst Avenue.

There was Larry at the kitchen table on the phone; a police officer was beside him. On the living room floor was Mother, already in a body bag. I sat on the couch and looked at the bag and wept like crazy, in part because the bag looked like it held a child and I suddenly realized how much Mother had shrunk over the years.

When I checked her bedroom, I found the heating pad still on warm.

Larry had come to the house because he got no reply when he telephoned, so he knew something was up. When he arrived, he found Mother on the floor in a brand-new dress she had recently purchased. She had got up at her regular time, around 5:30, had a bath, put on her new dress and died, not wanting to be found in any other way except well-groomed and looking wonderful. Obviously, she had planned her departure for some time.

When I lost my father, I was too young to appreciate the full significance of his passing. When Mother died, it was like a very familiar door had closed never to open again. But later I realized she left because it was time to do so.

Her relatives had all died and so had her friends and neighbours. More importantly, her boys had all survived and were enjoying successful lives. She had done what she had to do and had done it well.

For 53 years she'd kept her tiny house pristine clean and orderly. The memories it held came back to haunt me as I returned later to help Larry go through her things and to designate mementos for family members.

What struck me most was how few "things" she had. Mother had only bought out of necessity and anything beyond that was an occasional or seasonal gift from family or friends. She lived so simply there was nothing of monetary value in the house, and it struck me how true to her Newfoundland outport roots she had been. Her one tiny closet held all of her dresses, and three drawers in the dresser held her sweaters, blouses and "smalls." In all, there were only two bags of clothing to give to the Salvation Army Thrift Shop.

Most of the furniture was worthless; one of brother Jim's children fell heir to the dining room furniture.

As we went through things, I realized how extraordinary her life had been as it centred on people and not on things. Her joy came from cooking a healthy meal for family, not going out to a restaurant. She listened to the radio and watched a bit of TV; going to movies didn't interest her.

I realized, too, how much influence she'd had in shaping the values that I hold so dear.

CHAPTER 53

Formalized Work Ends

It doesn't matter what your status in life, you have to pay your dues. And I did that at NWI, where for long stretches I would work overnight shifts. These were more difficult than the seven days a week anchoring I did at Global for a spell because I was never able to get a solid night's sleep. What I liked about it, though, was the quiet work environment and the ability to take a bit of extra time on research and writing the copy.

I was a member of the Canadian Media Guild, and the CBC technicians had their own union, the Communication, Energy and Paper Workers Union (CEP). I always had a lot of time for the technical and operations people because I realized that while they didn't get the pay scales of the on-air talent or producers and writers, their work was vital to creating a fine product, which is what news is, despite how purists may decry using such a term.

At some point, the unions and management must have agreed to allow on-air people like me to operate our own teleprompters. That lessened the cost of production, as did employing remotely operated cameras.

I always found it a bit unnerving in the beginning of this low-cost era when I entered a cold studio, put on my own microphone, organized my teleprompter, and listened while the camera grunted and groaned into the perfect position for me. It was simply that I had grown into this business interfacing with in-studio people and that was comforting for me.

I mention all this because while my first five years at CBC were just great, the final years were not. I think it began to seriously erode with a technicians' strike in 1999. Management was assuring everyone that programming would continue if the technicians walked out, but in reality, they didn't, because unlike the management at, say, Global, which could operate the equipment if necessary, the CBC managers could not. The executives realized they had to get some people into management who had done some of this technical work, and they started that process after the 1999 strike.

The strike didn't affect the NWI newscasts but, in getting to work, we had to cross picket lines and I didn't like to do that. What I did do, though, was bring food and treats to the picketers, especially those on the overnight shifts. It was a small gesture, but it made the point.

After that work action, the atmosphere at the CBC was never the same. I still got along well with all of our crews and colleagues, but oftentimes you could cut the air with a knife when controversies arose. It just wasn't the same fun it had been before.

The sale of NWI coincided with my 65th birthday so it was a logical time for me to leave the CBC. The departure was memorable in that it was a quiet affair in the newsroom, but Peter Mansbridge dropped by to say "ciao" and that was appreciated.

What was also unexpected was some severance. The CBC was under no obligation to a freelancer to do so, but management did give me a modest severance and I really appreciated the gesture that was initiated, I'm certain, by Heaton Dyer, a senior manager, probably with the blessing of David Nayman.

A note about unions. I'm a believer in the movement partly because they allowed me to work in the trades as a youngster, making good money during the summers of my high school years. But I object to unions abusing their power or exploiting members. I certainly felt exploited when the Guild used members' dues to hire buses to go to Ottawa to protest against something with which I happened to agree. I also heard that one of the most iconic of the union leaders, Bob White, used to travel to Ottawa from Toronto return in an airline's first-class section. It's a one-hour flight and a waste of union funds.

The ultimate transgression, though, had to be the 2019 decision by Jerry Dias, head of the new union that included the old CEP and represented some 12,000 members in the media sector, to use large sums of members' dues to run television advertising berating the Conservative Party of Canada and its leader, Andrew Scheer, before the federal election had been called.

For journalists to be seen taking sides in an election makes a mockery of the profession and I'm quite frankly happy not to be involved any longer.

CHAPTER 54

That Guy Who Used to Be John Dawe

In the years following my departure from Global News, something happened on many occasions that I found curious. It happened on the East Coast, the West Coast, in other parts of Canada, and, even in the U.S. and Mexico: People would come up to me and say, "Didn't you used to be John Dawe?"

I swear that happened many times in many places, and Shirley was often witness to it. These people were not only reacting to my face but also to my voice. I had never considered my voice to be that distinctive, but many people did.

My response was always, with a smile, "I still am," after which there'd be a discussion about my days at Global, hosting the Santa Claus Parade, doing various telethons, and questions about some of my former colleagues, almost always Peter Trueman or Bob McAdorey.

I never took umbrage at these interruptions because I learned early on in the television news business that when people turned on Global News and invited you into their homes, you had a responsibility to treat them with respect; if you did that you would become one of their family, in a sense. They would listen to you while they were having dinner, for goodness sake. And I think people realized that I did reflect that old saying: "What you see is what you get."

So it was that Shirley decided to buy me a vanity license plate for my vehicle: USED2BJD. Even the Service Ontario clerk found that amusing and, yes, she remembered me, too, once she thought about it.

So, there I was: A used-to-be high profile person with no real plan for retirement. Thankfully, I didn't have to wait long for Shirley to swing into action to get me going. The first thing she did was purchase three cooking lessons for me with a friend of friends. I had always been interested in cooking and did quick meals with ease. I was also a baker of sorts, thanks to the legacy of my mother who was renowned for her cakes and pies. But these lessons would open up a significant new world to me.

The three lessons that year led to nine, the same number more or less that I attended every year for more than a decade. We were a small group with a few retirees and a few working women who relished a lengthy lunch hour of instruction and good food.

I have a loose-leaf book that's got to be four inches thick with just about every type of basic meal we would be interested in making, along with some special recipes for what have become signature dishes, such as boeuf bourguignon and coq au vin. One area I excel in is soups, especially puréed soups.

Those lessons and my growing interesting in cooking led me to try the new technology, and I quickly adopted "sous vide" cooking equipment and that wonderful Canadian invention, the Instant Pot. My son gifted me a Ninja Air Fryer to make French fries, among other things, without a lot of oil.

Those first cooking lessons were one of Shirley's best gifts to me in our more than 50 years of marriage. Another was membership in the Toronto Lawn Tennis Club.

Shirley had joined the Lawn in 2002 and at the time I told her I wasn't interested. My excuse then and in subsequent years was that I wasn't a club person and spending time in what I thought would be smelly men's locker rooms didn't appeal.

Still, she tried every year until, finally, in 2008 I agreed to join. You can't imagine the impact on me of almost daily bumping into people I had known for decades. Within three months or so I had come to know a few hundred people, mainly through tennis, and I became actively involved in club life – a lot more, even, than Shirley.

The Lawn has a biannual variety show called "Footfaults" that's produced by members for members. On my first appearance in the show, I was awarded a "best actor" accolade for my performance as Brian Mulroney in a political skit. My fondness for singing also came in handy for many performances. So that, too, opened new opportunities for meeting other members.

As my tennis game improved, I began to enter tournaments and play in House League, which added to my enjoyment. It got to the point where I was playing five or six hours of doubles tennis every week and socializing with some of the key tennis fixtures of the Lawn. There's no life like it.

We've made many friendships at the Lawn, me more than Shirley. Establishing friendships late in life is always a bit tricky but there's something about Lawn people that makes it easy and memorable. We all share a desire to keep our bodies in shape and to enjoy doing exercise to ensure that. And exercise for the brain is achieved in many ways, but mainly through bridge and scintillating conversation. When you've got such commonality of purpose, new challenges appear, and results are analyzed. One of my few regrets in life is that I waited so long to join the Lawn.

Prior to and after joining the Lawn, Shirley and I did some wonderful travel to far-off places. We were never ones to go on organized holidays, so the majority of our trips have been individual, relying on our own planning expertise. Read, Shirley's planning expertise.

In late 2005 we sold our home in South Rosedale where we had lived for more than 20 years. It was time since Jonathan (now known as Jack) had moved away and the house was simply too big for the two of us. Early the next year we bought a condo that still kept us in the 'hood we had come to love and cherish.

The sale of the home was highly emotional as anyone who has done it can attest. We had moved a few times before settling on Crescent Road, and while we couldn't guarantee the new owners that they would love it as we did, we hoped that would be the case. Silly, I know, but that's us.

The new owners were a young couple with two children about the same age as Jonathan when we had bought the house. And the owner's grandmother was a Dawe from Newfoundland. Not only that, they said they planned to continue providing the floral embellishment that Shirley had developed in the front of the house and which our neighbours just loved. As we drive by the house today, we can see it is being loved and cared for and that is just wonderful.

Moving into a condo, though, gave us the flexibility to do a lot of serious travel, something we had wanted to do but were forced to postpone because of work commitments or family commitments. A couple of those trips stand out.

Shirley is a long-time member of a women's group called the International Women's Forum, which encourages women's leadership throughout the world. She enjoyed attending their conferences and knew I would, too, so when an opportunity arose, we would go to the conference but take in more of the region we would be visiting.

When we attended the conference in Jordan, we spent time in both Israel and Egypt, for example. And we experienced that travel with dear friends from Toronto, Don and Jane O'Born. With the

O'Borns we also visited Argentina and Uruguay.

If I began writing about those trips I'd be doing so for the next five years, so that isn't going to happen. What I will say is that as a spouse attending these conferences, I found the topics of discussion fascinating, topical, and even provocative at times. I could fully understand why Shirley was so enamoured with the organization – so much so she headed the Canadian chapter on one occasion.

The women who organized things were fearless. In Jordan, the conference was held at a hotel that had been bombed some time earlier and, since Queen Rania would be speaking, there was a strong military presence close by.

We had also planned to go Egypt, knowing full well there had been attacks on tourists but, by golly, Shirley and Jane weren't going to let that stop them from seeing the wonders of the Nile. On our own!

The two of us did a remarkable trip to Bali to help a long-time friend of Shirley's celebrate an important birthday. For me this was one of the most moving trips I have ever done. To say I loved Bali and its people is an understatement. Never had I felt so at peace with the world and enjoyed so much spirituality on a daily basis.

There had been fundamentalist bombings targeting tourist areas in Bali a few years before we were there, but a repeat of that never entered my mind. I did read in early 2019 that the Muslim government of Indonesia was keen to diversify the population of Bali, which is more than 90% Hindu, but I trust that won't change the island's basic nature.

In 2010 an invitation to the wedding of the daughter of our friends, the Houssers, of Victoria and Salt Spring Island, took us on two remarkable journeys.

The first was to Vancouver and Stanley park for the Canadian wedding of their daughter Sarah to a young man from Lesotho,

Southern Africa, named Thabang Moshologu. We were there to witness but were moved beyond words by an impromptu spiritual event. As Sarah, accompanied by her father, walked down an incline to the waiting assembly of friends and relatives, a bald eagle came out of nowhere and soared over their heads twice. It was fantastic.

Some six months later we joined the Houssers at the traditional tribal wedding in the Moshologu home village in Lesotho. I do not have the language gift to describe that experience fully and in detail because it was a feast for the eyes and ears meant to be digested there and then.

After that remarkable experience, we joined the Houssers on a motor trip to Swaziland and then South Africa, where we went on safari at a private reserve outside Kruger National Park.

If you've been on a safari, you'll know what we experienced. We managed to see the "big five" animals in their natural habitat doing what they do best. We saw lions immediately on entering the park and, over the course of a few days, enjoyed seeing elephants, buffalo, leopard and rhinoceros. We also saw giraffes and hippopotamus, among others.

We had planned to go to Cape Town for several days, reaction for which I had no medication. Whatever it was, it affected my lungs and I had trouble breathing. I stayed in our tent for the better part of two days and it receded somewhat, but we decided to return home.

As this was happening, Shirley got word that her mother had entered hospital. She had been deteriorating for many years from the effects of dementia but now the end was near.

We were re-booked on South African Airways to New York and then Porter Airlines to Toronto, from where Shirley alone transited for Vancouver. She arrived minutes after her mother had breathed her last.

Anne Zitko's death was expected but still very sad. She had been a loving and sympathetic mother-in-law for more than 40 years and I loved her dearly. Shirley's father Ed had died many years before from the same affliction. Shirley was now head of the family with all that entailed.

My mood, meanwhile, had been dampened even more so by a nasty experience with Porter Airlines. Bearing in mind I had worked in the industry for 15 years, I knew what to expect when we changed flights to return home almost a week early. South African Airways charged us an extra $150 each for the flight change and that was perfectly acceptable. But when we got to Newark to check in for Porter, I was shocked to find that the extra amount on my return ticket, which I had booked separately from Shirley, would be $520. This for a one hour or so flight. I tried to reason with the staff but to no avail.

When I returned home, my first chore was to write a letter of complaint to Porter about this disgusting charge and general treatment, advising there was a compassionate situation involved. Porter's response was to send a form letter explaining the charges but offering four $50 vouchers applicable only to full-fare flights on Porter in the next 12 months. I scrapped all of it.

I mention this in detail because it was yet another sign of how much the world had changed and how service had deteriorated on so many fronts, in the airline industry especially.

As for me, my airline travel would become limited and, of course, I would boycott Porter because there are some things on which I just refuse to compromise.

Over the years we've done some wonderful motor trips to Florida to visit friends. And I drove to Myrtle Beach seven or eight times with buddies to play golf for a week.

Shirley and I visited Greece 12 times in the 60s and 70s and all those trips were to the islands. We had tried staying in Athens in

1968 but it was so unpleasant because of the diesel exhaust smell and general confusion, we lasted only one night and went immediately to the port city of Pireaus to find a ferry to the enchanted islands we'd read so much about. We chose the village of Lindos on the island of Rhodes for most of our visits.

We were very aware, though, that we had missed many wonders of the ancient world on the Greek mainland, so that became a target for adventure that we achieved a few years ago. As we experienced Greek culture, we realized what we had missed all those years in understanding the evolution of democracy and the preoccupation of early Greeks with the importance of having healthy minds and bodies. And as for Athens, our few days there were filled with wonder and delight and we could have spent another few weeks and not be bored.

The latest major airline trip we took together was to three Central Asia countries that had declared independence from the Soviet Union in 1991. We travelled in 2019 with a group to Uzbekistan, Kyrgyzstan and Kazakhstan and then did a post-tour trip to Dubai and Abu Dhabi. It was a journey to experience some of the wonders of the Silk Road and for the most part it lived up to expectations.

It was the year of my 80th birthday, and at a wonderful celebration Shirley spent weeks organizing, she told some of the whys that solidified her love for me and our partnership of more than 50 years.

One of them was my sense of curiosity and adventure and Shirley illustrated that by showing a blown-up photograph of me wearing a Kazakh traditional garment and hat and holding on my arm a 35- to 40-pound eagle against the backdrop of a glacial lake some 3,000 metres in the mountains above the city of Almaty.

I'm not certain what lies ahead in the years to come, but you can be certain that while I can still do the tennis and the trips and the dancing, I will be there.

CHAPTER 55

"Regrets, I've Had A Few"
"But then again, too few to mention."

That Paul Anka song, "My Way," gets a lot of play at parties for people retiring, having milestone birthdays or at celebrations of life. I'm nowhere near the final grouping, I hope, but for the purposes of this memoir the lyrics serve me well.

This project began as a legacy memoir to explain to my son and any other family that comes after me what kind of a person I was and what shaped my life. I will acknowledge there are gaps in the story, but I'm not going to apologize for leaving out details of my relationships or my feelings regarding people I've worked with and with whom I didn't get along or had no time for.

There are others I met early in life that had a huge impact on me only to leave us so quickly. The most important of these was David Graham, of Vancouver, the youngest child in what I would call the Graham Dynasty that resided on Point Grey. They were an intensely private family and I had met David by chance in Montreal through one of the characters I lived with at the Zeta Psi House, David Nunn, also from Vancouver.

David Graham agreed to be an usher at my wedding, and we enjoyed a strong friendship over the years before his passing in the

1994 at age 52.

He was a visionary and when he wanted to build a home on an impossible piece of land, he asked the renowned architect Arthur Ericson to design it. The 1963 David Graham House that was stepped on the rocky cliff overlooking the Pacific in West Vancouver was a masterpiece of wood and glass. It was demolished in 2007 much to the chagrin of the heritage community in B.C. I visited that house a few times and it was a marvel. Arthur Ericson said himself that it solidified his reputation as the architect you went to when you wanted to build on an impossible site.

At one point, David allowed a film company to use the house for billeting two extremely well-known actors while their film was being produced. Their behaviour in that house was so bizarre, along with the concomitant debasement of the home, that David soured on the house after that experience. He sold it and it was subsequently demolished.

On one occasion we joined David and his wife along with two other couples on a wet lease of a 75-foot ketch called the *Taormina*, based in Tortola, the British Virgin Islands. We sailed the Sir Francis Drake Channel for a week in all kinds of weather and it was one of the great experiences of my life, since I'm not a swimmer and always steered clear of sailing. On this occasion, though, I tethered myself and helped out during stormy weather and a subsequent race with another sailboat from Newport. I completely understood the sailor's passion.

My best ever fishing experience was down there as well. I went out for a half-day deep-sea experience and managed to catch every important fish there was to catch, including a mighty 40-pound dorado, which we brought back to our hotel and served to all the guests.

In 1992 when Jonathan was 14, we took him to Europe on a

holiday. We first went to France but our main destination was Dorset in England, where David now lived and where he was celebrating his 50th birthday.

David was joint master of the Cattistock Hunt. His partner was Viscountess Charlotte Townshend who, at the time was one of the richest women in Britain, owning 15,000 acres of property in Dorset and a big chuck of London centred on Holland Park. She also owns a swannery, which her ancestors bought from Henry VIII in 1543. She's the only person other than Her Majesty Queen Eilzbeth II who's allowed to own swans in Britain.

David's tented party was held on the lawns of her estate, complete with a jazz orchestra from London. The estate home was huge with one wing having been built a few hundred years before to house the Prince of Wales and his entourage who were coming for a weekend visit.

We were billeted with a charming couple who lived close by. It would be one of the final acts of hospitality in their house before giving it up as a result of the Lloyd's insurance crisis of the early 90s. Our host was what was called a "name" and he lost almost everything.

Among the people at the party was Kim Campbell, a Vancouverite and former Prime Minister of Canada who took a shine to Jonathan.

We enjoyed this short visit with our friend because we had seen much less of him after he moved from Canada to Britain on the strength of a European passport he was able to secure because of his British heritage.

So, it was all the more shocking when we received word of his death while on an annual visit to the Canyon Ranch in Tuscon, Arizona. At his funeral his brother Bill, a former Liberal Cabinet Minister and our MP in Toronto, told the story of David being on a trek. During a pause he sat on a log to partake of a bag of crudités the spa had sent with them. One of the other trekkers, according to

Bill, said: "Graham, you're carrying too much weight." Whereupon David quickly stood up, patted his stomach and declared it muscle. A nanosecond later he was felled by a massive heart attack and died on the spot.

Shirley couldn't go but I flew out for his funeral and was so distraught I stayed inebriated for a few days, and that, alas, was one of my few regrets because I made an ass of myself in front of many old friends and acquaintances. David was a long-time friend with whom we shared many good times and I missed him terribly.

As I reflect on David, I'm struck by how I could have been a better friend to, say, Hal Shaper. Often, he said to me over the phone or in writing that we had to go to South Africa and spend some time with him because we never knew how much time we had left. Hal had left Britain and returned home where he continued to work. He died before we got there and our later trip to spend time with his widow and children was thwarted by my safari illness and Shirley's mother's passing.

And there are still other situations where I could have done more, been more sensitive to the circumstances and allowed change to happen naturally and quietly, rather than suddenly and with malice.

My biggest regret in life, though, is not taking more time with my son during his formative years. When he was two years old, I had him on my knee at the end of my Christmas newscast at Global and my audience loved it. We did that for a few years. He also appeared playing violin once. And then there was the time he was one of the characters on the Russian float in the Santa Claus Parade.

All of that coupled with my celebrity turned him into what his friends called a "Name Brand Kid" in his teenage years. He was very popular but also prone to silly behaviour and developing foibles. Just like his father at that age, I thought.

After I left Global, I had a lot of time to spend with Jonathan.

We developed a strong relationship and tried to do some projects together. For instance, I got an idea for a screenplay and wrote it after consultation with Jonathan. I then gave my script to him to put into the street-ese that he was familiar with and used. The end result I thought was good and I sent it in to several script-writing competitions in California. It never won anything but one of the judges did write a positive response to the script.

Jonathan came up with the idea to Christianize the script because Christian movies were all the rage in the U.S. under the George W. Bush administration. He had a friend who was a "born again" and a writer, so we gave it to him to adapt. It, too, missed the boat because funding for that type of film dried up rapidly after George W. Bush left office.

We still have that script and I believe it has legs, but Jonathan has no interest in pursuing it. I'll get back to it one day because I believe it was meant to be.

What's fascinating to me is how so many of my conscious and unconscious dreams and aspirations have been actualized. It's almost as if the path I was on had already been chosen and it was mine to manoeuvre and to pace. I've always felt as though there was a guardian angel looking over me, but I couldn't ascertain if that was my late father or Shirley, whose influence over me has been strong.

Eating my mother's last banana led to a life lesson. Adopting the essence of the Golden Rule as a lifestyle led to meeting some extraordinary characters and keeping them in my life. Their stories will live on. This memoir will be published, then picked up and made into a movie and I'll have to revert to living the life I had when I was in television, that of a minor celebrity.

Mind you, if that happens, I'll have to lose my vanity license plate, and that would be a shame.

-30-

AFTERTHOUGHT

Aside from such influences as the Golden Rule, my mother, certain other people who have been well documented, or writers such as Khalil Gibran and Myles Connolly, the biggest influence on my life has been music and singing.

I believe it all started when my mother put me on either a chair or a table to sing "God Bless America." I was about eight at the time and that song was important to us because America had done so much to help end the war. The guests loved it and I guess I loved their reaction to me.

As I entered my teens, I didn't sing publicly – that would never do when you're trying to be cool, man – but I listened carefully and memorized a lot of great songs. They ranged from popular music such as "I'm Yours" that Don Cornell made into a hit in 1950 to jazz ballads such as "Pick Yourself Up" by Anita O'Day, which became my theme song for life.

My love for jazz developed as I watched my brothers, especially Larry, listen to the radio and identify which band was playing what and who was singing. His expertise impressed me and I emulated him thereafter, developing a broad knowledge of my own. Like Larry, my musical tastes were varied and my only weakness was classical music, which didn't interest me at the time but which became important in my twenties.

My first ever concert was a performance at Massey Hall by Pete Seeger in the mid-50s. He was alone on stage, sitting on a stool, singing passionately about lives and circumstances we knew little about but by which we were transfixed.

At one point he told the audience about his friendship with iconic folksinger Woodie Guthrie and how he admired him. He told the story of Woodie being asked by a Ladies Auxiliary if he would write a song for them. He agreed and penned some words that Pete sang for us that night:

> "Oh, the Ladies Auxiliary
> It's a fine auxiliary,
> The best auxiliary
> That you ever did see
> If you need an auxiliary
> See the Ladies Auxiliary
> It's the Ladies Auxiliary."

There were other verses but that opening had us in stitches and it wasn't long before I realized that folk music was all about regular people and their everyday struggles, especially with authorities.

Jazz was about people, too, but the music and words delved into the depth of their relationships with each other and bared their souls.

Thanks to a wonderful character named Johnny Armstrong, I got hooked for a while on Rhythm and Blues, specifically Black music and my root song for that genre was "The House of Blue Lights." My friend Dan Ghikadis liked the song, too, and we used to sing it at parties along with many, many others.

We never had a shower in our family home bathroom on Craighurst Avenue where I grew up, but when I moved to Montreal in 1960 to a place with showers, I had a ball practicing my favourite songs during my morning ritual, much to the chagrin of anyone who was close by.

I had begun to collect records, too, in the late 50s, mostly jazz but some vocals by people like Jackie and Roy Kral who were the best cabaret duo in the jazz world. They sang the most amazing songs and they were one of the few groups I had to see when they came to the Town Tavern in Toronto (where I had to use my brother's birth certificate to get in).

The 60s gave birth to the "British Invasion" of North America with The Beatles and The Rolling Stones, among many others, but in those early days I was still stuck on the folk songs of Joan Baez, Bob Dylan and others. My friend Al Scriggins liked them, too, but this pal at the Zeta Psi House in those early days also loved classical music, and he took me on a journey with that genre from which I've never veered. My love is most profound for jazz ballads and great rock and roll, but classical music, including opera, has been a strong inspiration over the years.

There are few works to compare with the "Second Piano Concerto" by Rachmaninoff, but I've often said that when I was feeling down for some reason, I'd take my *Blonde On Blonde* album out and play Dylan's "Sad Eyed Lady of the Lowlands" and would pop out of the mood in the seven minutes that it took him to tell that story. Today, I simply ask my Google Home to play it on Spotify … it's all so instantaneous.

I knew I'd never have a career in music when Eddy Cowan refused to sign me up for North Toronto Collegiate's "Maytime Melodies" show in 1954. But I wasn't afraid to sing with Dinah Christie on Global's News At Noon or with our provincial reporter Bill Bramah on another occasion. And when I joined the Toronto Lawn Tennis Club and was asked if I'd participate in its bi-annual variety show, "Footfaults," I readily agreed.

One year I did a solo, taking the great ballad "Every Time We Say Goodbye" and turning it into "Every Time You Double Fault" (a tennis term). I wore a white jacket, carried a glass of champagne and sang or spoke à la Noel Coward, as choreographed by our director. I was a hit.

All my work in television prepared me for this, with a special nod to all the telethon work I was involved in for many years. I remember doing the Variety Club Telethon for the first time, and when I introduced the next host, Johnny Lombardi, I sang "That's Amore" to welcome his segment. He loved it and began using it as his theme in subsequent years. The audience loved it when we were a bit goofy on telethons.

On several occasions I threatened to sing with Ronnie Hawkins on various charity shows but it never happened. I did sing with the Danny Marks Band, though. Danny has one of the best cover bands in this region and they performed at my 70th birthday celebration, during which I sang a few songs, much to the chagrin of some guests.

Years before, for fun, I entered the media Lip Sync Contests that were held back in the 80s. One year I sang an Eydie Gorme and Steve Lawrence song with my dear friend, fashion designer Marilyn Brooks, and we came second to a young upstart singer named John McDermott, who, of course, went on to much wide acclaim.

In our Montreal party days, singing is what we did, always. Well, four of us anyway: Me, Dan Ghikadis, Ian Henderson and Leanne Schwartz (later Sanders). We called ourselves Three Goys and a Gal. I don't know how our partners and other partygoers enjoyed it but we had a ball.

With the advent of tape and then discs, my extensive record collection seemed irrelevant, so I gave it away, but not before I was able to find CDs of my favourite albums. Today, of course, vinyl albums are making a comeback for the purity of the sound.

Sadly, I can't sing anymore. Something happened to my voice a few years ago and it's totally unreliable for anything but a few bars. I still sing to myself, and once or twice I've punished myself through a birthday greeting in song, but even that's difficult.

And I can't fathom much of today's music, especially the words. When I think of great tunes such as George Gershwin's "Love Walked In" or Cole Porter's "I've Got You Under My Skin," they just seem to have more meaning than "Hit Me Baby One More Time." Then again, maybe I'm not listening closely enough to Drake and these other pop stars. I heard Seal sing Joni Mitchell's "Both Sides Now" and was blown away. Maybe there's hope for me yet.

Marilyn Brooks created some wonderful scarves and tee shirts with the slogan "Music Is My Life." I have one and it always draws positive comment.

Whether you realize it or not, music is the most universal positive reality in our world (aside from love). It is totally and utterly ubiquitous. It's one of life's absolute necessities, like oxygen and water. And it's not only the music that's been written down and performed. It's the sound of life around us.

AFTERTHOUGHT II

Buying and cooking food takes up much of my time these days. Although I have the four-inch-thick cooking class menu binder and far too many cookbooks, I still make relatively few dishes. Most of my recipes are adaptations of ones from my cooking teachers. But one, a curried chicken dish that's so easy but unbelievably delicious, is an adaptation of a recipe given to me by an old friend from high school, Lynn Connell.

Shirley thinks some readers may be interested in one of these recipes, so I'm going to reproduce it here.

REALLY EASY CURRIED CHICKEN

Ingredients

- 1 kilo of boneless, skinless chicken cut into bite-sized cubes
- Patak Curry Paste – whatever heat you like
- Kitchen King Curry powder – one or two tablespoons to taste
- 1 can coconut milk (cream works, too, but is richer)
- 1 can artichoke hearts, preferably in water not oil
- 1 can hearts of palm in water
- 1 bag of fresh baby spinach

- Some asparagus spears if in season
- 4 or 5 tablespoons of olive oil (not strongly flavoured like Greek)
- Salt and pepper as you like

Method

- Heat the olive oil in a large frying pan, adding both curries as it heats up. Medium heat is fine.
- Add the chicken and take a few minutes to toss it to brown all sides.
- Add the coconut milk (cream).
- Drain and halve the artichoke hearts then drain the hearts of palm and cut into one-inch lengths. Add to the pan.
- Cut the asparagus into one-inch lengths and put them in.
- Make sure everything is mixed and keep the pan on medium heat for a few minutes.
- Remove from the heat and place the contents of the pan into a casserole dish. Cover and allow the flavours to mingle for as long as you have, be it minutes or hours.
- An hour before dinner, place the casserole in a pre-heated oven set at 350°F (180°C) for about 45 minutes.
- Carefully remove the lid on your counter and add the spinach, mixing it up as best you can. Replace the lid and let sit for a while.

While the chicken is cooking, I prepare some rice in my Instant Pot as well as preparing a simple salad with a citrus or rosemary vinaigrette, each of which takes just a few minutes.

Lynn calls this meal "shockingly wonderful" and I would agree.

ACKNOWLEDGEMENTS

A lot of people have had a role in shaping this memoir.

It was originally intended as a legacy piece for family to enjoy but turned into a full publishable memoir at the insistence of many people with whom I shared some of the stories. Foremost among these are my tennis and bridge pals at the Toronto Lawn Tennis Club. You know who you are and I'm eternally grateful for the nudges.

Among those I shared early drafts or excerpts with and who offered excellent comments are friends Barbara Orr, Joe Wright, Derek Nelson, Celese Fletcher and Sarah Varley.

Author Martin O'Malley got me on the right track after he read what I thought was my last big draft and recommended significant changes. I only hope he agrees that I followed his expert advice.

The creative team of Hilary Kelley and Stephen Sussman, long time friends, offered to design the cover and what a brilliant job they did.

The penultimate word has to be reserved for my editor, Penny Hozy. When my friend Nick Rundall recommended Penny for this project I had no idea what to expect from another wordsmith. I thought I was a pretty good writer but Penny made the stories sing with subtle changes, deletions and expansions. I am truly indebted to this thoughtful and sensitive writer who has four published books to her credit.

And the sharp-eyed reader will realize I have made no reference to the love of my life Shirley so far in this acknowledgement. For the first time in our more than 53 years of marriage, Shirley gave me plenty of leeway to write or not to write, was helpful in remembering some key dates and situations and, above all, did not pressure me to read the manuscript. In other words, she let me sink or swim on this project and for that I am truly grateful. Besides, the book gave me much to think about and work on during the 2020 pandemic, allowing her to concentrate fully on her own activities. I hope she likes the book.

CPSIA information can be obtained
at www.ICGtesting.com
Printed in the USA
BVHW030450290121
598917BV00025B/103/J